INTRODUCTION TO

STRATEGIC THOUGHT

INSIGHTS FROM THE GREATEST MILITARY THINKERS

INTRODUCTION TO STRATEGIC THOUGHT

Insights from the Greatest Military Thinkers

Col Harjeet Singh (Retd)

PENTAGON PRESS LLP

First published in 2023 by
PENTAGON PRESS LLP
206, Peacock Lane, Shahpur Jat
New Delhi-110049, India
Contact: 011-64706243

Typeset in Palatino, 11 Point
Printed by Aegean offset Printers, Greater Noida, U.P.

ISBN: 978-93-90095-85-8 (HB)

www.pentagonpress.in

Contents

1

Introduction

"The nation that will insist on drawing a broad line of demarcation between the fighting man and the thinking man is liable to find its fighting done by fools and its thinking done by cowards."[1]

—Sir William Francis Butler

War and Strategy

Times change. Warfare changes. War has remained a constant feature in man's existence and history books are filled with accounts of conflict. War and the fear of it have been by far the most powerful among the influences that have shaped the course of international relations over the centuries. Violence has been used to achieve political or personal aims, throughout history, and it has been studied with great earnestness, as conflict is the condition of all life. War is not a sporting event; it is not waged for the purpose of winning. Every military action has potential strategic implications, whether positive or negative. Victory, or a tolerable stalemate, is sought for political reasons. It is inherently difficult to craft the desired condition of peace with order out of war. Perhaps order with peace is the proper way to express the relationship. Moreover, war is the realm of chance and uncertainty. It can be so challenging to succeed militarily and strategically in war that the immediate demands of warfare consume creative energy and effort.

In a military context, commanders and planners attain strategic objectives through planning and executing operations and the employment of tactics. Militaries do not undertake tactical actions simply for their own sake, but to achieve objectives that can be translated into desired political conditions. Tactical actions, even successful ones, can also have negative strategic implications. The space between local or tactical actions and the effects of these actions at the strategic or political level may be very abrupt. While tactical actions have their own logic driven by battlefield geography and tangible physical objectives, sometimes a seemingly unimportant action by any participant (as senior as a general or as junior as a soldier) can have a powerful political impact. However, while discrete tactical actions can have strategic consequences, whether intended or unintended, a simple aggregation of tactical actions does not in itself constitute a strategy. Neither is a collection of operational plans a strategy.

At its most fundamental sense, strategy is the effective translation of military means (*force or the threat of force through military capabilities*) to political ends (*desired policy or political condition*). The military does not act for its own purposes; the application of military force is ultimately in the pursuit of political goals. Strategy is the method for translating those political goals into tangible military action. The origins of modern strategic thought lie with the classical strategists and their writings contribute towards our understanding of the subject. Their work is timeless in their context, irrespective of changes in technology over the ages. Studies of the works of strategists through the ages thus assumes great significance.

War is generally understood as armed conflict between two opposing military forces, waged with the goal of achieving some political purpose, such as conquest, independence, or acquisition of territory. War has certainly been a part of human history from the beginning of organised societies, as evidenced from our earliest written records. Over the course of history, warfare has become a more nuanced political tool, with a variety of motives. Also, written histories and analyses of the strategy of war, can be defined as the interaction of political, economic, and military activities to achieve the objects of war.

Because strategy encompasses both the political and the military realm, it also reflects changes in social structures, communications, technology, and popular opinion. Theories and strategies for warfare continue to develop today in light of such changes as the possibility of nuclear annihilation on the one hand and the growth of small-scale guerrilla warfare and terrorism on the other. If strategy is seen as the grand plan for war, tactics is the science of how battles are actually waged—how troops are organised, what weapons will be used, and the execution of battle plans. While strategy typically takes place at the highest level of command or with the political leadership, tactics most frequently are the decisions of commanders in the field.

The study of the tactics of war is also inextricably linked to advances in the tools of war—the science of weaponry.

How can military strategy evolve to battle combatants such as non-state-sponsored international terrorist movements that follow none of the traditional rules of war and makes no distinction between civilian and military targets? How can military tactics help us to understand and resolve ethnic conflicts within nations? It is certainly true that many of the lessons of modern warfare no longer seem to apply. The wars of the 21st century seem to have more in common, in some ways, with the localised, often brutal conflicts of the European Middle Ages, but with frightening new advances in technology and weaponry. Politicians need to create new strategic paradigms for why and how to engage in wars, and commanders need to create new tactics for fighting them, including the sciences of nation-building and counter insurgency efforts to win the hearts and minds of the local citizenry. Only history will tell if we have been wise enough to learn the right lessons and apply them to our 21st century challenges.

A grounding in the history of strategy will help understanding the discipline and to appreciate the linkages between issues of the day, the bigger picture, and their relationships, past and present, with political and military leadership. The nature of strategy is eternal. Regardless of time or place, those using military force for the purposes of policy will face the same complex phenomena. Strategy has always been, and will remain, a complex, non-linear, multi-dimensional, violent, and competitive activity. Thus, although every case of strategy in action displays unique features, each has something to teach us about dealing with its challenges.

In order to understand strategy we must look to history, for 'the only empirical data we have about how people conduct war and behave under its stresses is our experience with it in the past'.[2] There is an essential unity to all strategic experience in all periods of history because nothing vital to the nature and function of war and strategy changes.[3]

What is Strategy?

Strategy sprung from the need for people to defeat their enemies. The word strategy comes from the Greek *strategos* which means the art of generals. The concept of strategy is sometimes used interchangeably with the concept of tactics. Tactics, however, refers more precisely to the military means chosen in order to reach strategic goals. Subordinated to these goals, tactics can thus be reduced to the conduct of a battle, in limited time and space, according to strategic plans and specific circumstances

The term "strategy" originally referred to what we now know as "military strategy." The enormous number of rational and irrational factors that go into the creation of strategy in war, bereft of any certainty, was thought to be beyond systemic calculation by the average person, leading many to conclude that strategy and war were atheoretical. Strategy was initially believed to be an enigmatic art that could only be fully comprehended by military genius. In more modern times, the role of military genius has been downplayed, with military staffs, comprising experts and specialists, able to formulate strategy through a process that takes advantage of collective wisdom rather than singular genius.

The origins of "strategy" in its contemporary usage are derived from Paul Gédéon Joly de Maizeroy's reference to *"la stratégique"* in 1771, the general meaning of which has remained the same since.[4] In a translation of the writings of the Byzantine emperor Leo VI, Joly de Maizeroy noted that "in order to formulate plans, strategy studies the relationships between time, positions, means, and different interests, and takes every factor into account . . . which is the province of dialectics, that is to say, of reasoning, which is the highest faculty of the mind."[5] It suggests that strategy required a degree of reason rather than adherence to rules.

The term 'strategy' is frequently employed in such a way that it is not clear whether the author means military strategy or grand strategy. In the broad contemporary sense of the word, strategy is concerned with the totality of means available, not excluding violence, to reach a political goal. The latter embraces all the instruments of statecraft, including the military. Also, the tendency to restrict strategic studies to its military dimension can give a false impression that complex systems can be completely understood in terms of their components. Not only does it keep the attention of the strategist away from essential elements of the theatre of war but it also omits many other factors like ideological underpinnings (mis)informing strategic calculation. Military strategy is basically a plan that describes how military means and concepts of employment are used to achieve military objectives. Strategy is much more than a plan. A good strategy considers the potential effects of unexpected factors and the role of others who might disrupt one's strategy because of opposing interests.

There is also a relationship between war and warfare, which can be conflated without properly understanding its implications. War is a legal concept, a social institution, and is a compound idea that embraces the total relationship between belligerents. In contrast, warfare refers to the actual conduct of war in its military dimension. Warfare bears the characteristic, even defining, stamp of violence. States and other political communities wage warfare in order to prosecute their wars. However, the two concepts are vitally different. Historical illustration provides the clearest explanation of the distinction.

State survival and the pursuit of power are profoundly influenced by the strategic and military culture of the state. The nature of strategy is greatly influenced by the geographical and operational environment within which a state exists, and is a feature closely associated with that state's survival and pursuit of power. Strategy is indeed a key feature in the survival of states and their pursuit of power, a fundamental element of statecraft.

Strategy and military culture can characterise the state, and this narrative reveals how connecting the political objectives with the cultures of the people, the military, and the state, together as one, assist in the preservation of the state. The various examples of the importance of the geographic and operational environment provide understanding into the relationship between state survival and power, where gaining and maintaining territory shapes the operating environment and increases power, and equally how the uncertainty of chance in war can upset the best laid plans. We, therefore, need an insight into the importance of understanding the implications of the political objective, strategy and military culture, and geography and operating environment and their influence on the nature of strategy.

The Difference Between Strategy and Tactics

The complementary nature of strategy and tactics has defined their intertwined existence. In the military realm, tactics teach the use of armed forces in engagements, while strategy teaches the use of engagements to achieve the objectives of the war. In war, actions become strategic or tactical depending on whether they relate to the form or the significance of the engagement. With tactics, the soldier is forced to quickly apply the tools they have in the heat of battle. With strategy, the commander does not see most of the situation; he must guess and make assumptions, which decreases his confidence. As a result, the commander can become slowed by fear and rendered indecisive in just those moments that call for decisive action.

Just as the term "strategy" originated with the Greeks, so too did the term "tactics." The original meaning of "tactics" is "order"—literally the "ordering of formations on the battlefield." However, the current use of "strategic" and "tactical" stems from World War II. "Strategic" is associated with long-range aircraft and missiles while "tactical" has referred to shorter-range aircraft and missiles. Interestingly, there is no discussion of warships being either strategic or tactical. The current terminology comes from the rhetoric of proponents of air power in a two-step process of transportation. First, bomber aircraft that were used against industrial targets were called "strategic," to convey their ability to win wars on their own. This was opposed to mere tactical bombing in support of ground forces. The term "strategic" then became associated with the completely incidental quality of long range, which bombers might need to attack industrial targets in some geographic areas. In turn, that caused 'tactical' to acquire the meaning of short range.

American joint doctrine defines strategy as "a prudent idea or set of ideas for employing the instruments of national power in a synchronised and integrated fashion to achieve theatre, national, and/or multinational objectives." That same doctrine defines the strategic level of war as "the level of war at which a nation, often as a member of a group of nations, determines national or multinational (alliance or coalition) strategic security objectives and guidance, then develops and uses national resources to achieve those objectives." This definition highlights the role strategy plays in determining the outcomes for a state. Other definitions of strategy are:

- "the art of distributing and applying military means to fulfil the ends of policy."[6]
- "the direction and use made of means by chosen ways in order to achieve desired ends."[7]

Strategy seeks to balance the projected employment of resources against the availability of those resources to achieve the goals of a state, which is broader than just the use of military force alone. Policy implies "the political objectives that provide the purposes of particular historical strategies."[8] Policy is a product of politics; it provides the basis for the political objectives that underpin strategic ends.

One of the most commonly accepted frameworks for strategy is the one that Arthur F. Lykke Jr. and others at the US Army War College developed. This framework focuses primarily on the employment of instruments of national power in the pursuit of political (rather than purely military) objectives.[9]

Lykke saw strategy within a comprehensive continuum that encompassed the entire political environment, but that strategy had to be practical enough to enable a strategist to act toward achievement of the political goals involved, using four elements:

- **Ends** (*objectives*) explain "what" is to be accomplished. Ends are objectives that, if accomplished, create or contribute to the achievement of the desired end state at the level of strategy being analysed and ultimately serve national interests.
- **Ways** (*strategic concepts/courses of action*) explain "how" the ends are to be accomplished by the employment of resources. The concept must be explicit enough to provide planning guidance

to those who must implement and resource it. Since ways convey action, they often include the use of a verb, but ways are statements of "how" not "what" in relation to the objective of a strategy. A simple test for a way is to ask, "in order to do what?" That should lead to the real objective. Some concepts are now commonly accepted and their names have been given to specific strategies (e.g., containment, forward defence, assured destruction, forward presence). But note that in actual practice these strategies have specific political objectives and forces associated with them and the concept is better developed than the short title suggests.

- **Means** (*resources*) explain what specific resources are to be used in applying the concepts to accomplish the objectives. Means can be tangible or intangible. Examples of tangible means include forces, people, equipment, money, and facilities. Intangible resources include things like will, courage, and intellect.
- **Risk** explains the gap between what is to be achieved and the concepts and resources available to achieve the objective. Since war is a human endeavour that incurs chance and friction, and there are never enough resources or a clever enough concept to assure 100 percent success in the competitive international environment, there is always risk in any military operation. The strategist seeks to minimise this risk through the development of a strategy—the balance of ends, ways, and means.

In practice, Lykke's model is hardly as linear as a balance of ends, ways, means, and risk might suggest, and the notion of risk is often overlooked or given only cursory treatment. However, vetting a strategy realistically for risk is critical. An honest assessment of the other elements of a strategy will highlight where that risk exists.

Good strategy is as much a function of peace as its proper execution during war, and particularly so as several of the components comprising the make-up of strategy take shape during times of peace. Thus strategy has everything to do with putting in place the ends, ways and means of strategy being more a function of peacetime than of war.

Instruments of National Power

The instruments of national power are tools used by a state "to apply its sources of power, including its culture, human potential, industry, science and technology, academic institutions, geography, and national will," articulated as diplomatic, information, military, and economic instruments. Additional forms of national power are legal, intelligence, and financial.[10] These instruments are most effectively employed in combination to gain leverage to attain strategically decisive outcomes.

The diplomatic and military instruments of national power are typically directive in their employment, in that policymakers and their subordinates can direct the employment of these instruments towards the interests of a state. Diplomacy relies on other instruments of national power to provide credible coercive value, whether by military force or by economic sanction, while military power encompasses the available resources and actions taken in support of national security goals by the military and its associated organisations to coerce or compel another state or non-state actor to submit.

Five levels of military strategy have been developed for understanding the aspects of warfare that need to be addressed by a commander and his forces. These are:

1. *Technical*: weapon interaction.
2. *Tactical*: forces directly opposed fight one another; nature of terrain is pivotal.
3. *Operational*: struggle of minds; combat encounters.
4. *Theatre*: relates military strength to territorial space; the satellite view.
5. *Grand*: confluence of interactions that flow up and down the levels of strategy to determine outcomes.

Strategy in Context

In its current interpretation, strategy fits into a continuum ranging from policy down to tactics. Strategy—especially military strategy—is a servant to the goals that are necessarily a function of national policy, which are a broad course of action or statements of guidance adopted by the government at the national level in pursuit of national objectives.

In its practice, policy is an expression of politics within the external security environment, often bounded by the national interests at hand. While military forces do not directly make policy in practice, military leaders certainly exercise influence and must be cognizant of the dictates of that policy. At some level it has been described an "unequal dialogue" of civilian leaders dictating terms to military professionals that mostly execute civilian policy.[11] Thus strategy is a "bridge" or negotiation, whereby the strategic situation dictates a back and forth evolution of dialogue among civilian policymakers, military professionals, and other national security stakeholders. In general, policy is expressed as an action to be taken or a condition to be achieved.

Statements of policy rarely provide clear statements of strategic objectives that would achieve that condition. However, for militaries that are subordinate to civilian authority, strategists are obligated to develop strategies laid down by the dictates of policy guidance. As a result, the relationship of policy to strategy is inherently unequal; defective policy bolstered by even the most brilliant identification of ends, ways, and means is still defective. While policy necessarily governs strategy, good strategy that is consonant with policy goals can provide civilian leaders a clear statement of the full cost of that policy guidance.

While strategy and tactics may at first appear to be similar, their underlying logic is fundamentally different. Classically, strategy addresses the translation of national security objectives into a balance of ends, ways, and means. It is principally focused on doing the "right" thing. In contrast, tactics focus on employing the resources at hand (typically forces on the battlefield) to accomplish the tasks assigned it—with the premise of doing things "right." Bridging the two normally requires the conduct of operational art, which translates the abstractions of strategy into concrete tactical direction.

While good tactics give options to strategy, even the most skilful tactician cannot rescue bad strategy.[12] One of the most practically useful distinctions between tactics and strategy is that the "tactical thinker seeks an answer," whereas "the strategist will instead search for the right questions."[13] Instead of tactics' pursuit of culmination or victory, strategy seeks a favourable continuation of events. In that sense, so-called strategic "end states" are not termination; instead, they are really transition points to the next desired continuation of events whereby a country hopes to be in a position of advantage when compared to its adversaries.

The Limits of Strategy

The dependence of strategy on policy creates a number of challenges for the strategist. Tensions can and do develop between the demands of policymakers, who must factor in both domestic and foreign political considerations, and the reluctance of uniformed strategists to provide options without a full understanding of the costs, risks, and benefits for each option. The principals and agents frequently offer different perspectives on how to attain policy goals.

Strategists must also be prepared to develop strategy even in the absence of published policy. Those strategists will face a paradox between policy uncertainties and the need to express strategy with clarity to the tactical force, especially in ongoing operations. The best a strategist can hope for is an educated guess as to what might constitute policy guidance even when none is forthcoming, then develop strategy against that nominal guidance. Maintaining a dialogue with counterparts who may be privy to policy considerations becomes paramount, as it will better inform that educated guess.

Developing a strategy in the absence of policy guidance could be construed as military leaders impinging on the equities of policymakers. At the same time, the absence of policy guidance makes it virtually impossible to develop a coherent strategy of any kind. Both sides of the policy-strategy divide must be cognizant of the relationship between the two to empower both. Ultimately, it is incumbent on strategists, and especially military strategists, to provide appropriate context for the conduct of operations and the translation of that strategy into purposeful action.

The Paradox of Military Strategy

There are very few areas where the use of paradox is as valuable as it is in military strategy. A bad road is good. A rocky shore is a safe place to land. A night attack presents the best opportunity for victory. Paradoxes abound in the realm of military strategy. Very often, the much sought after element of surprise is shrouded in paradox. A bad road that is difficult to traverse may be the best choice because the enemy least expects an attack from that avenue. A rocky shore is a safe place to land troops because the enemy will have the fewest number of troops available to defend it. A night attack may be the riskiest for the attacker but the cover of darkness allows the enemy to be taken by surprise. An anecdote, perhaps apocryphal, relates the incident of a Roman general who led his army through a swamp, marching all night to the battlefield he knew was dry, so that he could reach there first and occupy the high ground before the battle. After the battle, he asked his troops...when did we win the battle? One said...when the infantry attacked! Another said.... When the cavalry broke through. No, said the general...it was won when we marched through the night and occupied the high ground!

Another example of paradox can be found in the relationship between the success of new, high-technology weapons and their eventual failure. Most enemies will put the majority of their resources behind ways to protect against the opposition's weapons that pose the greatest threat at that time. Therefore, less advanced or successful weapons may remain useful when the more advanced weapons have been countered and rendered ineffective by the enemy. The world's superpowers spent billions of dollars researching and developing nuclear weapons that could wipe out civilisation many times over. However, due to the other superpowers devoting resources to counter these weapons and the inherent danger of creating an endgame situation with no winners, recent military encounters have seen the use of less advanced weapons to fight wars.

Above all, deceit—in war and politics—if practiced wisely can lead to victory and avoid casualties. However, what has worked in the past does not necessarily conform to current challenges.

Understanding Strategy

Any understanding of strategy requires knowing what it is, where it fits, and the form it takes. Translating political guidance into military actions requires a method for taking the demands of policy and operationalising that guidance into tactical action. While strategy may take various forms, its application is hardly linear and rarely simple considering the nuances that come with its application, whether at the national or theatre level. Strategy and tactics, while seemingly similar, are merely cognates of each other and not interchangeable. Competent strategists can and must distinguish between the logic that governs strategy's selection of choices and the focus on task accomplishment that is at the heart of tactics. Knowing the dictates of strategy will guide tactics to the net strategic effect that will make those tactics relevant. In the end, what must guide the actions of the strategist is the attainment of the policy objective; it is that which should dictate how to use force.

Military strategy is the practice of reducing an adversary's physical capacity and willingness to fight, and continuing to do so until one's aim is achieved. It takes place in wartime as well as peacetime, and may involve using force, directly or indirectly, as a threat. Reducing an opponent's capacity and willingness to fight is always a relative matter; one can achieve it by building a quantitative or qualitative superiority in military power well before hostilities might commence.

The use of strategy has literally changed the map of the world and caused the rise and fall of many a nation and its people. Strategy is a never-ending holistic approach to anticipated future challenges in the light of our own ends, ways and means as well as the consideration of frictions and the behaviour of enemies, among others. Strategy has to be fluent, flexible, adaptive and non-linear. That's why strategy is not purely a science but rather an art, and more than a sequence of events leading to a desired outcome.

There are countless books on strategy and strategic theory. Throughout history, military strategists have described the practice in diverse ways. Each author has expounded views reflecting their time and the nature of warfare prevalent at the time. Some have been analytical while others have been trailblazers in opening up new avenues of thought. The intention in this volume is to explain the strategic thought put forward by the former through history. There is no overarching theory of military strategy to describe the relationships between individual military strategies. Even the definition of strategy lacks consensus, with various theorists defining it to suit their own purposes rather than addressing it in a rigorous, systematic way.

The choice of strategic thought in this book is eclectic but it serves the purpose of understanding the subject as it has developed over the ages.

This understanding of the value of studying history and theory in combination with practice is widely shared in military education systems throughout the modern world. At higher level more emphasis is given to study of history and theory in order to develop critical analysis and judgment. At the strategic level prescriptive doctrines no longer work as they do at lower military tactical and technical levels where situations are less ambiguous and often more predictable. Reading does not give all the answers, but it lights what is often a dark path ahead. [...] Ultimately, a real understanding of history means that we face nothing new under the sun'.[14]

The origins of modern strategic thought can be traced back to the classical strategists. An examination of their works shows that the basic questions with which they have grappled over the past two centuries have been remarkably constant. There are strategic principles that hold good for all times and for all arms—irrespective of changes in technology and strategies. Not only that, the historical background can help us to clarify and understand contemporary issues. To understand the present and the future we need to understand the past because events do not take place in a vacuum, they have their roots in history. We cannot understand what is happening in the world today if we do not know the past. History matters. This is especially true of the principles of war and military strategy. But history is not the only guide to the future. The present provides the patterns that can help identify the directions of change. These days one hears so much about 'change' and 'revolution' in almost every field—changes in world politics, the economy, the revolution in communications technology, and of course the revolution in military affairs—that the risk of losing sight of the continuities in human life is ever-present. Much has changed in our world, yet much remains the same.

FURTHER READING

- Lawrence Freedman, *Strategy: A History* (New York: Oxford University Press, 2013).
- Colin S. Gray, *The Strategy Bridge: Theory for Practice* (Oxford: Oxford University Press, 2010).
- Oliver Prescott Robinson, *The Fundamentals of Military Strategy* (Washington, DC: US Infantry Association, 1928).
- Antulio J. Echevarria, *Military Strategy: A Very Short Introduction* (New Delhi: Oxford University Press, 2017).
- Colin S. Gray, *Modern Strategy* (Oxford: Oxford University Press, 1999).
- Peter Paret, ed., *Makers of Modern Strategy: From Machiavelli to the Nuclear Age* (Princeton: Princeton University Press, 1986).

2

Sun Tzu

"All warfare is based on deception. Therefore when capable, feign incapacity; when active, inactivity. When near, make it appear that you're far away. When far away, that you're near. Offer the enemy a bait to lure him, feign disorder and strike him. Speed is the essence of war."[1]

—Sun Tzu

The Context, the Author

The Art of War is an ancient military compendium, written in China around the 4th century B.C., straddling the "Spring and Autumn" and "Warring States" periods. The work is attributed to Sun Tzu, a general, a strategist, a philosopher, who lived during the Zhou dynasty. Its thirteen chapters, in a manuscript impressed on a bamboo roll, is considered the oldest military manual ever written. *The Art of War*, remains a text which describes Chinese society, culture, philosophical roots, and political way of approaching reality, that no other book can do in such brevity.

The works of Sun Tzu were introduced to the Western world by a Jesuit missionary, Jean Joseph Marie Amiot, through his translation of the *Art of War*, as *Art Militaire des Chinois* in 1772. It is credited with influencing Napoleon, the German General Staff, and even the planning of Operation Desert Storm. Leaders as diverse as Mao Zedong, Vo Nguyen Giap, and General Douglas MacArthur have claimed to have drawn inspiration from the work.

Sun Tzu's *The Art of War* began to draw attention of the Russians in 1860, the British in 1905-1910 and the Germans in 1910. The English version began with Captain EF Calthrop's translation, which was subsequently improved upon by Lionel Giles and further brought up to more comprehensive form by Samuel B Griffith. Sun Tzu, in contemporary light, assimilates all view points and explores its relevance to modern warfare. As one of the oldest and most famous studies of strategy, it has had a huge influence on military planning, business tactics, and beyond.

The Book

The Art of War is composed of 13 chapters, each of which is devoted to one aspect of warfare, it has long been praised as the classic work on military strategies and tactics of its time.

CHAPTER 1: LAYING PLANS

This chapter focuses on the planning stage of war.

Sun Tzu states the five factors that determine the outcome of the battle. These are:

1. The Moral Law.
2. Heaven.
3. Earth.
4. The Commander.
5. Method and Discipline.

These factors can be grouped as follows:

Heaven and Earth as the external factors, Moral Law and Method and Discipline as the internal factors, the Commander as the leader.

Commander factor stands for the virtues of Wisdom, Sincerity, Benevolence, Courage, and Strictness. It symbolises a war commander or any other leader or manager influencing and manipulating an organisation.

External factors (Heaven and Earth) are the same for the two sides of the battle. As Sun Tzu said, the one who made more calculations regarding these factors, who adapt and take advantage of these factors, will be victorious.

In a modern interpretation of these factors Heaven is interpreted as the variable factors such as trends, weather, and current state of the economy. In making plans, the leader should consider the changing environment and be flexible to adapt and take advantage of the changes better than the opponents. Earth is interpreted as the constant factors such as geography, roads, laws and regulations. The plans should be in accordance with these factors. Together these two factors (Heaven and Earth) picture the current situation.

The internal factors are within the control of the leader. The Moral Law is what makes the leader and the followers believe what they do is right. According to Sun Tzu, if the leader has a right cause for fighting (and communicate this cause to the followers) the followers will follow the leader regardless of their lives, without loss of courage against danger.

Method and Discipline stands for the organisation and means to achieve the goal. According to Sun Tzu, method and discipline is the organisation of the army into subdivisions, appointing officers to ranks and building a supply network for the army and control of the army budget.

Since these five factors determine the winner and loser, every leader or manager should make plans and calculations regarding these factors. According to Sun Tzu, the one who makes more calculations before the battle will be victorious.

To predict the winning side of a battle, we should look at the following points:

1. Which of the two sovereigns is influenced with the moral law (Moral Law).
2. Which of the two generals has most ability (Commander).
3. With whom lie the advantages derived from heaven and earth (Heaven and Earth).
4. On which side is discipline most rigorously enforced (Method and Discipline).
5. Which army is stronger (Commander, Method and Discipline, Moral Law).

6. On which side are officials and men more highly trained (Commander, Method and Discipline).
7. In which army is there a greater constancy both in reward and punishment. (Commander, Method and Discipline).

According to these points, the one with the right cause, better leader, taking advantage of the external factors and manipulating the internal ones in the right way will be victorious.

In order to plan and act right, the leader should know the position of the opponent. Obtaining inside information of the opponent is explained in the 13th chapter, "the use of spies". It is emphasised to prevent the opponent making a good plan, good preparations or a gainful move is done by giving false impression and misleading him.

CHAPTER 2: WAGING WAR

The leader should know the negative effects of war beforehand. War is costly. If you prolong the battle it will drain your resources and exhaust your men. This gives your opponents an advantage. Therefore, victory should be gained quickly without long battles.

In this chapter there are also recommendations about the reward system. Sun Tzu states that the soldiers should share a common goal (in war, victory) in order to fight well. Also, if they achieve something valuable they should be rewarded in order to encourage them to achieve more.

CHAPTER 3: ATTACK BY STRATAGEM

In the art of war, the best achievement is breaking enemy's resistance and gaining the victory without fighting. In the case of battle, conquering the enemy territory without destroying it. There are two reasons for this:

1. War is costly and gain with minimum cost is more valuable.
2. Gaining a destroyed country isn't a real victory since it has no use for the victorious side.

Therefore, the highest point of leadership is to disappoint the enemy's plans, next is to prevent facing the enemy, next attack the enemy, worst is to siege a walled city.

Sieging is not recommended because it usually takes much longer than a field battle to come to a result. And the result isn't always guaranteed. Since it takes a long time, environmental factors can change and may turn against the attacker. The sieged city will close all connection to the outside; therefore, it will be much harder to get valuable information to consider during planning.

Sun Tzu suggests a rule for choosing the right strategy for attack (or not to attack):

- If our forces are ten to the enemy's one surround him.
- If five to one, attack him.
- If twice as numerous, divide our army in two.
- If equally matched, we can offer a battle.
- If slightly inferior in numbers, we can avoid the enemy.
- If quite unequal in every way, flee from him.

According to Sun Tzu there are three ways that a ruler can bring misfortune to his army:

1. By commanding the army to advance or retreat, being ignorant of the fact that it cannot obey. This is called hobbling the army.
2. By attempting to govern an army in the same way as he administers a kingdom, being ignorant of the conditions which obtain an army.
3. By employing the officers of his army without discrimination, through ignorance of the military principle of adaptation to circumstances. This shakes the confidence of the soldiers.

According to these three rules, the army should be led by a military professional, not the ruler himself since ruling an empire is different from leading an army. Lack of knowledge in the art of war will cause the ruler to give orders which are impossible to obey, not to see and consider the conditions of the battlefield and appoint wrong men to critical positions.

Sun Tzu states the five essentials for victory:

1. He will win who knows when to fight and when not to fight.
2. He will win who knows how to handle both superior and inferior forces.

3. He will win whose army is animated by the same spirit throughout all its ranks.
4. He will win who, prepared himself, waits to take the enemy unprepared.
5. He will win who has military capacity and is not interfered by the sovereign.

Since war is vital for the country the decision should be made after taking all factors into account. If there's no gain in entering a battle, the battle should be avoided.

Not every leader has the chance of leading a superior force. A small army can also win. Also, a large army can sometimes face an even larger army. In such cases the leader should be aware of the methods of leading both a superior and an inferior army in order to gain victory.

Communication and sharing the goal is essential for victory. In order to reach the goal of the organisation, each member should share the urge to achieve it.

The battle has two sides and all a leader can do is to prepare his own army for the battle. Victory depends on the preparation of the other side. As Sun Tzu said, the winner prepares himself and waits for a chance to attack and gain victory.

In the introduction of *Art of War*, an incident from the life of Sun Tzu was told:

> *In order to test his warfare skills, King Wu asks Sun Tzu to prepare some of the girls from his harem as soldiers. Sun Tzu divides the girls into two groups and appoints one girl as the commander to each group. He trained the groups for basic right and left turns. When the girls were ordered to turn, they laughed and did not obey the command. Sun Tzu said "if the orders are not clear and cannot be understood, the general should be blamed. But if the orders are clear and still not obeyed then the officers are to blame" and wanted to behead the two girls in the role of group leaders. King Wu interrupted and wanted Sun Tzu to spare the life of the two girls but Sun Tzu refused. After the execution of two girls, two other girls were appointed as leaders and this time all the girls obeyed the orders. After this incident, Sun Tzu was appointed as general in the army.*

Since ruling a country and leading an army is different, the general who is capable of leading the army should be left free in his job.

Since strategy is important, this chapter was summarised by Sun Tzu himself at the end:

> *"If you know the enemy and know yourself, you need not fear the result of hundred battles. If you know yourself but not the enemy, for every victory gained you will also suffer a defeat. If you know neither the enemy nor yourself, you will succumb in every battle."*

CHAPTER 4: TACTICAL DISPOSITIONS

Sun Tzu emphasises that a good fighter first secures himself, and then waits for a chance to defeat his enemy. This is because we can make preparations to secure ourselves; this is in our hands but we need a weak point to attack at the enemy's side. Therefore, protection can be guaranteed but victory cannot be.

In fact, standing on the defensive indicates insufficient strength, attacking excessive strength. A skilful general hides the strength of his army while standing on the defensive but when has the chance; he attacks like a flash and gains the victory. The way to victory is:

1. Measurement.
2. Estimation of quantity.
3. Calculation.
4. Balancing of chances.
5. Victory.

All these are connected to each other like a chain. Measurement is gathering data about the environment (Earth), Estimation of quantity is estimating the required resources. Calculation is based on the extent of resources determined in Estimation of quantity. Making many calculations, the leader takes every possible outcome into account and Balances the chances. After balancing the chances he chooses the best option that leads to victory.

CHAPTER 5: ENERGY

The control of a large force is the same principle as the control of a few men. The important point is to divide them into proper subdivisions and connect them with proper communication methods.

There are two methods in fighting; direct and indirect. In order to officially declare war, the general should attack directly but what gives the advantage is the indirect one. Since the art of war is based on deceiving the enemy, an indirect attack catches the enemy off-guard and inflicts much more damage. A skilful general uses these two methods in cycles and different combinations according to his own calculations and strategy.

In order to deceive the enemy, the skilful general cloaks the true strength and order of his army and gives a false impression of weakness and disorder. In some cases, giving sacrifices as baits can be useful to keep the enemy busy at wrong places and advance him to our trap.

It is emphasised that a clever fighter takes advantage of the harmony of his men. In this regard Sun Tzu suggests the utilisation of synergy instead of individual ability.

CHAPTER 6: WEAK POINTS AND STRONG

As the result of being prepared for the enemy, the army which is already at the battlefield has the advantage. This is also similar with the market entry barriers in the modern business world.

The clever fighter does not let the game be led by his opponent. Instead he imposes his will upon his enemy. He can either let an enemy get closer to the trap or keep the enemy distant according to the strategy. If the enemy is not responding his moves, he uses psychological tactics to prevent the enemy building and acting according to a strategy. After foiling the enemy's plans, he attacks an unexpected point to gain victory.

Against a skilful attacker, the enemy is never sure about what to defend. On the other hand, the enemy is never sure about what to attack against a skilful defender.

If plans are prepared in secrecy and all conditions are ready for the plan to put into action, we can attack or outrun the enemy. We can force our enemy to act the way we want him to by giving baits.

The attack plans must be kept secret in order to confuse the enemy about what and when to defend. In such case, the enemy will be forced to defend several points causing him to divide his forces. Trying to secure different places, the enemy will leave a weak point which gives us opportunity to attack.

The numerical advantage does not guarantee victory. By forcing the enemy to reveal his plans and leave a weak spot can bring victory to a smaller army.

One important point is not to repeat same tactics in different battles. Since secrecy and deceit are the key factors in victory, using the same tactics will be easy to defend for the enemy. Also, since every battle has its own conditions, using generic tactics will not bring victory. Instead the general should consider the internal and external factors for that battle and come up with an unpredictable plan to deceive the enemy.

Conditions may change during the battle. Therefore, in order to gain victory the tactics should be changed according to the changing conditions. In the battlefield the one who can adapt and respond to the changing conditions succeeds in winning.

CHAPTER 7: MANOEUVERING

Receiving the command from the sovereign and completing preparations for the battle, the general moves his army according to his plans and this tactical manoeuvring is the most difficult part of war.

With right manoeuvring the general can mislead his enemy and can reach the destination before the enemy army.

For the right execution of the manoeuvre, the army must be well organised, otherwise it will be impossible to move and maintain order.

Another challenge in manoeuvring is moving the heavy equipment quickly. A fully equipped army obviously cannot move as agile as a lightly equipped one but leaving equipment behind in order to gain speed and agility will weaken the army.

Longer movements than the capacity of the army are disadvantageous. Stronger men will reach the target but weaker ones will be lost on the way.

Before building alliances, we must know the plans of our potential ally. Before moving the army, the general should be aware of the dangers and know the characteristics of the terrain on the way. In this regard having local guides is useful. If there's no gain in moving the army, it's the best not to move. The movements should be made according to the circumstances.

Making changes are risky. Therefore, all data must be collected and taken into consideration before making such decision. Having a local guide is helpful.

In any possible action, the army should perform the best in order to gain advantage. Sun Tzu gives examples from nature for the level of best performances such as being rapid like the wind, compact like the forest, raiding like fire, being immovable like a mountain, making plans secret and impenetrable like the night, and being quick like a thunderbolt.

In order to move a large army in order, the general has to use gongs and drums, banners and flags. Sun Tzu emphasises the importance of control and communication.

The art of warfare is:

- The art of manoeuvring.
- The art of handling large masses of men.
- The art of studying moods.
- The art of retaining self-possession.
- The art of husbanding one's strength.
- The art of studying circumstances.

Therefore, a skilful general should:

- Know where to move and where not to move the army.
- Be capable of maintaining order of the whole army while manoeuvring.
- Understand the mood of both his men and the opponent and act in accordance with this mood.
- Be calm and patient.
- Be able to utilise his resources wisely.
- Be able to read the signs of the environment and the enemy and change plans accordingly.

CHAPTER 8: VARIATION IN TACTICS

Circumstances and environment limit the possibilities of the general. There are roads which must not be followed, armies which must not be attacked, towns which must not be besieged, positions which must not be contested and commands of the sovereign which must not be obeyed.

Sun Tzu underlines the responsibility of the general for making the right choices that will be advantageous for his army. These choices include not moving, attacking, besieging and obeying the sovereign. Refusing to obey the orders of the sovereign is risky but if the general is completely sure of his judgment and success in the battlefield, he can take the risk and apply his own plans.

The art of war teaches us to be prepared for enemy attack, to ensure our own safety, not relying on the chance of not being attacked.

There are five dangerous faults which affect a general:

1. *Recklessness:* which leads to destruction.
2. *Cowardice:* which leads to capture.
3. *A hasty temper:* which can be provoked by insults.
4. *A delicacy of honour:* which is sensitive to shame.
5. *Over-solicitude for his men:* which exposes him to worry and trouble.

To avoid these five faults, the general must make careful calculations of every detail, be brave in executing his plans, be calm and in control of himself, not give too much importance to his own honour and not to be too soft and worried about his men.

CHAPTER 9: THE ARMY ON THE MARCH

When fighting, the general should not place his army in a disadvantageous position regarding geographical obstacles. This can be done by knowing the terrain and its effects on the battle. The general should also use this knowledge to gain advantage over the enemy.

All armies prefer high ground to low and sunny place to dark. And the general should look for favourable conditions to execute his plans.

There are signs that reveal the intentions and feelings of both enemy and the general's own men. If the enemy is near but remaining quiet, he's relying on the natural strength of his position. When he keeps trying to provoke a battle, he's worried about the possibility of the other side to advance. Rising of birds may be a sign of an ambush plan. Humble words and increased preparations are signs of an advance, violent language and pretending to attack are signs of retreat. When soldiers are leaning on their spears, this shows that they are hungry.

In order to use punishment for discipline, the general should first gain the loyalty of his soldiers. Punishment is only useful on loyal soldiers.

A general should have trust in his men but always insist his orders to be obeyed.

CHAPTER 10: TERRAIN

Sun Tzu classifies terrain in six groups:

1. Accessible ground.
2. Entangling ground.
3. Temporizing ground.
4. Narrow passes.
5. Precipitous heights.
6. Positions of great distance from enemy.

Ground which can be freely crossed by both sides is called accessible. On this kind of ground, the general should occupy the positions with advantage before the enemy.

Ground which can be abandoned but is hard to re-occupy is called entangling. An attack from this kind of ground may be disadvantageous because in case of retreat it will be hard to cross an entangling ground.

Ground with the position that neither side will gain by making the first move is called temporizing ground. In such ground it is better not to be tricked and pulled into battle by baits. On the other hand, forcing the enemy to advance first will offer an advantage.

In case of the narrow passes, if we occupy them with strong forces, it will be advantage for us, but it's risky to follow an enemy escaping through a narrow pass. If the pass is heavily garrisoned by the enemy, it is best is to stay out.

In case of precipitous heights, it is advised to occupy advantageous locations before the enemy and not to follow an enemy which has already occupied these locations.

If there is a great distance between two armies, it is not wise to start a fight. In such cases the army should be advanced near the enemy, else it will be tired and may be exposed.

There are six faults that the general is responsible of:

1. Flight.
2. Insubordination.
3. Collapse.
4. Ruin.
5. Disorganisation.
6. Rout.

If two armies with an enormous difference in size meet, the result is the flight of the smaller one.

If the soldiers are strong but the officers are weak, the result is insubordination. In this case the soldiers will not respect and obey the officers.

If the officers are strong but the common soldiers are weak, the result is collapse. Since the victory will be gained through synergy, having a talented leader is not enough. There should be strong men under him to achieve the goals.

If the higher officers have problems with the leader and are insubordinate, they will not wait for orders or obey given ones. In this case the officers will act on their own account and the result is ruin.

If the general is not capable of leading, his officers will be disobedient. The result is disorganisation. In order to gain victory, all ranks should be occupied by talented members of organisation. Authority and discipline must be established before entering any battle.

When a general is unable to estimate the strength of the enemy and attacks a strong army with a weak one, the result is rout.

The geographical conditions are the most important factors in battle. The general make his calculations, estimates the power of enemy and prepares tactics to bring him victory.

Regarding the calculations, if the result will be victory then the general must fight even if the sovereign orders him to retreat. The general must not fight if the calculations show a defeat even if the sovereign orders him to attack.

Sun Tzu recommends that leaders regard their soldiers as their own children to make them emotionally connected to the leader and follow him to death. But if the leader is unable to establish his authority, these soldiers will be like spoiled children and are useless.

Conditions of own army, the enemy's army and the natural environment are three pillars of victory. A general should know each of them to be victorious. Sun Tzu said, "if you know the enemy and know yourself, your victory will not stand in doubt. If you know Heaven and know Earth, you may make your victory complete".

CHAPTER 11: THE NINE SITUATIONS

Sun Tzu classified the battlefield according to location in nine groups:

1. *Dispersive ground*: when a chieftain is fighting in his own territory, it is dispersive ground. It is not recommended to fight in dispersive ground.
2. *Facile ground*: when he is a little inside the hostile territory, it is facile ground. It is not recommended on facile ground to stop and fight. This slows down your speed into the country.
3. *Contentious ground*: the ground which gives a great advantage to holder is contentious ground. It is not recommended to attack from contentious ground since holding it is more advantageous.
4. *Open ground*: the ground on which each side has the freedom to move is open ground. On this ground it's not recommended to block the enemy's way, since the ground is easy on every side, blockage is meaningless.
5. *Ground of intersecting highways*: the ground which forms the key to three neighbouring states is ground of intersecting highways. The one who controls this also controls the others. On this kind of ground, it is recommended to make alliances with neighbouring states.
6. *Serious ground*: If the army penetrates deep into the hostile country leaving fortified cities behind, it is serious ground. In such ground it is recommended to gather the plundered resources from the captured towns to use in the future battles ahead.
7. *Difficult ground*: If the enemy territory is geographically challenging, it is called difficult ground. In this ground it is not recommended to halt and camp. The army should keep marching to get out as soon as possible.

8. *Hemmed-in ground*: the ground which is reached through narrow paths and hard to retreat is hemmed-in ground. This kind of ground can be used to camp and make our plans.
9. *Desperate ground*: the ground on which we can be saved from destruction by fighting without delay is desperate ground. There is no choice in desperate ground other than fighting.

The skilful general knows the point in the enemy army which he should attack. Attacking this point he splits the enemy army, and prevents the parts helping each other. A skilful general is capable of causing disorder in the enemy army. The skilful general only moves his army if there is gain in moving. If not, he keeps still.

In desperate situations, soldiers fight without fear. If there's no place to retreat, the soldier will do his best to survive. In such situations soldiers are perfectly loyal and trustworthy.

Omens and other superstitious thoughts discourage the army. The general should avoid them have effect on the soldiers. Until death itself comes, there's nothing to be afraid of.

The army led by a skilful tactician looks like a snake. If attacked at the head, it will attack with its tail. If attacked at the tail, the head will retaliate. If attacked in the middle, both head and tail will respond.

Even enemies can be allies in some conditions. It is the talent of the general to bring them together.

CHAPTER 12: ATTACK BY FIRE

According to Sun Tzu there are five ways of attacking by fire:

1. Burn soldiers in their camp.
2. Burn stores.
3. Burn baggage trains.
4. Burn arsenals and magazines.
5. Throw fire at the enemy.

All of them except the last one are indirect war. In the first four, attacking by fire weakens the enemy, decreases their supplies and breaks his courage. The last one is the usage of fire as a weapon.

In use of fire, the season and wind should be taken into

consideration. A dry summer is the ideal season. In attacking by fire, there are five possible developments:

1. When fire breaks out inside the enemy camp, also attack with fire from outside.
2. If there is an outbreak of fire but enemy's soldiers remain quiet, do not attack. Let the fire do more damage before it is noticed.
3. When the fire reaches its limit, attack the enemy camp as soon as possible. If it is not practical, stay where you are.
4. If it is possible to attack with fire from outside, do not wait for the inside fire, attack when possible.
5. When you start a fire keep the wind on your back. Do not get caught in the fire.

When attacking by fire, stealing some of the water from enemy is useful. If you steal all the water the enemy will understand that fire is coming and get prepared for it.

"Move if there is gain, if not, stay where you are".

CHAPTER 13: THE USE OF SPIES

Since war is costly and may last for a long time, the victory gained after a loss is not considered as victory.

The wise sovereign and good general strikes and conquers, achieves things beyond the reach of ordinary men, by foreknowledge. Foreknowledge cannot be obtained from spirits, or from experience and it cannot be calculated. Valuable information about the enemy is obtained from other men (spies).

There are five classes of spies:

1. *Local spies* are the inhabitants of a district.
2. *Inward spies* are officials of the enemy.
3. *Converted spies* are enemy's spies getting caught and used for our own purposes.
4. *Doomed spies* are those do things openly for purposes of deception and are expendable. (by reporting a doomed spy to the enemy, makes our other spy trustworthy for the him).
5. *Surviving spies* are those who bring back news form the enemy's camp.

Deploying all five kinds of spies is called "divine manipulation of the threads" and it's a very valuable advantage.

Sun Tzu recommends the use of spies also in businesses other than war. Since inside information is an essential part in attack and defence plans, use of spies adds great power to an army.

Comments

Sun Tzu summarised much in the following words: 'If you know the enemy, and know yourself; your victory will never be endangered. Know the ground, know the weather; your victory will be total.' Sun Tzu advised that battle should be avoided unless all considerations are favourable. The key to Sun Tzu's thought is that the ultimate victory is inducing a surrender without striking a blow. He believed that it is more important to kill the enemy's courage than to kill the enemy's soldiers. Sun Tzu advised against repeating tactics which have gained you one victory.

Sun Tzu's *The Art of War* possesses an enduring beauty, both in its language and in its simplicity. In a few pages it lays out the basic principles for planning and executing a military campaign, examines the qualities of good leadership, and sets criteria for judging whether the political ends justify the military means.[2] Sun Tzu believed that the strategy should not be a plan in the form of a pre-established list, but rather required prompt and appropriate actions in response to changing conditions.

Sun Tzu wrote that in general 'the best policy is to take the state intact; to ruin it is inferior to this. To capture the enemy's army is better than to destroy it. To subdue the enemy without fighting is the acme of skill. Those skilled in war subdue the enemy's army without battle. They capture his cities without assaulting them, and overthrow his state without protracted operations.[3] History shows that there is no benefit from a long, protracted war. So wars of attrition must be avoided. According to Sun Tzu, the perfect strategy would therefore be to produce a result without any serious fighting. The psychological action itself should be so effective that the enemy surrenders without any physical action being required.

Sun Tzu advised to take advantage of the enemy's unpreparedness, travel by unexpected routes and strike him where he has taken no precautions. He stressed the need for the use of an indirect route to close with the enemy. If you want to gain an advantage over an enemy, lull them into a false sense of security. Sun Tzu advised: 'The enemy must not know where I intend to give battle, he must prepare in a great many places.... And when he prepares everywhere, he will be weak everywhere. He identified the link between speed and surprise, and urged commanders to 'appear at points which the enemy must hasten to defend; march swiftly to places where you are not expected'. Sun Tzu believed that speed, mobility or rapidity and manoeuvre are the essence of warfare.

Furthermore, Sun Tzu's emphasis on deception in warfare underscores the importance of the acquisition and manipulation of information to one's advantage. Information warfare has become the latest buzzword in military establishments. Information warfare as a concept is not new—denying your enemy knowledge of your plans and actions is as old as warfare itself. Sun Tzu would have certainly considered the enemy's electronic nerves the perfect target; so do today's practitioners of information warfare.

FURTHER READING

- Sun Tzu *The Art of War*. Translated by Lionel Giles (London: Luzac and Company, 1910)
- *The Art of War*, Translated by Samuel B. Griffith (Oxford: Oxford University Press, 1963)
- *Sun Tzu, The Art of War*, Translated by Thomas Cleary (Boston: Shambhala Dragon Editions, 1988)
- *The Art of Warfare*. Translated by Roger Ames (Random House, 1993)

3

Kautilya

"The arrow discharged by an archer may or may not kill a single person; but skilful intrigue, devised by wise men, may kill even those who are in the womb." [1]

—**Kautilya, *The Arthaśāstra***

The Author

Ancient Indian tradition describes Kautilya (also known as Chanakya and Vishnugupta) as a native of Taxila (near Peshawar, in modern Pakistan) who had journeyed to Pataliputra (Patna), capital of the Nanda empire, in search of recognition of his learning. There he was insulted by Dhana Nanda, last of the Nanda rulers, and the irascible Brahmin swore vengeance. Pursued by Nanda soldiers, Kautilya escaped into the forests, where he met the young Chandragupta Maurya. Kautilya took Chandragupta to Taxila and schooled him under his tutelage. This was the time when Alexander's legions were invading northwest India. Alexander retreated from the Punjab in 325 B.C., and soon thereafter Chandragupta worked his dynastic revolution, killing Dhana Nanda and becoming the ruler. Indian tradition asserts that Kautilya had masterminded this revolution and continued as Chandragupta's counsellor.

Whatever the nature of accounts of his life, Kautilya was a historical figure and he was responsible for the compilation of a work on polity, which has exerted a profound influence on the development of political ideas in traditional India. The *Arthaśāstra* was believed to have been lost and was known only through references and quotations from it in subsequent works in Sanskrit. It was discovered and published in the 1920s and immediately provoked extensive discussion on the nature of its contents and their implications for understanding the traditional Indian polity.

In Ancient India, war was entirely the endemic reality; peace did not exist.[2] The *Arthaśāstra* is a manual of instruction on the administration of a state and ways to meet challenges to it. Kautilya was a consummate political realist and often gives the impression of being amoral. He viewed the state as a seven-limbed organism which grows in war and whose purpose is to destroy its enemies and extend territory under its control by all means, including aggression against and subversion of its opponents.

The central idea of Kautilya's doctrine, as enunciated in the *Arthaśāstra*, was the prosperity of king and country and the king's quest for victory against rival neighbouring states. The king had to try to defeat his enemies one after another. Kautilya identified seven factors of power, which reinforced his ability to do so. These were the qualities of the king, then of his ministers, his provinces, his city, his treasure, his army, and his allies. The aim of the *Arthaśāstra* was to instruct the king on how to improve the qualities of these factors and undermine those of his enemy's. He showed great understanding of the weakness of human nature while enunciating his doctrine.

The *Arthaśāstra* deals with the many facets of governmental administration and pays special attention to war, preparation for it, and its triumphant execution. The king is the central point of this political structure, and Kautilya's exhortation to him is to be on guard at all times. In its spirit of *realpolitik*, the *Arthaśāstra* deals with a system of politics or principles based on practical rather than moral or ideological considerations. In its elucidation of *machtpolitik*, the *Arthaśāstra* is vociferous in the use of power by a political state in the attainment of its objectives. It thus reveals an altogether surprising aspect of ancient Indian civilisation. Moreover, Kautilya begins his work with the statement that it is "a compendium of almost all the *Arthaśāstras* which have been composed by ancient teachers."[3] In its text are quoted opinions of previous authors and schools of thought.

Kautilya's *Arthaśāstra* is acknowledged by Indian scholars as the most important ancient Indian text on strategy.[4] It is a complex and subtle work, and as such is vulnerable to selective reading and interpretation. Kautilya (c. 350-283 BCE) is still an inspiration to modern Indian strategic and military thought. Some of the classic Indian teachings on strategy might surprise those accustomed to images of a democratic, inclusive, peaceful, modern India. These include mention in the *Arthaśāstra* on pursuit of power through *realpolitik*, the recommended use of offensive force, deception, espionage, treachery, assassination, and deceit, and the view that conquest and the establishment of hegemony is the appropriate policy of the "effective" leader.

A nation-state's strategic affairs have three dimensions – securing its existence (*kśema*), achievement (*yoga*) and promotion of its national goals pertaining to various cultural and politico-economic factors (*vivardhana*). Power, according to the *Arthaśāstra*, is the object of inter-state relations, and "dissension and force" are the natural state of international relations.[5] Power is relative and must be maximised both in absolute and relative terms, for survival and success.[6] However, the *Arthaśāstra* does not form the whole of Indian strategic tradition—there exists a more violent, less compromising tradition as well. Whereas the *Arthaśāstra* emphasises both political flexibility and military mobility, an older tradition represented by another Indian classic text, the epic *Mahabharata*, emphasises annihilation of the enemy through systematic attrition.[7]

The Book

The *Arthaśāstra* comprises fifteen *adikaranas* or books. A verse in the first chapter states that the *Arthaśāstra* has 150 chapters, 180 *prakaranas* (sections devoted to a specific topic) and 6000 verses. The *Arthaśāstra* is predominantly written in prose of the *sutra* (maxim) form with 380 *shlokas* (verses).

Book One involves the king, his training, appointment of ministers and officers of the state, safety and security. Book Two refers to the duties of various executive officers of the state and elaborates the role of the state in agriculture, mining and leisure activities. Book Three deals with law and administration of justice and provides a code of law. Book Four concerns detection and suppression of crime, and control over merchants, artisans, torture and punishment. Book Five is a miscellaneous collection of topics including the salary scale of officials and advice to the chief minister on ensuring continuity of rule on the demise of the ruling monarch. Book Six has two chapters; the first provides a theory of the constituent elements of a state, and the second chapter pertains to foreign policy.

Book Seven elaborates the mandala theory of the circle of states and the six methods of foreign policy that may be used in various situations. Throughout, the ultimate goal is set for the ruler—expansion of kingdom to ensure the well-being of the state. Book Eight enumerates the *vyasanas* or calamities, shortcomings or weaknesses that may affect the functioning of various constituents of a state adversely. Book Nine concerns preparation for war that includes the kinds of troops to mobilise for an expedition, precautions to be adhered to, and dangers to be guarded against. Book Ten is about fighting an enemy and describes the main battle camp, types of battle arrays and different modes of fighting. Book Eleven describes how a *vijigisu* or conqueror should subjugate *samghas* or oligarchies governed by a group of chiefs. Book Twelve shows how a weak king, when threatened by a stronger king, should frustrate the latter's design and ultimately overcome him. Book Thirteen concerns the conquest of an enemy's fortified capital by subterfuge or by fighting. It also describes how the conquered territories should be ruled. Book Fourteen enumerates secret remedies and occult practices. Book Fifteen defines and illustrates the thirty two *tantrayuktis* or methods of treating a subject

The *Arthaśāstra:* A Critique

The *Arthaśāstra* is similar to realist interpretations of *The Art of War* and the texts that communicate the Chinese strategic culture tradition. In the view of some Western scholars, Kautilya offered his treatise as a science of world conquest. According to this interpretation, one either conquers or suffers conquest. "[Kautilya] did not say to himself, 'prepare for war, but hope for peace: but instead, 'prepare for war, and plan for conquest."[8] As far as the means to that end, Kautilya's advocated making treaties (while planning to break them), as well as recommending the use of spies and secret agents to assassinate enemy leaders. On a first reading, there is little in the text that might clearly differentiate it from a *realpolitik* Chinese strategic culture. This leads some to focus on the worst in the classic texts and to overlook their warnings about the dangers of war and the need for prosperity, good governance, and legitimate rule to maintain power.[9]

Perhaps the most commonly cited idea from Kautilya is the concept of *mandalas*, or circles. Those closer in the circle, on the borders of the state, will be enemies. Those farther away will be allies. This discussion of natural enemies and natural allies is consistent with balance-of-power politics (or defensive realism) but is overly mechanistic, however. Kautilya's idea of concentric circles is not meant to be one of fixed geographic relationships. Rather, *mandalas* apply to relationships of power, influence, and interest, not only geographic proximity. Relationships are not so fixed that all border states must be enemies, although Kautilya believed that abutting states were more likely to be enemies or objects of conquest than not. He explicitly advocates conquest and holds the opinion that the best leader is a "conqueror" (*vijigisu*) who actively seeks to maximise power at all times, and constantly prepares for war either actively or passively.[10]

However, Kautilya counsels on matters broader than war alone. He avers that war is dangerous and uncertain, and that if there is no prospect of one's decline relative to an enemy, then peace (while continuing to maximise prosperity) is preferable to war.[11] Thus, generating and sustaining wealth and political legitimacy are critical.[12] Kautilya was also deeply concerned with the moral quality of leaders, welfare of the people, justice, and legitimacy of the regime.[13] Also, justice and legitimacy in foreign policy, as well as military prowess, were necessary for a leader's success.[14]

Most of the contents of the Kautilya's *Arthaśāstra* are distilled from the four *Vedas—Rig Veda, Sama Veda, Yajur Veda*, and *Atharva Veda* and what is regarded as the fifth *Veda*, the *Puranas*, featuring, among numerous stories, myths and legends, the two great epics—the *Ramayana* and the *Mahabharata*, which continue (to this day) to shape thinking and colour political discourse. Considering that India has long been associated with morality, spirituality and pacifistic other-worldliness, the hard-headed, no-nonsense and strictly ends-focused policy approach, packaged in the ancient texts and updated by Kautilya in his codex, is astounding in its clarity, suggesting an alternative basis for a worldview and policies that could serve the country's modern-day interests better. International relations are governed, say the *Vedas*, by 'the law of the fish' (*matsya nyaya*), i.e. of big fish swallowing the small fish until there remains only the hegemon or *chakravartin*, with a realm extending to 'the very ends uninterrupted (so as to) constitute one state and administration up to the seas'.[15]

The study of Kautilya is one of the significant ways in which we can become more conscious about the strategic culture of India. The importance of the concepts and the ways of thinking that the *Arthaśāstra* reveals is useful because in many ways the world which we face today (of multiple states, of several major powers, of an uneven but lumpy distribution of power among those major states, even while the system has one predominant military power), is similar to the world that Kautilya operated in when he built the Mauryan Empire to greatness.

The results of a Kautilyan analysis would not be very different from India's nuclear policy or policy towards other countries. While there are no exact parallels in history, there are certainly ways of thinking conditioned by context and similar circumstance. Though technologies and experiences may be very different from those Kautilya knew, human nature, politics and state behaviour do not appear to have changed so drastically as to be unrecognisable. While theories have multiplied and changed drastically, politics has not altered since Kautilya's time,. The idea of *mandalas*, of the basic functions of the state, of the necessity and justification for the use of force, and of raisons d'état, are part of the popular vocabulary and thinking on politics and international relations in India.

Kautilya underscored the importance of dynamism in the growth of a state. To him passivity was eccentric[16] and the objective of a State was power; not just to control outward behaviour but also the thoughts of one's subjects and one's adversaries. He outlined several precepts that governed the general power of a State:

- Every nation acts to maximise power and self-interest.
- Moral principles have little or no force in the actions amongst nations.
- Alliances are a function of mutuality.
- War and peace are to be considered solely from the perspective of what advantages they provide to the instigator.
- The *'mandala'* premise of foreign policy provides the basis of strategic planning of alliances and a general theory of international relations.
- Diplomacy of any nature is a subtle act of war, in contrast to the Clausewitzian view of war being a continuation of policy.
- Seeking justice is the last desperate resort of the weak.

Kautilya is mainly criticised for his techniques of warfare. He is considered immoral in his iteration of espionage and killing of enemies by secret agents as he did not consider victory by deceit unethical. So long as the ends were met, means deployed did not matter.

Kautilya envisaged various kinds of war to wage, and he advised the ruler to optimally utilise his resources (*prakritis*) in accordance with the *sadgunya* or six measures of foreign policy, selected as appropriate:

- making peace with a treaty (*samdhi*) containing conditions or terms;
- the policy of hostility (*vigraha*);
- the policy of neutrality (*asana*), remaining quiet and not overtly preparing or planning to proceed on a campaign;
- marching on an expedition (*yana*);
- seeking shelter or protection (*samsraya*) with another king or in a fort; and
- the dual policy (*dvaidhbhava*) of peace with one king and hostility with another at the same time.

Complementing these are the *upayas*. which overlap the six measures of foreign policy and can be adapted to any of them. These concepts are adopting a conciliatory attitude (*sama*), placating with rewards and gifts (*dana*), sowing dissensions among enemies (*bheda*), and using force (*danda*).

The kinds of war were:

(a) *Prakashyuddha*, i.e. Open War:[17] This was advocated to be fought in accordance with the norms of *dharmayuddha* or righteous war.

(b) *Kutayuddha*, i.e. Concealed War:[18] This was recommended in circumstances where the *vijigisu* is not superior to the enemy and the terrain and season were not favourable. Various forms of *kutayuddha* are mentioned in the *Arthaśāstra*. Here the conduct of the war involved the use of devious methods as opposed to *dharmayuddha*. It implied that there were no restrictions on its conduct and principles gave way to expediency. However, the conduct of the war still devolved on military principles.

(c) *Tusnimyuddha*, i.e. Silent War:[19] In this kind of war, the use of secret agents was recommended. This war was in sharp contrast to the previous two types of wars. The use of devious methods was its hallmark.

Two other types of war also find mention in Kautilya's *Arthaśāstra*. These are:

(a) *Mantrayuddha*, i.e. Diplomatic War:[20] This was a recommended method for a weaker ruler. It does not refer to actions on the battlefield but off it, and was to be conducted furtively. It involved the use of conciliation (*sama*) and gifts (*dana*) amongst diplomatic efforts as a prelude or precursor to actual fighting. The use of subterfuge was not ruled out.

(b) *Gudhayuddha*, i.e. Secret War:[21] This was a variation of *kutayuddha*. It involved employing irregulars to wage war while outwardly having regular diplomatic ties. It could be akin to cold war norms or proxy war where covert violence, assassination and other means were employed to weaken the enemy.

Kautilya's maxims on tactics and strategy are, at once, wise and sound. He insists throughout on the necessity for constant precaution, on avoidance of risks, on protection by means of energetic defensive measures and vigilant sentries. He emphasises the need for accurate topographical information and recommends the utilisation of natural features in battles, with attention to climatic and meteorological changes. He recognises the absolute necessity of having a reserve in battle. Without a reserve, he categorically maintains, the king should never attempt to fight, "for it is by the reserve force that dispersed troops are collected together."[22]

It should be noted, however, that Kautilya was no warmonger by temperament. If the end could be achieved by non-military methods, even by methods of intrigue, duplicity and fraud, he did not advocate an armed conflict. "When the advantages derivable from peace and war are of equal character, one should prefer peace; for disadvantages, such as the loss of power and wealth, sojourning and sin, are ever attending upon war."[23] Elsewhere, however, in an altogether different context, he says: "Whoever is inferior to another shall make peace with him; whoever is superior in power shall wage war."[24]

War must always serve the larger ends of policy and not be an end in itself; the statesman's objective must always be the betterment of the state as a result of war, not the mere defeat and destruction of the enemy. If war brings both parties to a common ruin, it is bankruptcy of statesmanship. War must be conducted by armed forces; but much more important than the force of arms is the high strategy which saps the enemy's morale and disrupts his forces and brings about his collapse, or takes him to the verge of collapse, before armed attack.

Defence versus Development

Kautilya was aware of the problems caused by financial constraints. National security demanded expansion in spending on infrastructure and in military capability. But an increase in taxes was considered counterproductive, as that would retard long-term economic growth, make taxpayers discontented and prone to be turned against the ruler. He argued that power breeds more power but the challenge was: how to initiate the process with limited resources. His genius lay in offering insights for maintaining independence and becoming prosperous:

- First, economic prosperity strengthened national security and brought happiness to people, but it was not sustainable unless the gains were distributed fairly.
- Second, he emphasised the role of good institutions for internal stability. The rule of law (and not rule by law), is essential for protection of private property rights and constraining the

predatory or extortionary behaviour of rulers and bureaucrats. Internal stability, in turn, is essential for acquisition of knowledge and accumulation of capital.

- Third, he emphasised good governance, i.e. clean, caring and competent administration so that resources were not siphoned off from building infrastructure to personal usage.
- Fourth, a judicious blend of moral and material incentives was necessary to elicit optimum effort from the king at the top to the herdsman at the bottom of the economic pyramid.
- Fifth, changes could be brought only through cooperation and coordination and not through confrontation and coercion.
- Sixth, it was a king's moral duty and in his self-interest to be a loyal servant to his people.

National Security

Kautilya averred that national security was not only important but was also very complex. He approached it meticulously and methodologically. He suggested spying both on foes and friends; making sure the nation was as powerful as any potential adversary (balance of power); provision of physical infrastructure; following a cost-benefit approach in economic matters (but not for national security); and paying enhanced wages to advisers and high ranking defence officers for ensuring honesty, efficiency, loyalty and most importantly, for following a pro-active and dynamic approach. Independence was the most precious thing and was to be defended by all possible means. A nation must be vigilant and well-prepared to defend itself at all times. He emphasised that any and every present or future threat to national security be eliminated at any cost, stating that, "an enemy's destruction shall be brought about even at the cost of great losses in men, material and wealth."[25]

His advice to a king was: "No enemy shall know his secrets. [The king] shall, however, know all his enemy's weaknesses. Like a tortoise, he shall draw in any limb of his that is exposed."[26] Accordingly, "a king shall have his agents in the courts of the enemy, the ally, the Middle and the Neutral kings to spy on the kings as well as their eighteen types of high officials."[27] He added, "He shall always station envoys and clandestine agents in all states of the *mandala*. They shall cultivate those acting against the interests of the conqueror (*vijigisu*) and, while maintaining their own secrecy, destroy repeatedly such inimical persons."[28]

Kautilya continues to warn present and future generations not to get complacent about national security. Clearly, if the adversary has full information and behaves in the same manner, then there would be an arms race. Therefore, Kautilya stated that, "When the degree of progress is the same in pursuing peace and waging war, peace is to be preferred. For, in war, there are disadvantages such as losses, expenses and absence from home."[29]

Kautilya labelled some emotions as 'obstacles' to achieving gains from campaigns. These were "passion, anger, timidity, compassion [leading to aversion to fighting], recoiling from awarding deserved punishment, a lack of higher values, haughtiness, a forgiving nature, thinking of the next world, excessive piety, meanness, abjectness, jealousy, contempt for what one has, wickedness, distrust, fear, negligence, inability to withstand harsh climate (cold, heat or rain) and faith in the auspiciousness of stars and days."[30]

The counsels of the *Arthaśāstra* are based on the assumptions that international politics is anarchical in nature, that rivalry and conflict are inevitable, and that the State's survival requires as much cleverness, dissimulation, deceit, and the employment of covert aggression as raw military and economic power. Undoubtedly, the social, political and economic institutions and conditions prevailing at the time of Kautilya during the 4th century BCE were markedly different from those of today. Yet, Kautilya's proactive, pragmatic and dynamic approach, his insights, concepts, and methodology are as relevant today as they were in his time.

From Kautilya's perspective, permanent peace among states was impossible. In fact, one of the most remarkable aspects of his thought was his view that a state of peace can go hand in hand with one of permanent enmity. Whereas in the Western liberal tradition peace and amity are generally seen as logical complements, Kautilya argued that peace and enmity are equally complementary and are as "natural" an expression of power politics as the forced complementarity of peace and friendship. A state may find it prudent to arrange a truce with an adversary of equal strength, so as to avoid a senseless war in which victory is impossible, but such a truce is temporary in nature and subject to revision according to the fluctuations of the balance of power.

Moreover, such "peace" need not imply a corresponding psychological condition of friendship. Underneath the political truce, enmity is to be continuously cultivated in the psychology of one's State and its long-term strategy, in preparation for the day when it may be possible to attack the unsuspecting adversary and destroy him. Similarly, a weak State may submit peacefully to the hegemony of a stronger one, or find itself courted by a stronger State seeking its support for containing a common adversary, but underlying such "peaceful" relationships is an element of convenience which can easily disappear given the ever-shifting patterns of international relations.

Unconventional/Asymmetric Warfare

Kautilya was well aware of the high costs and unpredictability of regular "open" warfare. Hence, much of his treatise offers detailed advice on how to carry out "covert" or unconventional warfare. It might be carried out in the context of a political strategy in which the statesman, playing the part of a snake charmer, would lull the adversary into passivity by means of a non-aggression pact or an agreement defining spheres of influence.[31]

No serious study of unconventional warfare can avoid the morally and politically problematical question of whether democracies should "answer fire with fire", i.e. engage in selective unconventional warfare of their own as a means of compelling an adversary to desist from its own unconventional warfare efforts. If economic and diplomatic sanctions have proven ineffective, if the mechanisms of international law and organisation are unavailable or have failed, if direct war and conventional military options are unadvisable because of their high costs, unconventional warfare may be the appropriate instrument with which a democratic society should defend itself against an adversary's strategies of violent peace. A resort to unconventional warfare under such circumstances serves the dual purposes of defence against the existing attack and deterrence to future ones.

World of Surveillance

Surveillance of the enemy is as old as humanity. From Sun Tzu's *Art of War* to Kautilya's *Arthaśāstra*, rulers have attached great significance to intelligence not only about the enemy but citizen attitudes towards power. The motivation of the rulers has not changed, but the means to conduct surveillance have changed dramatically and technological means to gather private and secret information have grown exponentially. The rise of terrorism has offered justification for expanded surveillance to the detriment of privacy of citizens. One of the unintended consequences of the globalisation in communications has been to empower individuals to expose secrets and attract attention to any issue that may trouble them. A leaf could be taken out of Kautilya's treatise on the principles involved.

Internal Security Management

Kautilya wrote that a state could be pushed into peril by four types of threats and challenges—internal, external, externally-supported internal and internally-supported external. He emphasised that of these four types, internal threats should be indispensably dealt with adequate and immediate attention. He averred that internal troubles, including revolts, rebellions, sabotages, subversions and so on, are far more serious and harmful than external threats and challenges. The most dangerous enemy is the enemy within. Kautilyan assertions on internal security and his views on a well-crafted grand strategy for the management of internal security affairs have great value in the changing domestic, regional and global scenarios of the 21st century. It is primarily based on the fact that relative freedom from insecurity germinated by harmful threats and challenges emanating from internal sources or conflicts—with or without outside support, is a necessity of every country and society.

An analysis of most insurgencies in the world shows that Kautilya was accurate in his belief that the greatest cause of insurgencies was societal discontent and he advocated that the state must attach great importance to the well-being of the people for, "if they become impoverished, they become greedy and rebellious." He also averred that "an internal rebellion is more dangerous than an external threat because it is like nurturing a viper in one's bosom."[32]

Kautilya described types of rebellions (insurgencies) and classified their seriousness based on the affected region and identity of their sponsors. Similarities in methods used today and those espoused by Kautilya are striking wherein he proposed the use of four instruments of state power—*Sama* or Conciliation, *Bheda* or Dissension, *Danda* or Force and *Dana* or Gifts, which are used by states even today. Although application of his principles would depend on the circumstances of a case, his codex gives us a basic framework for planning a counter-insurgency campaign.

A comparable peril against which a state must guard is the tendency to allow individual components of state power to fragment the making and execution of policy. For Kautilya, whose emphasis is on the integrated nature of state power, it would be an absurdity for the administrative, economic, military and intelligence assets of a state to be deployed without a proper coherent vision and understanding of the common goals they seek to achieve. The individual components of state power, if divided and operating at cross-purposes, would breed chaos and indiscipline within the state. The synthesising element is that of leadership coupled with political, bureaucratic, military, and intelligence assets. Without effective leadership, disorder will prevail within the state apparatus and gravely diminish the ability of the state to either control or effectively respond to challenges.

In situations of urban warfare (against a fortified enemy city), Kautilya explicitly stated that indiscriminate bombing (use of fire) would be counterproductive—"...fire shall not be used at all. For fire is a divine calamity whose effects are unpredictable; it is a destroyer of uncountable numbers of people and wealth. Even when captured, such a fort would only give rise to further losses." The applicability to modern-day urban counter-insurgency is implicit—use of firepower would not work in an urban environment as a military victory would leave a combat zone broken and the population distraught.

Military Organisation and Administration

Chandragupta Maurya had a large standing army and an efficient war office supervised it. It was divided into four arms i.e. *padati* (infantry), *ashva* (cavalry), *ratha* (chariots) and *hasti* (elephants). These four components headed by their respective *adyakshas* or superintendents were together called the *chaturangabala*, or the four-limbed army. This organisation has little relevance today as modern armies have many more components and organisations. Even the command and administrative structure has metamorphosed, though the hierarchal system remains. What remains of interest is that Kautilya, in his time, had delineated the responsibilities of commanders at each level for maintaining discipline, training and equipping as well as the disposition of forces in battle formations, according to the envisaged tactics.

Kautilya recognised that an army is dependent on finance for its upkeep. He averred that finance is necessary to undertake any state endeavour and is the chief means for both *dharma* (righteous duty) and *kama* (enjoyment). He attached importance to the necessity for regular and liberal scales of pay for the army. Also, an army must feel that it enjoyed an honourable place in society; otherwise, its morale would suffer and it could not remain efficient.

Kautilya warns against calamities which adversely affect the army like not giving due honours, insufficient salaries and emoluments, low morale, etc. He makes an incisive observation that an unhonoured army, an unpaid army, or an exhausted army will fight if honoured, paid and allowed to relax but a dishonoured army with resentment in its heart will not do so.

Warfare implies systematic military operations. It is distinguished above all by one identifying characteristic—organisation. Kautilya's most striking doctrine is his discussion of planning a campaign. He describes the factors to be considered before the king decides that it is in the state's interest to commence a campaign:

(a) Relative strengths of power, place and time.
(b) Seasons for marching on a campaign.
(c) Employment of troops.
(d) Revolts and possibility of a rebellion in the rear.
(e) Calculation of losses, expenses.
(f) Likely dangers of treachery.
(g) Assessment of dangers.
(h) Overcoming of dangers.

Kautilya regarded the period before the actual fighting began as critical to the outcome. It was vital that the ruler and his advisors be able and willing to undertake a dispassionate and rational appreciation of the total assets of their state in relation to the enemy (or enemies), modified by the contributions of allies.

Kautilya understood the rationale for strong armed forces and enunciated many military strategies. He does not make much distinction between military strategy and statecraft as he believed that warfare is an extension and an integral part of statecraft.

In today's world, the challenges of global security are no different from those that vexed the Mauryan Empire in 300 BCE. A cogent and dispassionate analysis of the *Arthaśāstra* reveals stark similarities between the problems faced by Kautilya's ideal state and the modern scourge of terrorism and insurgencies. Present day warfare adheres to ancient patterns. The truism that "those who forget the lessons of history are condemned to repeat it" applies in military affairs. If a society seeks to live in peace, it should be prepared for war; a unilateral desire for peace cannot ensure peace.

The *Arthaśāstra is* testimony to the constant and unchanging nature of war. Studies of military history show that certain features of conflict and warfare constantly recur; that relationships between type of action and success often remain the same; that certain circumstances and moments have, time and time again, proved decisive. The past being a prologue underscores the relevance and significance of the *Arthaśāstra*. It also underscores an ancient verity with regard to the relationship of a state and its society—that nothing can be crushed by a blow from without until it is ready to perish from decay within.

Conclusion

There is a palpable tendency for foreign policy to lag behind its rapidly expanding economic interests. A realist analysis of foreign policy and security strategy suggests that a country must live up to its potential. The general exclusion of the military from decision-making hinders a nation from becoming a power and the use of the military as an instrument of policy.

India's history highlights that a crucial requirement for developing a grand strategy is an integrative, coordinative state. Recognising grand strategy lessons from a country's history will assist defence reform initiatives. There is need for a critical investigation of the *Arthaśāstra* with an objective of making it relevant to today's conditions. It would bring out the true worth of the *Arthaśāstra* and also situate it at its rightful place in the body of strategic thought.

FURTHER READING

- Kautilya, *The Kautilya Arthaśāstra*, edited and translated by R. P. Kangle, *Part* 2. (Delhi: Motilal Banarsidass, 1965)
- R.P. Kangle. *The Kautiliya Arthasastra, Part 3, A Study* (Delhi: Motilal Banarsidass, 1965)
- Somnath Dhar, *Kautilya and the Arthaśāstra* (New Delhi: Marwah Publications, 1981)
- T.N. Ramaswamy, *Essentials of Indian Statecraft: Kautilya's Arthaśāstra for Contemporary Readers* (New Delhi: Munshiram Manoharlal, 1962)
- Kautilya. *The Arthaśāstra.* Edited and translated by L.N. Rangarajan (New Delhi: Penguin Books, 1992)

4

Machiavelli

"That which is good for the enemy harms you, and that which is good for you harms the enemy."[1]

—**Machiavelli, *The Art of War***

The Author

Niccolò Machiavelli (1469-1527) was a Florentine historian, politician, military strategist, and humanist. He is best known today for his political treatise, *The Prince*. In it, he wrote about the ways an aspiring prince might build a principality and how an existing prince might maintain control. While perhaps a lesser-known work, his *Art of War* (*Dell'arte della Guerra*) places Machiavelli among other well-known military theorists, such as Sun Tzu and Carl von Clausewitz, whose writings about military theory and practice have many similarities with Machiavelli's. There are also remarkable similarities with the *Arthaœstra* in his writings.

Niccolò Machiavelli's *Art of War* is one of the world's great classics of military and political theory. Praised by the finest military minds in history and said to have influenced Frederick the Great and Napoleon, the *Art of War* is essential reading for anyone who wants to understand the history and theory of war—and for readers of *The Prince* who seek to explore more fully the connection between war and politics in Machiavelli's thought.

The works of Niccolò Machiavelli are *The Prince, Discourses on Livy,* and the *Art of War*. Machiavelli dedicated his treatise *The Prince* to the ruler of Florence, Lorenzo de Medici. This work is the first detailed analysis of the art of power. Regarding the qualities required of the Prince, Machiavelli wrote that he should be merciful, lenient, humane, honest and religious, but most important of all is to look like he possesses all these qualities.

Niccolò Machiavelli, along with Carl von Clausewitz, Antoine Henri de Jomini and Basil Liddell Hart are the doyens of the continental school, which is concerned with ground warfare between armies and has historically been the major instrument of geopolitical, military strategy. It has also been the main influence on the shape of warfare in the 20th century. Machiavelli, Jomini and Clausewitz are described as the strategists of 'offensive war.'

On military strategy, Machiavelli said that if diplomacy failed, war was a natural extension of the policy. The *Art of War* also stresses the need for state militia and promotes the concept of an armed citizenry. Machiavelli believed that the whole society, religion, science, and art were based on security.

Machiavelli is said to have laid the foundations of military strategy. The politico-strategic environment before Machiavelli was characterised by personal wars of kings and princes, temporary private armies, poorly trained soldiers who were often mercenaries, the wars of the Crusades, endless sieges and inconclusive battles. Writing in an era of 'might is right', when every large state believed in the expansion of its territory and power by the use of force, Machiavelli was the first political thinker to grasp the competitive nature of the global system. He saw politics as a struggle for survival between growing and expanding nations in which wars were natural and necessary. He concluded that the existence of a nation depended on its capacity for war. He believed that political institutions must be organised in such a way as to create favourable preconditions for the functioning of the military. This theme dominates all of Machiavelli's works. In the *Art of War* he disassociated warfare from religious and ethical inhibitions and related it to constitutional, economic and political factors. The defence of a state was the responsibility not of a special privileged group or the ruler but the concern of all of society was the first lesson Machiavelli drew from his study of warfare in the Middle Ages. His advocacy of conscription assigned Machiavelli a prominent place in the development of military thought. Thus he foresaw what would happen in the future.

The Book

The key elements of Machiavelli's thought are: [2]

- War is an important activity in political life.
- Struggles and uncertainties shape the character and methods of war.
- The aim of war must be the total defeat of the enemy.
- Wars must be short and sharp. They must be ended as quickly as possible with the attainment of a definite result.
- Since everything depends on the outcome of the battle, everything possible must be done to ensure victory, including the full use of forces even if the enemy seems to be of inferior strength.
- A decisive battle should be the aim of every military campaign, and every military campaign must be a planned and coordinated operation.
- Command must be in the hands of one person.
- Military success depends on order and discipline.
- There should be a close and harmonious relationship between the political and military authorities and institutions.
- Mercenaries cannot ensure victory; a state must have its own 'proper army'.

The book has core of place and history. The problems Machiavelli discussed are not bound to any historical period. For example, during the French Revolution, military organisations and the conduct of war assumed new forms due to the growth of engineering and technology. But still Machiavelli's ideas—the establishment of military institutions and conducting war in accordance with rational, valid rules—retained their vitality. It is noteworthy that Clausewitz, who was extremely critical and contemptuous of other military writers, conceded that Machiavelli 'had a very sound judgement in military matters.'[3] Despite the new features that Clausewitz introduced, and which were outside the framework of Machiavelli's thought, he agreed with Machiavelli that the validity of any analysis of military problems depended on a correct conception of the nature of war.

The *Art of War* describes how an army should be trained and organised. Machiavelli was one of the first writers who talked about size, composition, weapons, moral and logistical capabilities of the army. The work is focused on the following elements:

- Selection of soldiers.
- Preparation of the army.
- Ways to maintain order.
- Leading battles.
- Clothing during war.
- Troops strength.
- Qualities and actions of the commander.
- Leadership of the army.
- Provisions.
- Encampment of troops.
- Methods of attacking and defending fortifications.
- General rules of warfare.
- Possible penalties.
- Secrecy in writing and transmission of letters and others.

Art of War was published in 1521, nearly a decade after the mercenary captain Fabrizio Colonna led troops backed by the Spanish house of Aragon to victory over Florence in 1512. Medici rule was restored, wresting power away from Machiavelli's political patron, Piero Soderini. Machiavelli was subsequently tried for conspiracy, tortured, and imprisoned. In 1513, he wrote *The Prince*, which was dedicated to Lorenzo di Piero de' Medici, grandson of the great arts patron, Lorenzo "the Magnificent" de' Medici.[4] After his release from prison, Machiavelli joined a political discussion group that met in the *Orti Oricellari*, the Rucellai family gardens. These gardens were an important meeting place for young Florentine humanists and aristocrats.

The *Art of War* opens with a gathering of friends to discuss politics, philosophy, and literature. Book I outlines the deplorable condition into which the military had fallen. In Book II, Fabrizio examines the training, organisation, and arming of his proposed citizen's militia. In Book III, a description of classical battle formations and methods is outlined. Included is the examination of a model battle following the lessons from a previous description of Ancient Greek and Roman Methods. The topics of Book IV are tactics and planning during and after a battle. The Order of March is covered in Book V, encampment and the welfare of troops is the topic of Book VI, and the defence and attack of towns is outlined in Book VII.

Machiavelli used a classical-style literary device in which four young nobles took turns asking questions to a primary spokesman, who exercised the role of the wise master. This functioned much like the discussions between Socrates and his students in Plato's *Republic*. The four young interlocutors in *Art of War* were Cosimo Rucellai, Luigi Alamanni, Zanobi Buondelmonti, and Battista della Palla.[5]

As the principal interlocutor, Machiavelli chose Fabrizio Colonna as the "wise master" to lead the dialogue. The choice of Fabrizio is somewhat puzzling given Fabrizio's conquest of Florence in 1512 and Machiavelli's resultant loss of status and imprisonment. In addition, Fabrizio was a well-known *condottiere* (mercenary captain). One of the primary themes of *Art of War* is the preference for citizen-soldiers over mercenary troops. Machiavelli wrote dialogues for Fabrizio that expressed emphatic opposition to the use of mercenary troops and great disdain for foreign powers meddling in Italian affairs. According to Fabrizio's character in Book I, "So a well-ordered city ought to want this study of war to be used in times of peace for training and in times of war for necessity and for glory, and the public alone left to use it as an art, as Rome did. And any citizen who has another end in such a practice is not good; and any city governed otherwise is not well ordered."[6] One would not expect the real Fabrizio to condemn his own occupation as a *condottiere* in such a way.

Machiavelli, through the subjects covered in the *Art of War*, attempted to revive classical military thought. His objective, as mentioned, was to strengthen a weak and prostrate Italy.

The *Art of War* by Machiavelli describes how an army should be trained and organised. Machiavelli was one of the first writers who talked about size, composition, weapons, moral and logistical capabilities of the army. On military strategy, Machiavelli averred that if diplomacy failed, war was a natural extension of the policy.

To Machiavelli, war is simply a means to a political end. War becomes an arm of the political machine. The *Art of War* is the summarisation of Machiavelli's political doctrine. In it he defines a functional unity between politics and war. Machiavelli evidently believed that the basic relationships between war and politics are:

1. Military power is the foundation of civil society.
2. A well-ordered military establishment is an essential unifying element in civil society.
3. A policy of military aggrandisement contributes to the stability and longevity of civil society.
4. The military art and the political art possess a common style.
5. A military establishment tends to reflect the qualities of the civil society of which it is a part.[7]

The Prince

Machiavelli's *The Prince* is a scientific book because it conveys a general teaching that is based on reasoning from experience which sets forth that reasoning."[8] The text is meant to teach. Its message is meant for the rulers of the Italian peninsula in general and Lorenzo de Medici in particular.

The Prince is structured in four parts:

1. The different kinds of principalities.
2. The prince and his enemies.
3. The prince and his subjects or friends.
4. Prudence and chance.

The book opens as a scientific treatise, detached from its subject matter but ends with a call to arms, very much connected to its goal—the strengthening of the Italian princes and states to drive out the invaders. *The Prince* is a blueprint for the liberation of Italy. Machiavelli is a patriot and the teachings of *The Prince,* no matter how repulsive, are meant to achieve this goal. The end justifies the means holds true throughout the text. It is also one of the early books on educating the leader. Machiavelli was not the leader but was the educator of the leader.

Art of War

To liberate Italy was to conquer Italy and the conqueror, according to Machiavelli, must spare no means to attain this end. A policy of iron, poison, and treachery must be followed. In essence a revolution on thinking about right and wrong must begin and Machiavelli hoped to spark this revolution with the text. Many means are suggested to reach the end.

The fundamental point of *The Prince* was concerning the prophets in general, Machiavelli remarks that all armed prophets have conquered and the unarmed prophets have failed.[9] This coincides directly with the ultimate message of *The Prince* which is that the end justifies the means in creating a strong Italy.

Machiavelli's treatment of the relationships between war and politics, civilians and the military, and technology and tactics is incisive. Clearly laying out the fundamentals of military organisation and strategy, Machiavelli marshals a veritable armoury of precepts, prescriptions, and examples about topics such as how to motivate your soldiers and demoralise the enemy's, avoid ambushes, and gain the tactical and strategic advantage in countless circumstances.

Machiavelli used ancient sources to find fundamental continuities in human behaviour and political balances of power. *Art of War* is replete with such connections. In addition, the work follows a great tradition of classical military manuals, some of which Machiavelli read and used as background to write *Art of War*.

From all of these sources, and from his own experiences, Machiavelli derived that war is an art. It is a specialised type of knowledge and expertise that Machiavelli believed was vital. Machiavelli recommended that a prince should make the art of war his principal art. Politics is also an art. The prince's study of the art of war is thus a fusion of the two arts.

In the preface of *Art of War*, Machiavelli makes it clear that his primary aim in writing his military treatise was to show a link to both arts and their effect on civilian and military lives. The bulk of *Art of*

War is Machiavelli's attempt to explain the link between war and politics. One might say that Machiavelli's understanding of the interconnectedness of war and politics is a truth now recognised across time and around the world.

Comments

Like Sun Tzu's Moral Law, Books I-II of Machiavelli's *Art of War* describe the link between citizens and the military, civic virtue, a well-ordered principality or republic, and the raising and training of the troops. Like Heaven and Earth, Books III-V describe the spatial arrangement of a battle, including geography and logistics. Machiavelli accomplished this with a description of a mock battle in Book III. While Machiavelli discussed issues similar to Sun Tzu's 'The Commander' in Books I-II, 'Method and Discipline' are the key topics of Books VI-VII of Machiavelli's work, wherein he discussed encampment of troops, specific methods of attacking and defending fortifications, and general rules of warfare. While there is no conclusive evidence to show that Machiavelli read Sun Tzu's *Art of War*, the similarities are quite striking.

Perhaps the similarities between Machiavelli's and Sun Tzu's treatises testify, at least in part, to the universality of warfare and the link between war and politics. Nearly echoing Sun Tzu, Machiavelli wrote that one should seek "to honour and reward the virtuous, ...to esteem the modes and orders of military discipline, to constrain the citizens to love one another," and other such actions that made the ancients praiseworthy.[10] Like Sun Tzu, Machiavelli wrote about the qualities of a good ruler and the relationship between the ruler and his subjects in a republic or principality. *The Prince* was his most obvious attempt at this. Machiavelli commanded the Florentine army against Pisa, giving him first-hand experience in both war and politics, as well as with the relationship between ruler and subject. As if taking advice from Sun Tzu, Machiavelli used his well-trained infantry to checkmate the Pisans, winning as a result of military strategy and organisation rather than a major battle. It was a military and a political victory.

In the first book of *Art of War*, Fabrizio distinguishes between two meanings of *art of war*: the "practice" of war on the one hand, and the "profession" of war on the other hand. To make war into a profession,

Fabrizio declares, is no way to live honestly, and no republic or well-ordered kingdom would consent to "any of its citizens or subjects" turning war into a profession. Thus in a well-ordered city, the art of war is not a career or profession but solely a *practice* or an *exercise*.[11]

Machiavelli effectively used, and advocated through Fabrizio's dialogue, what we now call mobile infantry warfare. This mode of warfare successfully combined the tactics of the Roman legions with the artillery available in the early 16th century. In the mock battle in Book III of *Art of War*, Fabrizio arrayed his army in much the same way the Romans would have. However, Fabrizio took into account the light and heavy artillery, such as arquebuses (an early form of long-barrelled personal gun) and cannons. Of the cavalry's method of dealing with an enemy that uses guns, Fabrizio stated, "The best remedy for [arquebuses] is to come to hands quickly; and if in the first assault some die, some always die. And a good captain and a good army do not have to fear."[12] Machiavelli employed infantry in coordination with artillery to take Pisa in 1509.

Two centuries after Machiavelli's death, Prussian military strategist Carl von Clausewitz wrote at length about the influence of the "political object" on the "military object," the relationship between war and politics. Clausewitz's famous axiom, "war is nothing but a continuation of political intercourse with an admixture of other means," expressed his understanding of the link between war and politics.[13]

One of the most challenging political and military powers with which Machiavelli had to contend was the Church. Machiavelli blamed the increased use of mercenary troops in Italy on the Catholic Church's effort to make the papacy a temporal power. In *The Prince*, he explained: "Thus Italy having fallen almost entirely into the hands of the Church and a few republics, and the priests and other citizens not being accustomed to bear arms, they began to hire foreigners as soldiers."[14] The Church was an ever-present social and cultural force in Florence and throughout Europe as a consequence of the importance of religion in European society, but its temporal authority was great enough to make it a formidable military and political power as well. Rather than viewing the Church as only a spiritual force, Machiavelli included the Church in his military and political calculations. The pope who reigned at the time *Art of War* was published was Giovanni di Lorenzo de' Medici, reigning as Leo X. The Medici family loomed large as a political, economic, and military force, with connections throughout Europe. Leo X granted indulgences to those who donated to rebuild St. Peter's Basilica, he extended the Spanish Inquisition into Portugal, and he excommunicated Martin Luther. From Machiavelli's perspective, Leo's papacy was more about politics and power than about religion.

The mixture of religion into the dynamic of war and politics was nothing new for Machiavelli who believed that the function of religion was to serve politics, inspiring politically constructive attitudes and behaviour, civic virtue, and military valour. Machiavelli's advice in *The Prince* is to rule through cruelty, miserliness, and deception if necessary. Machiavelli stated that it is better for the prince to be feared than to be loved, when only one of them is possible, so long as the prince avoids being hated.[15]

Machiavelli's view of religion in relation to war and politics was no doubt created by the condition of Italy before and during his lifetime. In reference to the expansion of mercenary soldiers due to the pope's quest for a temporal kingdom, Machiavelli felt that arms did not dignify the pope as a man of religion.

The key events that shaped Machiavelli's life found their way into his analysis of the military and civilian spheres of life in *Art of War*. Experience taught him that the citizen-soldier was preferable to the mercenary as a means of mitigating the dangers to society posed by foreign interference. Classical texts, particularly from the Romans, provided examples of civic virtue that were sorely lacking in Machiavelli's time. As a humanist, Machiavelli felt a connection to the classics, so he used them to make sense of his own time and to develop strategies to make the best of his situation. Just as the writings of Julius Caesar, Sun Tzu, Clausewitz, and others were unique to their particular historical era and geographic location, and can be best understood in that context, Machiavelli's *Art of War* is best understood in the context of Italy in the early 16th century. *Art of War* represents Machiavelli's effort to make sense of his world, the complex interaction of war, politics, and humanism in Renaissance Europe, as well as his effort to use classical texts to encourage his readers to learn from the ancient examples and return to the classical modes of warfare, statecraft, and civic virtue.

The main theme of the lengthy combat report is that battles are won by bodies in motion, bodies that can spread out, return to the flanks, envelop and entrap their opponents, enmesh them in their own plans, and overcome them through superior control over movement. Machiavelli's successful army does not have the largest number of troops or the best equipment; rather, it controls and governs the battlefield through the soldiers' bodies and their location in space. Fabrizio's troops manage and orchestrate the space of the battlefield. What seals the outcome is the asymmetry between the control over bodies in space and the adversaries' lack of mobility and proper orchestration of their movement. Thus, battle choreography requires not only command skills but a sensibility for what bodies can do and how they move in space.

Machiavelli remarks that he has just composed a little work on princes—a "whimsy"—and thus lightly introduces arguably the most famous book on politics ever written, the work that was to give the name Machiavellian to the teaching of worldly success through scheming deceit.

Presciently, Machiavelli warns that,

> *"It ought to be remembered that there is nothing more difficult to take in hand, more perilous to conduct, or more uncertain in its success, than to take the lead in the introduction of a new order of things. Because the innovator has for enemies all those who have done well under the old conditions, and lukewarm defenders in those who may do well under the new. This coolness arises partly from fear of the opponents, who have the laws on their side, and partly from the incredulity of men, who do not readily believe in new things until they have had a long experience of them.*[16]

Some Quotes of Relevance

Some quotations at the end of the dialogue, in Book 7, from *Dell'arte della guerra—Art of War,* are worthy of note:

- No proceeding is better than that which you have concealed from the enemy until the time you have executed it. To know how to recognise an opportunity in war, and take it, benefits you more than anything else.

- Nature creates few men brave; industry and training makes many.
- Discipline in war counts more than fury.[17]
- A prince must have no other objective, no other thought, nor take up any profession but that of war, its methods and its discipline, for that is the only art expected of a ruler.[18]
- The two most essential foundations for any state, whether it be old or new, or both old and new, are sound laws and sound military forces. Now, since the absence of sound laws assures the absence of sound military forces, while the presence of sound military forces indicates the presence of sound laws as well, I shall forego a consideration of laws and discuss military forces instead.[19]
- Whoever is more vigilant in observing the designs of the enemy in war, and endures much hardship in training his army, will incur fewer dangers, and can have greater hope for victory.
- Never lead your soldiers into an engagement unless you are assured of their courage, know they are without fear, and are organised, and never make an attempt unless you see they hope for victory.
- It is better to defeat the enemy by hunger than with steel; in such victory fortune counts more than virtue.
- To know how to recognise an opportunity in war, and take it, benefits you more than anything else.
- If some on the side of the enemy desert to come to your service, if they be loyal, they will always make you a great acquisition; for the forces of the adversary diminish more with the loss of those who flee, than with those who are killed, even though the name of the fugitives is suspect to the new friends, and odious to the old.
- It is better in organising an engagement to reserve great aid behind the front line, than to spread out your soldiers to make a greater front.

- He is overcome with difficulty, who knows how to recognise his forces and those of the enemy.
- The virtue of the soldiers is worth more than a multitude, and the site is often of more benefit than virtue.
- New and speedy things frighten armies, while the customary and slow things are esteemed little by them: you will therefore make your army experienced, and learn (the strength) of a new enemy by skirmishes, before you come to an engagement with him.
- Whoever pursues a routed enemy in a disorganised manner, does nothing but become vanquished from having been a victor.
- Whoever does not make provisions necessary to live (eat), is overcome without steel.
- Whoever trusts more in cavalry than in infantry, or more in infantry than in cavalry, must settle for the location.
- If you want to see whether any spy has come into the camp during the day, have no one go to his quarters.
- Change your proceeding when you become aware that the enemy has foreseen it.
- Counsel with many on the things you ought to do, and confer with few on what you do afterwards.
- When soldiers are confined to their quarters, they are kept there by fear or punishment; then when they are led by war (they are led) by hope and reward.
- Good Captains never come to an engagement unless necessity compels them, or the opportunity calls them.
- Act so your enemies do not know how you want to organise your army for battle, and in whatever way you organise them, arrange it so that the first line can be received by the second and by the third.
- In a battle, never use a company for some other purpose than what you have assigned it to, unless you want to cause disorder.
- Accidents are remedied with difficulty, unless you quickly take the facility of thinking.
- Men, steel, money, and bread, are the sinews of war; but of these

four, the first two are more necessary, for men and steel find money and bread, but money and bread do not find men and steel.

- The unarmed rich man is the prize of the poor soldier.
- Accustom your soldiers to despise delicate living and luxurious clothing.

Though Niccolò Machiavelli is best known for *The Prince*, his guidebook on ruling an Italian city-state, for a long time after his death, his *Art of War* was better known and more influential (alongside his *Discourses on Livy*, both of which were written after *The Prince* but published before). *Art of War* is often deemed a technical manual rather than a conceptual engagement with the question of war. The further the work goes on, the more the text becomes specialised and seemingly esoteric, which has led some scholars to dismiss *Art of War* as dull and tedious. Yet hidden underneath lies a significant rethinking of war and of the politics-war nexus.

Contrary to *The Prince*, which frames the relationship between war and the art of the state in abstract and sometimes stipulative terms, *Art of War* puts forward what we might call a sociological lens that renders war as a social practice. Through such lessons as how to set up an encampment or on how wide the ditch around a fortification ought to be, *Art of War* shifts attention to the spatial coordinates of warfare, its scales and proportions. The emphasis on the seemingly esoteric details of military organisation indicate that if the art of war is "the only art of concern to one who commands," then it is not because war teaches a prince how to command, but for other reasons.

The universal acknowledgment of the *Art of War*'s status as a classic of strategic thought is tempered by criticism of its speciûc military analyses and prescriptions. Critics attribute to its author countless errors of military judgment, most of which relate to technology, battleûeld tactics, and military professionalism. Virtually all of the criticisms are based on the assumption that Machiavelli was the unwitting victim of three related prejudices: an uncritical preference for all things ancient (and especially Roman), a dread of any form of military professionalism, and the quaint conviction that gunpowder technology—and technological innovation in general—was a factor of negligible signiûcance or a pernicious trend to be resisted. However, for Machiavelli, innovations in military technologies were useful and necessary, but they did not obviate the need for human excellence.

FURTHER READING

- Christopher S. Celenza, *Machiavelli: A Portrait* (Cambridge, MA: Harvard University Press, 2015).
- Marcia L. Colish, "Machiavelli's *Art of War*: A Reconsideration," *Renaissance Quarterly* 51, no. 4 (Winter 1998), pp. 1151-1168. http://www.jstor.org/stable/2901963
- Christopher Lynch, Interpretive Essay on *Art of War*, by Niccolò Machiavelli, 179-226. (Chicago: The University of Chicago Press, 2003).
- Niccolò Machiavelli, *Art of War*. Translated and edited by Christopher Lynch (Chicago: The University of Chicago Press, 2003).

5

Clausewitz

"No one starts a war—or rather, no one in his senses ought to do so—without first being clear in his mind what he intends to achieve by that war and how he intends to conduct it."[1]

—Carl von Clausewitz, *On War*

Introduction

Libraries are filled with works and critiques analysing, examining, deconstructing, explaining, glorifying or reviling Prussian General Carl von Clausewitz's seminal work *On War*. The work is based on rigorous analysis of the wars of the 18th and early 19th century, which were wars between nation-states. With the rise of intra-state conflicts, civil wars and terrorism in the last three decades, some consider *On War* as a relic from the past. According to this school violent conflicts emerge less between states; and the lines between state and non-state actors are blurred.

On War is a standard source for those interested in war and armed conflict. Most scholars agree that *On War* can generally be characterised in two diametrically opposed but accurate ways. First, it is seen as 'the one truly great book on war yet written'[2] and second, as 'often quoted but little read'.[3] Overall, in spite of its flaws and sometimes contradictory insights, it is one of the very few books that seeks to present a theory of war.

On War was written by Clausewitz (1780-1831) after the Napoleonic wars between 1816 and 1830 and published posthumously by his wife in 1832. It is an important military treatise and has a significant impact on strategic thinking. The book contains a range of historical examples in which Frederick the Great and Napoleon are central figures.

'War does not belong in the realm of art and science; rather it is a part of man's social existence', wrote Clausewitz.[4] According to him, war should never be seen as an end in itself but as an instrument of politics: "War is not merely a political act, but also a real political instrument, a continuation of politics by other means". He associated "strategy" with art and "tactics" with science. Clausewitz argued that the main task of an army is to enter into battle and destroy the main forces of the enemy in a decisive battle. Thus, the overall strategy must be focused on the destruction of the opposing army.

A Historical Perspective

Carl von Clausewitz's legitimacy as an astute observer of war emanates from his extensive experience both on the battlefield and in academia. Born in 1781, he was the son of a Prussian lieutenant. At the tender age of twelve, he was introduced to the bleak realities of war while serving in the Prussian army as a lance corporal. Prussia was engulfed in a war with France that would last twenty-three years and would leave an enduring impression on his mind.

One of the prevailing lessons he learned early on was that war had no single standard of excellence or set of rules to follow, but rather, was a matter of chance, fraught with outside influences, but dominated by politics. In his writing, he would insist that the political aspect of war should never be forgotten when planning a campaign; indeed, the political aim should hold prominence in every aspect of planning.

In the latter half of the 1790's, as part of a regiment that included a member of the royal family, Clausewitz was granted access to the library of Prince Henry, brother of Frederick the Great. Clausewitz's intellectual prowess, combined with this exposure, sparked a passion to learn as well as to be an educator.

In the early 1800's, Clausewitz graduated from Berlin's War College at the head of his class. There, he met his future intellectual mentor and teacher, Gerhard Scharnhorst, who would shape Clausewitz's ideas about social and political interplay in war. Scharnhorst, a renowned scholar, soldier and politician, would guide Clausewitz's assertion that the theorist wishing to understand the state and the nature of war "must never allow his thoughts to diverge far from the element central to each—power in politics, violence in war."[5]

Clausewitz would also gain insight and maturity of vision from studying the works of other noted theorists. He recognised their contributions, studied their writings, contemplated their strategic genius, but still felt that existing theory lacked sufficient emphasis on the elements of human intelligence and will.

First published in Germany in 1832, *On War*, consists of eight books with more than seven hundred pages. He gathered, read and studied widely until 1825 when he had completed six of his eight books and drafted the remaining two. In 1827, however, he began to expand and refine much of his manuscript, finishing only the first chapter of Book One.[6] He was intimately involved in development of his thoughts and coalescing of ideas when he died of cholera, while still editing and revising his work. His untimely death, brought an abrupt end to a work that has been unrivalled in the West. Perhaps his continual inner struggle to provide a theory that could not be wrapped in a strict formulaic model gives Clausewitz that human quality that allows the modern student of war theory to identify and find relevance in *On War* and that same struggle gave his work timelessness. Clausewitz is perhaps cited more often than any other theorist of war. His combination of experience and analytical rigour has allowed him to speak with an unaltered voice throughout the ages.

Clausewitz was one of a rare breed of soldiers. Not only was he a synthesiser and innovator in matters relating to warfare and its conduct but also, he was a practitioner. His military career was remarkable both for its longevity (almost 43 years) and for the breadth of its experience. More important, it spanned two remarkably different eras of warfare. As a young ensign, he was part of the army that had been brought to the pinnacle of perfection under the tutelage of Frederick the Great for use in what has been termed the age of limited warfare. Armies of this period represented an investment of capital and manpower that monarchs could ill afford to squander in large, set-piece battles. Manoeuvre in lieu of battle and the use of the military for limited gains had, therefore, come to be the overriding characteristics of warfare during this era.

In 1806, as an adjutant of an infantry battalion, Clausewitz fought in his "first great Napoleonic battle, an experience so shatteringly different from the tedious marches of his youth that it was hard for him to comprehend them both belonging to the single activity, war."[7] During the battles of Jena and Auerstedt (in Prussia) and the subsequent pursuit, the Prussian army was virtually destroyed, and Clausewitz was captured. After several months as a prisoner of the French, he returned to Prussia and became the personal assistant to Gerhard von Scharnhorst, a senior officer who was deeply involved in the attempt to reform and reconstruct Prussia's army.[8]

This part of his life contained a number of unexpected benefits. His early campaigning in the 1790s included experience in linear warfare and operations against French partisans in the Vosges mountains, gave him knowledge of the "small wars" or "wars of detachments" that most Prussian officers never acquired. Along with this practical learning, Clausewitz was exposed to a broad-ranging education in history, literature, and professional subjects due to intensive schooling within his regiment and later as a student at the War College in Berlin, from 1801 to 1803. He also began to write on military theory.

Clausewitz remained involved in the struggle against Napoléon as a reformer in Prussia and as a staff officer in the Russian army. After the Prussian monarch sided with Napoléon 1812, many of the reformers—including Clausewitz—sought commissions from the Czar. Due to his inability to speak Russian, Clausewitz was appointed as a staff officer. In this position, he was present at the battle of Borodino and the crossing of the Berezina River (both in Russia) in 1812, two instances of violence and tragedy that were to affect him greatly. He continued service with the Russians until 1814 when he was finally readmitted to the Prussian army. During the Waterloo campaign of 1815, Clausewitz once again served as a staff officer. This time he was chief of staff in the Prussian III Corps, the unit that held the attention of Marshal Emmanuel de Grouchy long enough for Napoléon to be defeated at Waterloo by Marshal Gabbard von Blücher and the Duke of Wellington.

Subsequently, Clausewitz was appointed to the largely administrative post of the director of the War College in Berlin. With time on his hands, he returned seriously to theoretical work (at approximately 36 years of age). He began to consolidate, from his vast collection of handwritten manuscript pages, a collection of a comprehensive theory that sought to define universal, permanent elements in war. This was later to become his most influential work, *On War*. Other noteworthy publications of his are, *Two Letters on Strategy* and *Principles of War*.

Perhaps the most important factor affecting *On War*, however, was Clausewitz's personality. He was always an introvert; solitary, bookish, shy, intellectually arrogant. Yet, based on letters written to his wife, we also know that he was sensitive to the sufferings inherent in war. Thus, he paid far more attention to the human side of warfare than did many of his contemporaries.

His intent with *On War* was "to write a book that would not be forgotten after two or three years, and that might possibly be picked up more than once by those who are interested in the subject."[9] Clausewitz planned to accomplish this purpose by penetrating "by means of logical analysis to the essence of absolute [or 'ideal'] war ... [in order] to understand war in the various forms it actually takes, as a social and political phenomenon, and in its strategic, operational, and tactical aspects." Unlike many of his contemporaries, Clausewitz felt that war was inevitable and an "integral part of the world order" and so was something that was to be analysed and understood, not shunned.[10]

The Book

During Clausewitz's lifetime, the conduct of war had been transformed. In order to come successfully to grips with this change, he needed to re-examine the subject thoroughly. We can see the direction of Clausewitz's analysis in *On War* as it was organised for final publication, in eight books. The first book, "On the Nature of War," defines war and its place in the world order. It also identifies those elements that are always present in war. Book Two, "On the Theory of War," discusses the possibilities and shortcomings of theory. Books Three through Seven are: "On Strategy in General," "The Engagement," "Military Forces," "Defence," and "The Attack." They discuss aspects of war at what today would be termed the operational and tactical levels. It is here that he goes into a detailed discussion of the themes developed in the first two books. The final book, "War Plans," once again takes up the themes of the dual nature of war and, in theoretical and historical essays of great originality, looks at "the political character of war and the interaction of politics and strategy." This organisation "does not, however, constitute a sure guide for the reader" because the "distinctions between the parts are less important than is the network of themes and arguments that links them." Clausewitz regarded only Chapter 1 of Book 1 as completely finished. The unfinished nature of the work has led to much discussion about what Clausewitz meant on a number of issues.

The first, and most important, problem was to define war and its nature. Clausewitz attempted to develop a concept of war as "a duel on a large scale, an act of force to compel our enemy to do our will."[11] War, then, tended to become a series of "reciprocal actions" as each contestant attempted to overwhelm the other by the use of force. Once begun, this contest led to extremes (in theory) in that there was no "logical limit" to the application of force.[12] The aim of this violence, at least from a theoretical standpoint, was to bring about the complete overthrow of the enemy.[13]

Clausewitz felt that the role of theory was to assist in the comprehension of reality and, more specifically, history. However, his historical studies convinced him that this view of war as always moving to an absolute form was incorrect, because war was "often far removed from the pure concept postulated by theory."[14]

The opposite of the "pure" form of war and the other part of its "dual" nature was war constrained by limits. The primary factor that limited conflict was its subordination to politics, for the "political object ... will ... determine both the military objective to be reached and the amount of effort it requires."[15] War was not a complete, untrammelled, absolute manifestation of violence (as the pure concept would require), [for otherwise] war would of its own independent will usurp the place of policy the moment policy had brought it into being."[16] Another factor that acted to force war further from its ideal form was the play of chance and probability.[17] "No other human activity is so continuously or universally bound up with chance. And through the element of chance, guesswork and luck come to play a great part in war."[18]

Thus, Clausewitz identified the three dominant tendencies of war (or paradoxical trinity as he called them): war's "primordial violence;" its subordination to policy; and chance. In order to be completely understood, wars must be fully analysed using these elements, for this "trinitarian definition still contains a decisive innovation—it alone is valid for real wars and it is valid for all real wars."[19]

Yet, to take advantage of this framework and not overwhelm it with the mass of available data, Clausewitz realised that the principal detail[s] must be grouped and abstracted. Accordingly, he developed other concepts to help explain specific operational characteristics or general ideas. It is here that soldiers have tended to focus their reading because Clausewitz offers certain ideas and convictions that are presented "like small nuggets of pure metal."[20] Two of the most intriguing and interesting are the concepts of friction and the culminating point.

War and Policy

Clausewitz states, "war is not merely an act of policy but a true political instrument, a continuation of political intercourse, carried on with other means."[21] This sentence may be the most quoted passage of Clausewitz's work which represents "the primacy of policy" and is usually regarded as his core message. There are numerous other passages where he has emphasised the primacy of policy such as: "the political object is the goal, war is the means of reaching it, and means can never be considered in isolation from their purpose," or "war should never be thought of as something autonomous but always as an instrument of policy" and "policy, then, will permeate all military operations and have a continuous influence on them."[22]

However, the primacy of the policy should not be understood as political determinism. While "political purpose remains the supreme consideration," it is "not a tyrant. It must adapt itself to its chosen means." Policy permeates all military operations; however, it does "as far as their violent nature will admit." Clausewitz' statement "war has its own grammar, but not its own logic,"[23] can be understood as the summary of the relationship between war and policy. War has its own restrictions as grammar does on speech, but this does not change the fact that it is merely a political instrument.

The scale of the political objective determines the scope of the military aim. However, another factor which determines the military aim is the enemy's response. In the very beginning of *On War*, Clausewitz begins by going straight to the heart of the matter and states:

> *War is nothing but a duel on a larger scale. Countless duels go to make up war, but a picture of it as a whole can be formed by imagining a pair of wrestlers. Each tries through physical force to compel the other to do his will; his immediate aim is to throw his opponent in order to make him incapable of further resistance. War is thus an act of force to compel our enemy to do our will.*[24]

The enemy's role is at the centre as it captures the essence of war, simply because war is a bilateral use of violence rather than a unilateral use; violence met by violence. The fact that "war is a duel" has a number of impacts on the entire theory of war. For instance, the military objective of the war may vary depending on the type of war. In an unlimited war, as in the Second World War, a military objective might be rendering the enemy totally defenceless while in a limited war a military objective can be coercing the enemy to affect his will.

Once the interaction begins, both sides start a series of activities to make a judgement about enemy's character, their institutions, and general situation, and this can only be made by using the laws of probability in the real world. Because of the imperfect knowledge of the situation, and usually unreliable intelligence, any given situation requires that probabilities be calculated in light of the circumstances. This is why, "no other human activity is so continuously or universally bound up with chance." Through the element of chance, guesswork and luck come to play a great part in war.[25] Chance, together with danger and courage, from the very start requires the interplay of probabilities and possibilities. As Clausewitz noted, "so-called mathematical factors never find a firm basis in military calculations. In the whole range of human activities, war most closely resembles a game of cards."[26]

All of these may sound commonplace, but it is crucial to know that history is replete with cases where actors underestimated the strength of their opponents; worse, they did not even take their opponents into consideration before they embarked on their military operation. The US's "War against Global Terrorism" may represent a good example of an actor who does not pay attention to their enemy and the dire consequences. Clausewitz's idea that escalation was not determined by the laws of necessity, but by the laws of probability, was also truly a revolutionary one in the military theory of Clausewitz's day.[27]

The Nature versus Character of War

According to Clausewitz, war has two natures: objective and subjective. The objective nature of war represents those qualities common to all warfare in all periods.[28] *On War* is a quest for objective knowledge, namely, the universal and eternal nature of war. On the contrary, the subjective nature of war corresponds to the actual, dynamically changeable, highly variable detail of historical warfare, as it is valid only for a specific time and place. Military forces, their doctrines, and the weapons that are used in each war are examples of this subjective nature. In today's language, the objective nature of war is called "the nature of war" while the subjective nature of war is called "the character of war."[29]

So, what is the nature of war? What are the common features of all warfare in all periods? If we are to follow Clausewitz, all wars are driven by unstable relations among three forces: "passion and enmity," "chance and creativity" and "policy and reason." He wrote:

> *War is more than a true chameleon that slightly adapts its characteristics to the given case. As a total phenomenon its dominant tendencies always make war a paradoxical trinity—composed of primordial violence, hatred, and enmity, which are to be regarded as a blind natural force; of the play of chance and probability within which the creative spirit is free to roam; and of its element of subordination, as an instrument of policy, which makes it subject to reason alone.*[30]

Danger, physical exertion, uncertainty and chance are four elements that comprise the "climate of war" that is common to all wars.[31] They can also be grouped into a single concept of general friction, which is one of the unique concepts invented by Clausewitz. Friction can be described as "the factors that distinguish real war from war on paper." Clausewitz states "Everything in war is very simple, but the simplest thing is difficult. The difficulties accumulate and produce a kind of friction that is inconceivable unless one has experienced war." In theory, everything may seem reasonable and flawless, however in practice; every individual has the potential to cause problems. Danger and physical exertion can aggravate any problems to such an extent that they must be ranked among its principal causes.[32]

In summary, the nature of war rests on the fundamental cause–effect relationships involving the forces of purpose, chance, and hostility. These principal elements, though always present, are constantly in flux, both influencing and influenced by one another. The interaction of these forces occurs in an atmosphere of war where danger, physical exertion, chance, uncertainty and friction reigns.

Limited versus Unlimited War

In *On War*, Clausewitz first describes absolute, ideal, or what has become known as "total" war, wherein the full resources of a nation are committed to waging war. Having established the idea of total war as a theoretical construct that cannot be attained in reality, he demonstrates how, in practice, warfare departs from the absolute. In so doing, he develops the concept of "limited" war, wherein a nation wages war with less than its full resources, and with aims other than the complete annihilation of one's enemy. Still, in limited war, as with all war, victory is achieved when one's enemy has been compelled to do one's will and one's political objectives have been met.

Clausewitz again describes the nature of war in dual terms when discussing aims. War, he states, may either be (1) "waged with the aim of completely defeating the enemy, in order either to destroy him as a political organism or to force him to accept any terms whatever"; or (2) "waged to acquire territory in order to retain the conquest or to bargain with the occupied land in the peace negotiations."[33]

All wars can be considered limited in some aspects because they are generally constricted to a specific geographic area, to certain kinds of weapons and tactics, or to numbers of committed combatants. These distinctions are the factors at work in a particular conflict, not its fundamental strategic classification. Another common error is the assumption that limited wars are small wars and unlimited wars are big ones. This confuses the scale of a war with its military and political objectives. Large-scale wars can be quite limited in political and/or military objectives, while a relatively small conflict may have unlimited political and military objectives.

The strategic pitfall in characterising wars as limited or unlimited is that such a label may lead to adoption of an incorrect strategy. This is particularly true in the case of limited wars. There are always temptations to limit the military means employed, even when the political objectives demand a strategy of annihilation. Such inclinations stem from the psychological and moral burdens involved in the use of force, the desire to conserve resources, and often a tendency to underestimate the enemy or the overall problem. Strategists must correctly understand the character and the resource demands of a strategy before they choose it.

The Clausewitzian Trinity

Determined to make this the main theme of this work Clausewitz began to redraft the whole work again, and completed the first chapter to his satisfaction. But even as he redrafted yet another idea came to him: that of war as a 'remarkable trinity', in which the directing policy of the government, the professional qualities of the army, and the attitude of the population all played an equally significant part. His mind was so fertile in ideas and analogies, his quest for precision so exacting that, even if he had been able to complete his revision, it is unlikely that he would ever have been satisfied with it. However long he lived he would probably have bequeathed to posterity only 'a collection of materials from which a theory of war was to have been distilled'. But he could still with reason claim that an unprejudiced reader in search of truth and understanding will recognise the fact that [the contents] for all their imperfection of form, contain the fruit of years of reflection on war and diligent study of it. He may even find they contain the basic ideas that might bring about a revolution in the theory of war. [34]

One of the most important theories espoused in *On War* is the famous Clausewitzian "Trinity". According to Clausewitz, there are three factors at play in war:

1. primordial violence, hatred and enmity which are natural forces;
2. chance and probability which exist in the creative spirit; and
3. war's subordination as an instrument of policy which make war subject to reason.

He goes on to relate these factors to the people, the commander and his army, and the government, respectively.[35] People will tend towards violence when faced with ideas differing from their own; the commander must use his creative genius when faced with the unknowns of war; and the government must ensure that the people and the commander are following the established guidelines (policy) most beneficial to the people. In establishing his Trinity, Clausewitz gives credence to the idea that, at any given time, one element may play a more dominant role than the other two, but that all three sides must be considered when formulating effective strategies for defeating one's enemy. Clausewitz argues that in guerrilla wars the "people" element of the triad takes precedence over the other two.[36]

Summarising the environment within which war and strategy are made, Clausewitz described it as being dominated by a "remarkable trinity" that is—composed of primordial violence, hatred, and enmity, which are to be regarded as a blind natural force; of the play of chance and probability within which the creative spirit is free to roam; and of [war's] element of subordination, as an instrument of policy, which makes it subject to reason alone.

The first of these three aspects mainly concerns the people; the second the commander and his army; the third the government. These three tendencies are like three different codes of law, deep-rooted in their subject and yet variable in their relationship to one another. A theory that ignores any one of them or seeks to fix an arbitrary relationship between them would conflict with reality to such an extent that for this reason alone it would be totally useless. Our task therefore is to develop a theory that maintains a balance between these three tendencies, like an object suspended between three magnets.[37]

Clausewitz concluded that the strategic environment is shaped by the disparate forces of emotion, chance, and rational thought. At any given moment, one of these forces may dominate, but the other two are always at work. The actual course of events is determined by the dynamic interplay among them. The effective strategist must master the meaning and the peculiarities of this environment.[38]

According to Clausewitz, these three tendencies are present in every war and yet vary in their relationship to one another. He maintains, "Our task therefore is to develop a theory that maintains a balance between these three tendencies, like an object suspended between three magnets." The weight of each tendency depends on the context of each war. More importantly, the remarkable trinity demonstrates that war's nature is inseparable from the historical and socio-political contexts in which that war arises, so therefore, war cannot be examined in isolation as a thing-in-itself.

He attributes objective (unchanging) tendencies to subjective ones (ever-changing): namely, he attributes passion and enmity to the "people," chance and probability to "the commander and army," and political reason to the "government." However, this should not be understood as a rigid, inflexible, and mutually exclusive relationship, as he does not equate them exactly. "The government" in this case stands for any ruling body; any "agglomeration of loosely associated forces;" the military represents any warring body in any era, while the "populace" suggests the population/citizenry of any society or culture in any period of history. For example, policy may be the responsibility of the government, but in the modern world it is likely to be influenced by a public opinion that could prove volatile. Additionally, policy can be influenced by those military commanders who are shaping strategy, in a process of dialogue with politicians.

Centres of Gravity

Another important theory raised by Clausewitz in *On War* is his idea of centres of gravity. According to Clausewitz, "one must keep the dominant characteristics of both belligerents in mind. Out of these characteristics a certain centre of gravity develops, the hub of all power and movement, on which everything depends. That is the point against all our energies should be directed."[39] In describing centres of gravity, Clausewitz devotes much attention to the importance of major, i.e. large scale, battles. According to Clausewitz, "the major battle is therefore to be regarded as concentrated war, as the centre of gravity of the entire conflict."[40]

A more nuanced reading of Clausewitz, however, reveals his belief that in wars akin to popular uprisings, the centre of gravity resides in the leadership's charisma and its effect on public opinion.[41] According to Clausewitz, once the centre of gravity is identified, the strategist must ensure it is attacked continually without giving the enemy time to recover: "Blow after blow must be aimed in the same direction, as ...only...by constantly seeking out the centre of his power, will one really defeat the enemy."[42] When attacking an enemy's centre of gravity, speed, focused consistency of effort, and ongoing re-evaluation are imperative.

The Nature of Politics and War

Before we can usefully discuss the making and carrying out of military strategy, we must understand the fundamental character of politics and the violent expression of politics called war. Let us start by analysing Clausewitz's description of war as both an instrument of policy and of politics with the addition of other means.[43]

War is a social phenomenon. Its logic is not the logic of art, nor of science or engineering, but rather the logic of social transactions. Human beings interact with each other in ways that are fundamentally different from the way the scientist interacts with chemicals, the architect or engineer with beams and girders, or the artist with paints. The interaction that concerns us when we speak of war is political interaction. The "other means" in Clausewitz's definition of war is organised violence. The addition of violence to political interaction is the only factor that defines war as a distinct form of political interaction— but that addition has powerful and unique effects. The two different terms we have used, policy and politics, both concern *power*. While every specific war has its unique causes, war as a phenomenon is fundamentally concerned with the distribution and redistribution of power.[44]

Power is sometimes material in nature: the economic power of money or other resources, for example, or possession of the physical means for coercion (weapons and armed personnel). Power is just as often psychological in nature: legal, religious, or scientific authority; intellectual or social prestige; a charismatic personality's ability to excite or persuade; a reputation, accurate or illusory, for diplomatic or military strength. Power provides the means to attack and the means to resist attack. Power in itself is neither good nor evil. By its nature, however, power tends to be distributed unevenly in ways that vary greatly from one society to another.

Power manifests itself differently and in different places at different times. In Japan, during the 16th through 19th centuries, real political power was exercised by the shogun, who was formally subordinate to the emperor. Later, senior Japanese military leaders were for a time effectively controlled by groups of fanatical junior officers. King Philip II of Spain, whose power was rooted in a landed aristocracy, was surprised to discover the power that Europe's urban bankers could exercise over his military strategy. American leaders were similarly surprised by the power of the disparate political coalition that forced an end to the Vietnam War. One of the major problems of strategy is to determine where and in what form real power lies and to identify those relatively rare points where military power can be applied effectively.

Politics is the process by which power is *distributed* in any society: a family, an office, a religious order, a tribe, a state, a region, the international community. The process of distributing power may be fairly orderly—through consensus, inheritance, election, or some time-honoured tradition—or chaotic—through assassination, revolution, or warfare. Whatever process may be in place at any given time, politics is inherently dynamic, and not only the distribution of power but the process by which it is distributed is under constant pressure for change.

A key characteristic of politics is that it is interactive—a cooperative or competitive process. It cannot be characterised as a rational process because actual outcomes are seldom what was consciously intended by any one of the participants. Political events and their outcomes are the product of conflicting, contradictory, sometimes compromising, but often adversarial forces. That description clearly applies to war.

Policy, on the other hand, can be characterised as a rational process. The making of policy is a conscious effort by a distinct political body to use whatever power it possesses to accomplish some purpose—if only the mere continuation or increase of its own power. Policy is a rational subcomponent of politics, the reasoned purposes and actions of individuals in the political struggle. War can be a practical means, sometimes the only means available, for the achievement of rational policy aims—that is, the aims of one party in the political dispute. *Hence, to describe war as an "instrument of policy" is entirely correct. It is an act of force to compel our opponent to do our will.*

Do not, however, confuse rationality with intelligence, reasonableness, or understanding. Policies can be wise or foolish: they can advance their creators' goals or unwittingly contradict them. They can be driven by concern for the public good or by the most craven reasons of self-interest. Rationality also implies no particular *kind* of goal, for goals are a product of emotion and human desire. The goal of policy may be peace and prosperity, national unity, the achievement of ideological perfection, or the extermination of some ethnic minority or competitor.

Remember too that policy, while it is different from politics, is produced via a political process. Even the most rational of policies is often the result of compromises within the political group. Such compromises may be intended more to maintain peace or unity within the group than to accomplish any external purpose. They may, in fact, be irrelevant or contrary to any explicit group goal. Policy is therefore often ambiguous, unclear, even contradictory, and subject to change or to rigidity when change is needed.

Clausewitz's reference to war as an expression of politics is therefore not a prescription, but a description. War is a part of politics. It does not replace other forms of political intercourse but merely supplements them. It is a violent expression of the tensions and disagreements between political groups, when political conflict reaches a level that sparks organised violence. Thus war—like every other phase of politics—embodies both rational and irrational elements. Its course is the product not of one will, but of the collision of two or more wills.

To say, then, that war is an expression of both politics and policy with the addition of other means is to say two very different things to strategy makers. First, it says that strategy, insofar as it is a conscious and rational process, must strive to achieve the policy goals set by the political leadership. Second, it says that such policy goals are created only within the chaotic and emotional realm of politics.

Therefore, the military professional who says, "Keep politics out of this. Just give us the policy, and we will take care of the strategy," does not understand the fundamentals of strategy. Strategists must operate within the constraints of policy and politics. The only alternative would be for military strategy to perform the functions of policy and for military leaders to usurp political power, tasks which are generally unsuited to both military strategy and military leaders.

The quality of determination is different from mere obstinacy. It is rooted in intellectual insight and composed of a rare blend of intellect and moral courage. The whole question of the relationship between determination, firmness, obstinacy, and strength of mind, between those familiar opposites of 'character' and 'intellect' that were to cause so much pedagogical debate and still sometimes do, was discussed by Clausewitz with a shrewdness and a precision that gives to these pages an intrinsic value far transcending their military context,

> *A government must never assume that its country's fate. its whole existence. depends on a single battle, no matter how decisive ... No matter how small and weak a state may be in comparison with its enemy. it must not forego these last efforts, or one would conclude that its soul is dead. They are even more desirable when help can be expected from other states that have an interest in our survival. A government that after having lost a major battle is only interested in letting its people go back to sleep as soon as possible. and, overwhelmed by feelings of failure and disappointment, lacks the courage and desire to put forth a final effort is, because of its weakness, involved in a major inconsistency in any case. It shows that it did not deserve to win. and possibly for that very reason was unable to.*[45]

This passage, which epitomizes much of his political writings, helps explain why Clausewitz was so unpopular with the cautious and conservative advisers of Frederick William III.

The Genius of the Commander (and the 'Art' of Negotiation)

A military Commander operating in today's complex environment must be, perhaps more so today than at any time in modern history, able to solve complex geopolitical problems by using good judgment while negotiating with a wide range of civilian leaders and governmental and non-governmental foreign and domestic agencies. Today's operational field is global in nature, and therefore, it is critically important that military commanders be skilled at the art of negotiation as well as the art of war. Moreover, senior military officers, junior officers and even enlisted personnel must be as familiar with the strategy and tactics of negotiating as they are with the application of military force on the battlefield.

Clausewitz advises those thinking of embarking on war first consider what they hope to achieve: "*The first, the supreme, the most far-reaching act of judgment that the statesman and commander have to make is to establish by that test the kind of war on which they are embarking; neither mistaking it for, nor trying to turn it into, something that is alien to its nature.*"[46]

Also, the emotional attachment to one's objective must be removed, a rational assessment of the problem must be made, and an adaptable view of what constitutes an acceptable terminating point must become the primary focus. Instead of fixating on "winning", the negotiator focuses on creating and attaining value through assessing 'common ground'. Still, to maximise the likelihood that negotiations will end in success, the negotiation warrior must make every effort to understand what his opponent seeks to achieve.

If leaders were attentive to Clausewitz's theories they would glean that success on the battlefield depends to a large degree on genius – what Clausewitz termed 'coup d'œil': an ability to assess a situation quickly and correctly. This ability relies heavily on the Commander's innate intuition. Successful strategic negotiators must be acutely aware of their "terrain", and the most successful have an almost uncanny ability to sense their opponent's course of action and respond quickly, whether through experience or innate ability. Instead of considering victory in unilateral terms, the mature negotiator must adeptly sew his thoughts and desires together to convince others to willingly make the garment that he desires even when it is not in their interest to do so.

> *A prince or general who knows exactly how to organise his war according to his object and means, who does neither too little nor too much, gives by that the greatest proof of his genius. But the effects of this talent are exhibited not so much by the invention of new modes of action, which might strike the eye immediately, as in the successful*

final result of the whole. It is the exact fulfilment of silent suppositions, it is the noiseless harmony of the whole action which we should admire, and which only makes itself known in the total result.[47]

Friction

War is characterised by the interaction of both moral and physical forces. The physical characteristics of war are generally easily seen, understood, and measured: hardware, technology, physical objectives seized, force ratios, losses of material or life, terrain lost or gained, prisoners or material captured. The moral characteristics are less tangible. (The term *moral* as used here is not restricted to ethics—although ethics are certainly included—but pertains to those forces of psychological rather than tangible nature, to include the mental aspects of war). Moral forces are difficult to grasp and impossible to quantify. We cannot easily gauge forces like national and military resolve, national or individual conscience, emotion, fear, courage, morale, leadership, or esprit. Yet moral forces exert a greater influence on the nature and outcome of warfare than do physical. In warfare we must either destroy the enemy's *ability to resist* or destroy his *will to resist*. The distinction between the two approaches is that attacking hostile ability is the *direct approach* aimed at physical forces and attacking hostile will is the *indirect approach* aimed at moral forces.

Clausewitz identifies an additional concept that is crucial to the strategist's understanding of war: *Friction*. According to Clausewitz, "the conduct of war resembles the workings of an intricate machine with tremendous friction, so that combinations which are easily planned on paper can be executed only with great effort."[48] Friction is "the force that makes the apparently easy so difficult."[49]

Nevertheless, Clausewitz knew that war even in its moderated form is not a pleasant affair; it is brutal and violent, and right from the start, he makes that point clear to the reader.[50] The accumulated effect of factors, such as danger, physical exertion, intelligence or lack thereof, and influence of environment and weather, all depending on chance and probability, are the factors that distinguish real war from war on paper.[51] Clausewitz brought these together in the concept of friction. 'Everything in war is simple, but the simplest thing is difficult.'[52]

Importantly, friction exists not only at the tactical but at the strategic level. It describes not only the difficulty associated with waging war, but also of assessing the effectiveness of one's own strategy and reformulating new strategies as the war unfolds. Owing almost entirely to friction the who, what, where and how questions become increasingly difficult to answer as a war progresses. Who is the enemy? How do we negotiate for the greatest good? Who is the target? What is their ultimate political aim? What is their trinity? What is the enemy's centre(s) of gravity? How do we target it? These questions may be a simplified version of what the modern strategist is asking, but the subject is complex and the answers are elusive, multi-layered and most importantly, ever changing.

In the chapter of *On War* titled *Strategy*, Clausewitz addresses the idea of planning strategy: "*Since most of these matters have to be based on assumptions that may not prove correct, while other, more detailed orders cannot be determined in advance at all, it follows that the strategist must go on campaign himself. Detailed orders can then be given on the spot, allowing the general plan to be adjusted to the modifications that are continuously required.*"[53]

He could not be more correct. The genius of the Commander and his ability to employ operational art is nowhere more critical than when faced with the tyranny of Friction. The guerrilla tactics used by insurgents, for example, demand that the Commander be constantly reassessing strategic options and remaining consistently flexible. He must be able to adjust his strategy quickly and apply nuance to a general plan, in order to suit the type of threat encountered. One thing remains certain, if we are to defeat the enemy, there must be a continual attempt to adjust the strategic plan and assess the who, what, where and how questions with speed, intelligence, and discernment.

War is the realm of uncertainty and Clausewitz therefore asserts that a 'sensitive and discriminating judgement is called for; a skilled intelligence to scent out the truth'.[54] This places a premium on knowledge that can only be obtained 'through the medium of reflection, study and thought'.[55] This knowledge should be combined with experience from life itself and must become a capability through 'absorption into the mind'.[56] The knowledge required is not easy to apply[57] and the difficulty becomes most extreme at the level of the strategic leader.[58]

Jomini believed that there was a common formula underlying the successes of both Napoleon and Frederick the Great that could be summarised as 'directing the mass of one's forces successively on the decisive points in the theatre of war, and as far as possible against the communications of the enemy without disrupting one's own': an object that could best be achieved by the mastery of what he termed (as everyone else has ever since) 'interior lines'.

Clausewitz denied the validity of such formulations, not so much because they were oversimplifications, but because they ignored what he saw as the essence of war:

> *They aim at fixed values; but in war everything is uncertain, and calculations have to be made with variable quantities. They direct the inquiry exclusively towards physical quantities, whereas all military action is intertwined with psychological forces and effects. They consider only unilateral action, whereas war consists of a continuous interaction of opposites.*[59]

No theory could be of any value, he maintained, that did not take account of these interconnected elements—the uncertainty of all information, the importance of moral factors, and, lending emphasis to both of these, the unpredictable reactions of the adversary. The element of uncertainty arose very largely from the impossibility of gauging enemy intentions and reactions, something that was particularly difficult when there were no overmastering political incentives to determine his military decisions. At best one could only work on probabilities, and in doing this, however good one's judgement, there would always be a substantial element of sheer luck. Even the best generals were successful gamblers who had the nerve to back their judgement. No amount of theory could, in a moment of crisis, tell them what to do.

> *Everything in war is very simple, but the simplest thing is very difficult.... Countless minor incidents – the kind you can never really foresee—combine to lower the general level of performance, so that one always falls far short of the intended goal ... The military machine ... is basically very simple and very easy to manage. But we should bear in mind that none of its components is of one piece: each part is composed*

of individuals, every one of whom retains his potential of friction ... A battalion is made up of individuals, the least important of whom may chance to delay things and sometimes make them go wrong.

This inherent tendency for things to go wrong was compounded by external and even less controllable factors, such as the weather.

Fog can prevent the enemy from being seen in time, a gun from firing when it should, a report from reaching the commanding officer. Rain can prevent a battalion from arriving, make another late by keeping it not three but eight hours on the march, ruin a cavalry charge by bogging the horses down in mud, etc.

In short,

Action in war is like movement in a resistant element. Just as the simplest and most natural of movements, walking, cannot easily be performed in water, so in war, it is difficult for normal efforts to achieve even moderate results.

It was this friction, said Clausewitz, that 'distinguishes real war from on paper', and an understanding of its importance had to be the starting-point for any theorist.

The second requisite, said Clausewitz, was the capacity, having taken a decision, to stick to it: determination. Everything would conspire to convince the general that his decision had been wrong: conflicting intelligence or, worse, the absence of any intelligence at all; the doubts of his subordinates; and the gradual exhaustion of the forces under his command, the decline in whose moral strength had to be made up for by the greater exertion of his own.

So long as a unit fights cheerfully, with spirit and elan, great strength of will is rarely needed: but once conditions become difficult, as they must when much is at stake, things no longer run like a well-oiled machine. The machine itself begins to resist, and the commander needs tremendous will-power to overcome this resistance. As each man's strength gives out, as it no longer responds to his will, the inertia of the whole gradually comes to rest on the commander's will alone. [60]

Clausewitz's Theories and Modern Warfare

Have improvements in modern warfare through technology rendered Clausewitz's theories obsolete? *On War* did not apply to all the wars fought in the past nor would they cover all wars to be fought in the future. Clausewitz's goal was to explain war as a universal phenomenon.[61] His theory on war involved universal principles that could apply to war itself. In this sense the theory holds true regarding modern warfare.

Clausewitz viewed war as a tool to accomplish political goals; technology has not altered this reality in modern warfare. In Book Eight, Chapter Two of *On War* Clausewitz states, "the overthrow of the enemy is the natural end of the act of war; and if we would keep within the strictly philosophical limits of the idea, there can be no other in reality."[62] The theory holds true regarding modern warfare and changes in technology; the objective has not changed, and new technology cannot be relied on as strategy. Technology may create a dynamic of its own but it has failed to eliminate "friction" in modern warfare.

Conclusion

Clausewitz has been condemned, maligned, misunderstood, praised, and hailed as a genius. Often without realising it, writers are pursuing the goals indicated by Clausewitz: the defining of means, ends, and implications, so that they can be used theoretically and applied in the formulation of policy. What is certain is that Clausewitz has come to mean more in the present era than he did to his own. Today's military officers and students of military matters should study Clausewitz and draw their own conclusions.

To truly benefit from Clausewitz's insights into the nature and effective conduct of war, policymakers must read *On War* carefully, and with an eye toward avoiding interpretations inspired more by hope than ground realities. Carefully studied, however, *On War* provides innumerable, uncannily accurate insights into the nature of war using soft and hard methods. Clausewitz warns of the pitfalls that await policymakers who ignore war's inherent characteristics and the admonitions to policymakers elucidated by Clausewitz possess a prescience that is unparalleled.

Clausewitz is a unique and complex individual whose wisdom has a timeless quality because he wrote from his experience, both as a scholar and a soldier. No policymaker should plan a war without reading his famous words: "*No one starts a war, or ought to, without first being clear in his mind what he intends to achieve by that war and how he intends to conduct it.*"

Clausewitz's theories continue to influence modern warfare, and as shown they have also influenced all branches of the military. Technology and advances in weaponry may change over time. However, Clausewitz's theory on war has proven to be the anvil from which strategy is forged. Elements of his theory can be seen in every conflict of the modern age, proving his theory has stood the test of time.

On War can be seen as a conceptual model, a framework for understanding the complexities of war. It's way of reasoning through proposal and counter proposal, using rhetorical questions and answers and comparing theory with reality makes *On War* today a stimulating work for the education of strategic leaders. The mere fact that the work is unfinished and neither a fully developed theory nor a checklist actually contributes to its value because it forces the reader to interpret before applying the ideas to reality and 'any theoretical work of this type that is devoid of apparent or real contradictions could never represent a realistic analysis of the real world of war'.

Much of the discussion about *On War* revolves around the issue whether the nature of war has changed or rather the ways in which war manifests itself. Based on both Clausewitz's text as well as recent studies, it can be concluded that at this point in time the nature of war has not changed but that its manifestations indeed have. The continuously new and changing forms of war in the 21st century will most likely generate intense study and debate, but as Clausewitz taught us, we should take our time before being overawed by first impressions.

FURTHER READING

- Peter Paret, "Clausewitz," in *Makers of Modern Strategy: from Machiavelli to the Nuclear Age,* eds., Peter Paret (Princeton, New Jersey: Princeton University Press, 1986).
- Hew Strachan, *Clausewitz's On War* (New York, NY: Grove Press, 2007).
- A.J. Echevarria II, *Clausewitz and Contemporary War* (Oxford: Oxford University Press, 2007).
- Michael Howard, *Clausewitz: A Very Short Introduction* (Oxford: Oxford University Press, 2002).

6

Jomini

"Correct theories, founded up on right principles, sustained by actual events of wars, and added to accurate military history, will form a true school of instruction for generals."

—Jomini, *Précis de l' Art de la Guerre, 1838*

The Author

Antoine-Henri Baron de Jomini (1779-1869) was a Swiss infantry general, who served in the armies of France and Russia, who grew up on the French frontier in the late 18th century. He observed the French Revolution and Napoleon's epic battles at close range which were so influential on him that he gave up his banking apprenticeship to pursue the study of strategy and a military career. It was for his writings on strategy that he is most known, as he served on staffs, but never commanded in war. "Jomini, more than Clausewitz, deserves the dubious title of founder of modern strategy."[1]

His principles, which at some point formed the basis for military education, influenced teaching in European and North American military academies through the 19th century. A Swiss of French extraction, Jomini received first-hand experience in the Napoleonic Wars (1805–1814) serving in various capacities as a staff officer beginning in 1805, first as a volunteer. He was quickly promoted, and by the end of 1810 Jomini had become brigadier general and was given the title of Baron of the French Empire. At that time, he was also a renowned military theorist; his first two editions of *Treatise on Grand Military*

Operations, published between 1805 and 1811, embraced the campaigns of Frederick the Great and Napoléon in Italy and compared 18th century warfare with the new Revolutionary combat doctrine.

In 1812–1813, Jomini served with Napoléon's *Grande Armée*, where he headed various offices on the lines of communications and as a chief of staff of one of Napoléon's corps. However, being disillusioned by the entire course of war, in August 1813, he joined the Allied forces organising against France. Admitted to the Russian service, he withdrew from the active duties in early 1814 when the Allies violated Swiss neutrality. After several years of retirement and literary work, in 1823 Jomini resumed his post in the Russian army. He served as an advisor during the Russo-Turkish War (1828–1829). He is also credited with the creation of the Russian Military Academy on General Staff in 1832. Jomini retired from the active service and settled in Belgium, where he continued his works on military writings. In 1853, Jomini was once-again called to the Russian service to act as a military adviser to Tsar Nicholas I during the Crimean War (1853–1855). After the peace he settled in Switzerland; in 1858, however, Napoléon III requested Jomini to furnish plans for his campaign in Italy. Jomini moved to Paris, where he continued his military writing until his death.

From 1784 onwards, French armies crushed their European opponents, began to transform the political structure of Europe and brought Napoleon Bonaparte to power in France. These were the times of great upheaval. Napoleon's military successes provided valuable lessons for the understanding of military operations. Napoleon's genius at the strategic and operational levels of war was a major catalyst for the development of the continental school of strategic thought throughout the 19th century. Under his leadership the French produced the first mass army in modern history and other European powers were forced to follow suit. Foremost among the military authors to emerge during the Napoleonic era were Jomini (1779-1869) and Clausewitz (1780-1831), who had an everlasting influence on both military theory and popular conceptions of warfare.

Jomini's systematic attempt to define the principles of warfare made him one of the founders of modern military thought. In 1800, after the peace of Amiens, he wrote his *Traité de grande tactique*, later titled *Traité des grandes opérations militaires* (5 vol., 1805; *Treatise on Grand Military Operations*, 1865). In 1837, when he was military tutor to the tsar's son Alexander, he wrote his greatest work, *Précis de l'art de la guerre* (1838; *Summary of the Art of War*, 1868). As a critic of military policy, Jomini succeeded for the first time in fixing divisions between strategy, tactics, and logistics. Primarily interested in strategy, he found the central problem in successful planning to be the choice of correct lines of operation by which a general could dominate the zone of operations in which he is engaged.

The Book

A study of Jomini's *Summary of the Art of War* (1838) reveals a considerable amount of basic military theory. He wrote of the tactical and strategic method, and also appreciated the great importance of morale. For Jomini, simplicity in battle planning was a cardinal virtue because he believed that 'the simpler a decisive manoeuvre is, the more certain will be its success'. Like Clausewitz, he emphasised the destruction of enemy forces as the key objective of a military operation and was fully aware of the value of surprise and the advantages of the strategic initiative while emphasising the need to concentrate forces upon the 'decisive point' of battle. He was an outstanding proponent of the idea that war could be conducted on the basis of a small number of permanently valid principles.

Summary of the Art of War, consists of six parts:

1. State military policy.
2. Strategy or the art of properly directing the masses in the development of military action of defend and attack.
3. Basic tactics.
4. Logistics or the art to move armies.
5. Engineering—attack and defence of fortifications.
6. Small tactics.

For Jomini, strategy was at the heart of the art of war. Of the six distinct branches that he theorised constituted the art of war, two-thirds were grounded in strategy. Jomini divided generic strategy into four levels of analysis—statesmanship, strategy, grand tactics and minor tactics.[2] He described statesmanship in policy terms, i.e., of the various political objectives for which a war might be waged. According to Jomini, states went to war:[3]

- To reclaim certain rights or defend them.
- To protect and maintain the great interests of the state, as commerce, manufactures, or agriculture.
- To uphold neighbouring states whose existence is necessary either for the safety of the government or the balance of power.
- To fulfil the obligations of offensive and defensive alliances.
- To propagate political or religious theories, to crush them out, or to defend them.
- To increase the influence and power of the state by acquisitions of territory.
- To defend the threatened independence of the state.
- To avenge insulted honour; or,
- From a mania for conquest.

Jomini's construct of statesmanship in terms of political objectives also served as the basis for his typology of war.[4] Regardless of the political objective or type of war, however, Jomini advocated that war was to be waged in accordance with the principles of war, though some latitude was afforded to context and specific circumstances.

Jomini realised the importance of just war, with wars to reclaim rights the most just of all. He deemed wars of conquest a crime against humanity. He viewed wars of opinion—that is, conflicts over political and religious dogma—as deplorable due to the cruelty and vindictiveness perpetrated by both sides against the other. Jomini astutely observed that dogma was usually only a pretext for some underlying political objective. Nonetheless, the intensity of the passions evoked by dogma was such to make for fearful and bitter conflicts. Rather than engaging an overly excited and exasperated people, Jomini advised waiting for passions to calm down before taking military action. In his words, "it is better to await the explosion and afterward fill up the crater than to try to prevent it and to perish in the attempt".[5] Wars of opinion also belonged to another class of war, wars of intervention, as they resulted from one state seeking to impose its doctrine on another, or alternately, to crush another state's heretical dogma. Additionally, he also viewed wars of opinion as sharing characteristics with national wars and civil wars, though he never made the distinction between the types of wars clear.

This ambiguity within Jomini's typology was also reflected in his statesmanship-level strategic prescriptions. For example, in attempting to distinguish strategies for wars of opinion and national wars, Jomini averred that the military precepts for such wars are nearly the same as for national wars, differing, however, in a vital point. In national wars the country should be occupied and subjugated, the fortified places besieged and reduced, and the armies destroyed; whereas in wars of opinion it is of less importance to subjugate the country; here great efforts should be made to gain the end speedily, without delaying the details, care being constantly taken to avoid any acts which might alarm the nation for its independence or the integrity of its territory.[6]

Thus, Jomini described two different statesmanship-level strategies for two very similar types of war, without providing any clear-cut distinctions between the two. In fact, Jomini went on to describe the French Revolution as at once "a war of opinion, a national war, and a civil war,"[7] further confounding his statesmanship-level typology and prescriptions.

Similar to Sun Tzu's word of advice to "know thy enemy," Jomini also advocated comprehensive intelligence of the adversary's military policy, to include "the passions of the nation to be fought, their military system, their immediate means and their reserves, their financial resources, the attachment they bear to their government or their institutions, the character of the executive, the characters and military abilities of the commanders of their armies, the influence of cabinet councils or councils of war at the capital upon their operations, the system of war in favour with their staff, the established force of the state and its armament, the military geography and statistics of the state which is to be invaded, and finally, the resources and obstacles of every kind likely to be met with, all of which are included neither in diplomacy or strategy".[8]

Jomini defined strategy as "the art of properly directing masses upon the theatre of war, either for defence or for invasion,"[9] or, alternately, as "the art of making war on the map".[10] The output of strategic planning resulted in a campaign plan. He was very explicit in the steps to be followed in crafting strategy, which he described as:[11]

- The selection of the theatre of war, and the discussion of the different combinations of which it admits.
- The determination of the decisive points in these combinations, and the most favourable direction for operations.
- The selection and establishment of the fixed base and of the zone of operations.
- The selection of the objective point, whether offensive or defensive.
- The strategic fronts, lines of defence, and fronts of operations.
- The choice of lines of operations leading to the objective point or strategic front.
- For a given operation, the best strategic line, and the different manoeuvres necessary to embrace all possible cases.
- The eventual bases of operations and the strategic reserves.
- The marches of armies, considered as manoeuvres.
- The relation between the position of depots and the marches of the army.
- Fortresses regarded as strategical means, as a refuge for an army, as an obstacle to its progress: the sieges to be made and to be covered.
- Points for entrenched camps, *têtes de pont* (A work erected at the end of a bridge nearest the enemy, for covering the communications across a river; a bridgehead), etc.
- The diversions to be made, and the large detachments necessary.

Contrary to his discussion of statesmanship, Jomini was very clear in defining terms associated with campaign planning, resulting in a lexicon that still survives in military planning, in many respects, to this day. He also took care in distinguishing the relationships and differences between concepts, as illustrated in his distinction between grand tactics, logistics and strategy:[12]

Grand Tactics is the art of posting troops upon the battlefield according to the accidents of the ground, of bringing them into action, and the

> *art of fighting upon the ground, in contradistinction to planning upon a map. Its operations may extend over a field of ten or twelve miles in extent. Logistics comprises the means and arrangements which work out the plans of strategy and tactics. Strategy decides where to act; logistics brings the troops to this point; grand tactics decides the manner of execution and the employment of the troops."*

With regard to the principles of war, Jomini placed the "fundamental principle," described as throwing the mass of one's forces upon the decisive point, as the most important one. It was the hallmark of Napoleonic warfare. As one might expect, his description of the fundamental principle fit perfectly within the construct of annihilation, described by Clausewitz, also a student of Napoleonic warfare. In order to comprehensively articulate the fundamental principle, Jomini further described it in four maxims:[13]

1. To throw by strategic movements the mass of an army, successively, upon the decisive points of a theatre of war, and also upon the communications of the enemy as much as possible without compromising one's own.
2. To manoeuvre to engage fractions of the hostile army with the bulk of one's forces.
3. On the battlefield, to throw the mass of the forces upon the decisive point, or upon that portion of the hostile line which it is of the first importance to overthrow.
4. To so arrange that these masses shall not only be thrown up on the decisive point, but that they shall engage at the proper times and with energy.

Jomini distinguished between several types of decisive points associated with his fundamental principle of war. First, he described decisive strategic points as those "which are capable of exercising a marked influence either up on the result of the campaign or upon a single enterprise. All points whose geographical position and whose natural or artificial advantages favour the attack or defence of a front of operations or of a line of defence are included in this number; and large, well-located fortresses occupy in importance the first rank among them"[14]. He described all capitals as strategic points as they served as both the centres of power of states and centres of communications.

Decisive geographic points and lines consisted of permanent features of a country the possession of which would confer control of large areas, such as valleys, and the chief lines of communication in a country. He also described decisive points of manoeuvre as "the flank of the enemy upon which, if his opponent operates, he can more easily cut him off from his base and supporting forces without being exposed to the same danger".[15] Finally, Jomini described decisive political points, which could be found in the bindings of coalitions or that otherwise dwelled in the operations and plans of cabinets. Jomini was, however, circumspect of this type of decisive point, as he felt it was often pursued for irrational reasons, resulting in strategic mistakes.

While Jomini consistently referred to the fundamental principle (also referred to as the general principle) in nearly all of his writings, he was criticised for a lack of clarity and inconsistency in describing the rest of them.[16] Responding to criticism by Napoleon's Chief of Staff, Alexander Berthier, Jomini published a separate conclusion in the 1807 edition of his *Traité de grande tactique*, entitled, "*Resumé of the General Principles of the Art of War*," in which he listed ten principles that supported the fundamental principle:[17]

1. The first means is to take the initiative of movement. The general who succeeds in gaining this advantage is the master of the employment of his forces at the place where he chooses to take them. On the other hand, the general who waits for the enemy can make no strategical decision since he has subordinated his movements to those of his adversary and since he does not have time to stop the troops that are already in motion. The general who takes the initiative knows what he is going to do; he conceals his movements, surprises and crushes an extremity or a weak point. The general who waits is beaten at one point before he learns of the attack.
2. The second means is to direct movement against the most important weak point of the enemy's forces. The selection of this point depends upon the position of the enemy. The most important point will always be the point that offers the most favourable opportunities and the greatest results: for example, positions that may lead to the severing of the line of

communications between the enemy force and his base of operations.

3. The result of the preceding truths is that if preference is given to the attack of the extremities of a line, then care must be taken not to attack both of the extremities at the same time.
4. In order to be able to act in a combined effort on a single point, it is important to hold your forces in an area that is very nearly square so that they will be highly dispatchable. Large fronts are as contrary to good principles as broken lines, large detachments and divisions isolated beyond supporting distance.
5. One of the most efficacious ways to apply the general principle is to make the enemy commit errors that are contrary to the principle.
6. It is very important when one takes the initiative to be well informed of the positions of the enemy and of the movements that he is capable of undertaking. Espionage is a useful means.
7. It is not sufficient for success in war to skilfully bring masses to the most important points; it is necessary to know how to employ them there. If a force arrives at a decisive point and is inactive, the principle is forgotten; the enemy can counterattack.
8. If the art of war consists of bringing the superior effort of a mass against the weak points of the enemy, it is undeniably necessary to pursue actively a beaten army.
9. In order to make superior shock of a mass decisive, the general must give care to raise the morale of his army.
10. By this rapid review, it is seen that the science of war is composed of three general activities, which have only a few subdivisions and few opportunities of execution. The first is to hold the most favourable lines of operations. Second is the art of moving masses as rap idly as possible to the decisive point. Third is the art of simultaneously bringing the greatest mass to the most important point on the field of battle.

Later, in the 1816 edition of his *Traité*, Jomini added two additional principles:[18]

11. Orders of battle, or the most suitable dispositions for conducting troops to combat, should have for their object to secure at the same time mobility and solidity.
12. In ground difficult of access ... the defensive order of battle should be composed of troops deployed in two ranks, and covered by numerous companies of riflemen. But troops intended for the attack, as well as the reserve, should be arranged in columns of attack on the centre.... [F]or the reserve having to fall up on the enemy at the decisive moment, it should be done with force and rapidity, that is to say, in columns. A part of the reserve can be kept deployed until the moment of falling on the enemy, for the purpose of imposing up on him an appearance of numbers.

Jomini's major contributions were not necessarily in the realm of what we today call strategy. He sought the nature of strategy in the lines of operation and tested the advantages of the inner and outer lines of operation. Instead, he contributed by providing a language of operations and campaign planning, along with some principles of war.

Jomini remained insistent that the basic principles of war exemplified by Napoleon, and codified by Jomini himself, would survive all technological change—a point of view that has been thoroughly vindicated by events. All good armies today profess to base their doctrine and operational methods upon ' principles of war' similar to those Jomini identified.

Lines of Operations

Central to the design and conduct of campaigns and major operations concerns use of lines of operation to define the directional orientation of a force in relation to an enemy. This reference to lines of operation is one of the few surviving remnants of the military theory of Jomini.

Jomini's concept of interior lines of operations refers to one side striving for a position within separated enemy forces, making it possible to independently to strike elements of the enemy force. Jomini hoped to provide the army commander with a practical manual that would guide him in the task of directing operations in the midst of the noise and tumult of battle. For him, warfare revolved around his basic ideas that: 'Strategy is the key to warfare; all strategy is controlled by invariable scientific principles; and, that these principles prescribe offensive action to mass forces against weaker enemy forces at some decisive point, if strategy is to lead to victory'. He believed that these principles could be disregarded only with the greatest danger.

The Role of Logistics or Supplies

For Jomini, supply or logistics was a serious problem; his writings show that he understood the important place of logistics in mobile and expansive warfare. Jomini's experience in the Peninsular campaigns and in the Russian invasion convinced him of the difficulty of waging a successful war against a nation resorting to what we currently call 'the scorched earth' policy. Modern field commanders are still struggling with the problem that worried Jomini: how to keep supplies abreast of rapidly moving troops.

In this respect he was much more practical in his appreciation of logistics than Clausewitz, who tried to separate military supplies from the business of war. Clausewitz believed that matters that do not relate to the act of fighting but only to the maintenance of equipment and care of the sick are not important. But for Jomini, supply was closely connected with the entire pattern of war and helped determine the outcome of military operations.

Jomini 'saw war largely in personal, heroic terms, controlled by the masterful commander'.[19] To Jomini, the examples set by Frederick the Great and Napoleon suggested that wars should be fought by rulers, who combined in their own persons, political and military leadership. He had very little to say about the relationship between political and military authorities. But as democracy, bureaucracy and meritocracy began to transform the military by 1800, the political relationship became problematic. However Jomini did not address this problem. Soldiers could find what they wanted in Jomini's writings: good arguments against strict subordination to political authority. Jomini believed that once a war started the political leadership must leave the military commander free to wage war according to scientific principles that the military had identified.[20] In other words, Jomini was against any political interference in military matters.

Comparison with Clausewitz

A careful comparison of Jomini's *Summary of the Art of War* (1838) and Clausewitz's *On War* (1831) discloses a considerable amount of common basic military theory. Both wrote of the tactical and strategic method, and each appreciated the great importance of morale. Clausewitz advocated simplicity of plans and emphasised the 'friction' of war. For Jomini, simplicity in battle planning was a cardinal virtue because he believed that 'the simpler a decisive manoeuvre is, the more certain will be its success'. Both frequently referred to the 'drama' of war; which was something fluid, changing and subject to chance. Both emphasised the destruction of enemy forces as the key objective of a military operation. Both were primarily concerned with land warfare. Both were fully aware of the value of surprise and the advantages of the strategic initiative. Both emphasised the need to concentrate forces upon the 'decisive point' of battle. Both were the strategists of offensive war. Clausewitz's *On War* simply reinforced Jomini's emphasis on the massive, aggressive use of force.

Despite several similarities in the works of Jomini and Clausewitz the outlook of the two men was very different. They looked upon each other as competitors or rivals in the field of military writing. While it is not certain if the two ever met; it is known that they disagreed in print for years. For Jomini, historical events formed the basis of his own grasp of the strategic principles of war. But Clausewitz disagreed sharply with a number of Jomini's specific historical judgments and charged him with two faults—theoretical bias and inadequate knowledge. Clausewitz read Jomini's *History of the Major Military Operations*, published in 1804-5, and considered it good, but felt that Jomini had not sufficiently distinguished the incidental from the essential. Jomini, in turn, regretted that Clausewitz had not lived to read his *Summary of the Art of War*, believing that this might have converted Clausewitz to Jomini's point of view.

While Jomini insisted on the supremacy of military leadership, Clausewitz insisted that the political leadership had to have the last word, because the nature of policy determined the nature of war and political circumstances shaped strategy. Thus Clausewitz brought out the political nature of war, in that it was a means to an end, not an end in itself. War should be brought to an end as soon as the objective is achieved. In other words, war is essentially subordinate to politics. A close integration of politics and war is a central thesis of the Clausewitzian perception of the war. Perhaps that is why he is more popular than Jomini in this age of democracy.

Some key points of difference are:

- The fundamental difference between the two is that while Jomini wrote principally as a practitioner of war, Clausewitz wrote as a philosopher of war.[21]
- Clausewitz wrote *On War* as an intellectual exercise to satisfy himself, while Jomini wrote in order to publish his works and further his career.
- Clausewitz explored the philosophical components of war and the basic nature of war. Jomini was more concerned with the practical aspects of war and thus sought to construct a theoretical system for winning wars. Therefore, it is said that Clausewitz wrote at the strategic level of war while Jomini wrote at the tactical and operational levels of warfare. For example Jomini's doctrine focused on the importance of manoeuvre, the use of interior lines, the role of intelligence and careful planning, and the need for strategic reserves to determine victory.
- Jomini's key objective was to identify principles and rules that would enable a commander to wage wars successfully. Jomini believed that there was one principle underlying the success of both Napoleon and Frederick the Great: 'the concentration of one's forces successively on the decisive points in the theatre of war, and as far as possible against the communications of the enemy without disrupting one's own'. This objective could best be achieved by the mastery of what he called 'interior lines'.[22]
- Jomini's principles were prescriptions for strategic choices. For example where to fight, for what purpose and in what force. In fact, strategic choice remains a basic problem even in contemporary war planning. In Jomini's view most military commanders made the wrong strategic choices because they did not understand the principles of strategy. Those principles he summarised in one sentence as 'bringing superior force to

bear on a point where the enemy is both weaker and vulnerable to crippling damage'.

- Clausewitz denied the validity of such formulations because they were oversimplifications; and because they ignored what Clausewitz saw as the essence of war. He said that Jomini's principles 'aim at fixed values; but in war everything is uncertain ... all military action is intertwined with psychological forces and effects'. While Jomini was adamant that Napoleon's success came from the application of these scientific principles, Clausewitz was not convinced. For Clausewitz there were no laws or rules that could determine success on the battlefield. For him, in war 'many roads lead to success'. Clausewitz was more concerned with philosophical analysis than prescription and he sought to penetrate 'the essence of absolute war [and] ... to understand war in the various forms it actually takes, as a social and political phenomenon, and in its strategic, operational and tactical aspects'. His theory is as successful in presenting the calculating and rational side of war as in analysing its non-rational and unpredictable qualities.
- Clausewitz put more stress on the importance of morale and psychological factors in warfare than did Jomini's theory of 'scientific warfare'. Clausewitz did recognise certain definite principles of war, which he considered simple common sense. Unlike Jomini he did not try to develop a 'system' for waging war. He felt that war was 'too complex to be reduced to a neat system of rules and diagrams'.[23] No theory of war can be intellectually correct and complete.
- Jomini's idea of massive strikes against the enemy's decisive point was dismissed by Clausewitz, who saw it as an attempt to 'reduce the whole secret of the art of war to the formula of numerical superiority *at a certain time in a certain place*'.[24]
- On the surface, Jomini's own formulation does not look very different from that of Clausewitz—'the best strategy is to be very strong; first in general, and then at the decisive point'.[25] But in reality there is some difference. Whereas Jomini wrote many chapters analysing where and what that decisive point might be, Clausewitz saw the main problem as a moral one;

i.e., the capacity of the commander to maintain his determination and will against all odds and then concentrate his forces against the decisive point. Anyone undertaking a war enters the realm of chance.

- For Clausewitz war was a messy affair that could not be reduced to a set of lessons and laws. There is no strategy that will always succeed. Military commanders have to live by their wits as much as by their intelligence. Courage alone is not enough. What is required is an intelligent application of force at the right time, at the right place. Thus Clausewitz sought to destroy the formalistic strategy of manoeuvre that was in vogue during this period, largely due to Jomini's influence.

Appraisal

For Jomini it mattered where the battle was fought and how the battle was fought. He stressed the manner in which the general conducted campaigns. Through the selection of the appropriate line of operation to attack at the decisive point along the flank of the opponent, the campaign would be decisive. However, if the commander failed to plan his campaign properly, the result would be a costly and indecisive battle.

Jomini believed that the key to the conduct of the operational art in war could be reduced to four maxims. These simple truisms included the use of strategic movements to manoeuvre the mass of the friendly army against decisive points in the theatre of war. In this manner the commander could aggressively engage fractions of the enemy's force at the critical time with the bulk of his own army. The choice of the correct line of operation was the primary means of achieving this goal and the fundamental idea in a good campaign plan.

This concept was at the core of the Jominian writings on strategy. This framework began with the theatre of war which encompassed the entire space in which the two opposing groups of states might come in conflict. Jomini then subdivided this into potential theatres of operations. The theatre of operations included the territory through which the opposing armed forces could attack or must defend. Every theatre of operations had a base of operations and an objective point to attack or defend. To advance from the base of operations to the objective point, armies moved through a zone of operations along a line of operations.

Jomini emphasised the importance of several types of key points within the theatre of operations. The most important was the objective point. The aim of the war, as defined by the political circumstances, drove the selection of the objective point. These could be either a manoeuvre point or a geographic point depending upon the political objectives and the relative military capabilities of the two sides. The manoeuvre point was force oriented and gained its importance from the relative positions of the opposing forces. A geographic objective point was terrain-oriented and could be anything from a capital city to a terrain feature which supported further operations. Proper selection of these objective points greatly aided the operational commander in the destruction or dislodgment of the enemy army.

Two other types of points Jomini discussed were strategic points and decisive points. Strategic points were any point of the theatre of war which had major military significance. This might include a communications centre or major military concentration. However, all strategic points were not necessarily decisive points. To be a decisive point, the point had to be capable of exerting a major influence upon the results of the campaign or major operation. Decisive points could also be either geographic or force oriented. Geographic oriented decisive points might include significant terrain features or communication centres. Manoeuvre decisive points resulted from the relative position of the troops on both sides. This was most frequently an exposed flank but could also include weak areas in the opponents front of operation.

From the selection of decisive and objective points, Jomini believed the commander then chose the lines of operation on which his army would operate. Within a theatre of operation, a line of operation extended from an army's base of operation through the decisive points to the objective point. While decisive points provided some directional orientation for the force, lines of operation were more than a simple route between two points. More generally, a line of operation was a mobility corridor which was broad enough to accommodate the force as well as allow some lateral shifting of forces to permit necessary manoeuvre.

Jomini wrote that selection of the proper line of operation was critical to the success of an operation. The correct line could enhance the magnitude of a victory or minimise the effects of a defeat. To support this contention, he described an entire series of different types of lines of operation including strategic, interior, exterior, double, simple, concentric, divergent and accidental lines. Within this vast variety of choices, Jomini believed that simple and interior lines enable a general to bring into action by strategic movements upon the important point a stronger force than the enemy.

However, he qualified this assertion by writing that interior lines lose their advantage when the masses become so large that the size of the mass hinders mobility and makes it more vulnerable.

FURTHER READING

- Crane Brinton, Gordon A. Craig, and Felix Gilbert. "Jomini." In *Makers of Modern Strategy*, edited by Edward Mead Earle (Princeton, N.J., 1943), pp. 77–92.
- Howard, Michael, "Jomini and the Classical Tradition," in *The Theory and Practice of War*, 3–20 (Bloomington, Ind., 1965).
- John Shy, "Jomini," in *Makers of Modern Strategy*, edited by Peter Paret (Princeton, N.J., 1986), pp. 143–185.
- John R. Elting, "Jomini: Disciple of Napoleon?," *Military Affairs*, Spring 1964, pp. 17–26.

7

Mahan

"It is then particularly in the field of naval strategy that the teachings of the past have a value which is in no degree lessened. They are there useful not only as precedents, owing to the comparative permanence of the conditions. This is obviously true as to tactics, when the fleets come into collision at the point to which strategic considerations have brought them. The unresting progress of mankind causes continual change in the weapons; and with that must come a continual change in the manner of fighting—in the handling and disposition of troops or ships on the battlefield."

—**Mahan, *The Influence of Sea Power upon History***

The Author

Rear Admiral Alfred Thayer Mahan (1840-1914) was a United States Navy officer, naval strategist, and educator, widely considered the foremost theorist of sea power. Born at West Point, New York, he went to Columbia University for two years, then against his parents' wishes, transferred to the Naval Academy, where he graduated in 1859, second in his class. He served on various ships during the American Civil War. At an early age he developed a strong interest in history and began to explore the role and importance sea power played on the grand strategy of a nation. He was appointed commander of the new United States Naval War College in 1886.

In 1890 Mahan published his college lectures as *The Influence of Sea Power upon History, 1660–1783*. In this book he argued for the paramount importance of sea power in national historical supremacy. The book, which came at a time of great technological improvement in warships, won immediate recognition abroad. In his second book, *The Influence of Sea Power upon the French Revolution and Empire, 1793–1812* (1892), Mahan stressed the interdependence of the military and commercial control of the sea and asserted that the control of seaborne commerce can determine the outcome of wars. Both books were avidly read in Great Britain and Germany, where they greatly influenced the build-up of naval forces in the years prior to World War I.

His work *The Influence of Sea Power upon History 1660-1783* is important as it revealed Mahan's thoughts on sea power; elevated his status as America's greatest theorist on sea power and gained him respect in other countries, especially in England. Mahan's views were shaped by 17th century conflicts between the Dutch Republic, the Kingdom of England, the Kingdom of France, and Habsburg Spain, and by the naval conflicts between France and Spain during the French Revolutionary and Napoleonic Wars. British naval superiority eventually defeated France, consistently preventing invasion and an effective blockade. Mahan emphasised that naval operations were chiefly to be won by decisive battles and blockades. Popular support for Mahan's theory reached a zenith with the United States victory over Spain, Japan's defeat of China in 1894, and the 1904-1905 war between Japan and Russia.

In the 19th century, the United States sought greater control over its seaborne commerce in order to protect its economic interests which relied heavily on exports bound mainly for Europe. Mahan's work propagated the need to revitalise U.S. sea power, and is a broader account of the relationships between the ocean, trade, and national strength. Its account of Atlantic imperial rivalries is also an estimate of the effect of sea power upon the course of history and the prosperity of nations. As an analysis of purely naval strategy, it is also a thesis emphasising concentrated battle fleet engagements as a means of achieving command of the sea. Most importantly, however, it is an outline of a grand strategy bound up in a national outlook towards the maritime world.

Mahan wrote *The Influence of Sea Power upon History 1660-1783* in response to the somewhat ironic position of the United States and its navy in the international system in the 1880s and 90s. The incongruity was chiefly with respect to the gap between growing U.S. economic power and the comparative weakness of the United States Navy which was going through a period of continuous change. Mahan had visions of the oceans as highways for both commerce and war. With an arms race beginning to heat up in December of 1896 Mahan wrote concerning the preparations for an impending conflict that the creation of materials for war, under modern conditions, requires a length of time which does not permit the postponement of it to the hour of impending hostilities. "To put into the water a first-class battleship, fully armoured, within a year after laying of her keel, as has been done in England, is justly considered an exhibition of the nation's resources for naval shipbuilding; and there yet remained to be done the placing of her battery, and many other matters of principle detail essential to her readiness for sea. This time certainly would not be less for ourselves, doing our utmost."[1]

Mahan contended that with the command of the sea, even if local and temporary, naval operations in support of land forces could be of decisive importance. He also believed that naval supremacy could be exercised by a transnational consortium acting in defence of a multinational system of free trade. His theories, expounded before the submarine became a serious factor in warfare, delayed the introduction of convoys as a defence against the Imperial German Navy's U-boat campaign during World War I. By the 1930s, the U.S. Navy had built long-range submarines to raid Japanese shipping; but in World War II, the Imperial Japanese Armed Forces, still tied to Mahan, designed its submarines as ancillaries to the fleet and failed to attack American supply lines in the Pacific. Mahan's analysis of the Spanish-American War suggested to him that the great distances in the Pacific required the American battle fleet to be designed with long-range striking power.

Mahan believed first, that good political and naval leadership was no less important than geography when it came to the development of sea power. Second, Mahan's unit of political analysis insofar as sea power was concerned was a transnational consortium, rather than a single nation state. Third, his economic ideal was free trade rather than economic independence as a national policy. Fourth, his recognition of the influence of geography on strategy was tempered by a strong appreciation of the power of contingency to affect outcomes. This was a profound geopolitical insight based on an understanding of the impact of geography on history.

In 1890, Mahan prepared a secret contingency plan for war between the British Empire and the United States. Mahan believed that if the Royal Navy blockaded the East Coast of the United States, the US Navy should be concentrated in one of its ports, preferably New York Harbour with its two widely separated exits, and employ torpedo boats to defend the other harbours. This concentration of the U.S. fleet would force the British to tie down such a large proportion of their navy to watch the New York exits that other American ports would be relatively safe. Detached American cruisers should wage "constant offensive action" against the enemy's exposed positions; and if the British were to weaken their blockade force off New York to attack another American port, the concentrated U.S. fleet could capture British coaling ports in Nova Scotia, thereby seriously weakening British ability to engage in naval operations off the American coast. This contingency plan was a clear example of Mahan's application of his principles of naval war, with a clear reliance on Jomini's principle of controlling strategic points.

Mahan became Rear Admiral in 1906 by an act of Congress promoting all retired captains who had served in the Civil War.

The Book, *The Influence of Sea Power upon History, 1660-1783*

As a matter of naval strategy, Mahan's argument is relatively straightforward. The purpose of a navy, Mahan notes, is to protect trade routes and seaborne communications between points assuring: "(a) our own goods and services are safe, and (b) that an enemy's are not." Mahan believed (and used history to demonstrate) that navies are best able to provide this protection through a decisive, concentrated engagement with an adversary fleet. Mahan disagreed with many of his contemporary thinkers who argued for comparably cheaper investments in coastal defence technologies and commerce raiding ships. These ideas, Mahan insisted, were dangerously misguided. Fragmented groups of ships dispersed across the sea were vulnerable to attack and destruction by a larger, unified fleet. His reading of history also demonstrated, time and again, that attacks on adversary merchant vessels by raiders were never as effective as a decisive battle with the enemy that drove his force from the sea or at least allowed it "to appear only as a fugitive." Toward that end, the construction of a fleet of armoured battleships was an essential condition of national power.

Mahan's broader theory of sea power was that commerce, shipping, overseas possessions, and the means to protect them was the basis of national prosperity and influence. As a grand strategist, he argued that Britain's "sea power" underwrote its rise to strategic preponderance in the European system from 1650 to 1780.

Mahan believed that national greatness was inextricably associated with the sea, with its commercial use in peace and its control in war; and he used history as a stock of examples to exemplify his theories, arguing that the education of naval officers should be based on a rigorous study of history. Mahan's framework, derived from Jomini, emphasised strategic locations (such as choke points, canals, and coaling stations), as well as quantifiable levels of fighting power in a fleet. Mahan also believed that in peacetime, states should increase production and shipping capacities and acquire overseas possessions, though he stressed that the number of coal fuelling stations and strategic bases should be limited to avoid draining too many resources from a country.

The primary mission of a navy was to secure the command of the sea, which would permit the maintenance of sea communications for one's own ships while denying their use to the enemy and, if necessary, closely supervise neutral trade. Control of the sea could be achieved not by destruction of commerce but only by destroying or neutralising the enemy fleet. Such a strategy called for the concentration of naval forces composed of capital ships, not too large but numerous, well-manned with crews thoroughly trained, and operating under the principle that the best defence is an aggressive offense.

The books' premise was simple, namely that in the contests between France and England in the 18th century, domination of the sea via naval power was the deciding factor in the outcome, and that control of seaborne commerce was critical to domination. In the 21st century this may seem obvious, but the notion was radical in Mahan's time, especially in a nation entirely obsessed with land expansion to the west.

In the decade before World War I, many naval officers in Britain preferred a simple strategy of a decisive battle over the enemy fleet which was at the base of Mahan's theory. To illustrate this concept, Mahan wrote in his *The Influence of Sea Power upon History 1660-1783*:

> *Nevertheless, a vague feeling of contempt for the past, supposed to be obsolete, combines with natural indolence to blind men even to those permanent strategic lessons which lie close to the surface of naval history. For instance, how many look upon the battle of Trafalgar, the crown of Nelson's glory and the seal of his genius, as other than an isolated event of exceptional grandeur? How many ask themselves the strategic question, 'How did the ships come to be just there?' How many realise it to be the final act in a great strategic drama, extending over a year or more, in which two of the greatest leaders that ever lived, Napoleon and Nelson, were pitted against each other? At Trafalgar it was not Villeneuve that failed, but Napoleon that was vanquished; not Nelson that won, but England that was saved; and why? Because Napoleon's combinations failed, and Nelson's intuitions and activity kept the English fleet ever on the track of the enemy, and brought it up in time at the decisive moment. The tactics at Trafalgar, while open to criticism in detail, were in their main features conformable to the principles of war, and their audacity was justified as well by urgency of the case as by the results; but the great lessons of efficiency in preparation, of activity and energy in execution, and of thought and insight on the part of the English leader during the previous months, are strategic lessons, and as such they are still remain good.*[2]

In the above quote, Mahan illustrates his belief in the strategic importance of seeking out the enemy fleet and precipitating a decisive battle and the relationship a decisive battle like Trafalgar had on the grand strategy of England. Mahan wrote a two-volume biography of Lord Nelson but the British experience at sea versus Napoleon infused all his work. "For any navy, naval officer, sailor, or academic, Trafalgar will have meaning. Because of this, it has a unique place in the development of naval history and maritime strategy."[3]

Mahan had previously displayed a propensity for historical scholarship when he did a historical analysis of the navy in the Civil War. Mahan began studying historical examples to use while he was at the Naval War College. Mahan wrote in his autobiography about this experience:

> *I cannot now reconstitute from memory the sequence of my mental process, but while my problem was still wrestling with my brain there dawned upon me one of those concrete perceptions which turn inward darkness into light—give substance to shadow. The Wachusett was lying at Callao, the seaport of Lima, as dull a coast town as one could dread to see. Lima being but an hour distant, we frequently spent a day there; the English Club extending us its hospitality. In the library was [Theodor] Mommsen's* History of Rome, *which I gave myself to reading, especially the Hannibalic episode. It suddenly struck me, whether by some chance phrase of the author I do not know, how different things might have been could Hannibal have invaded Italy by sea...instead of by the long land route; or could he, after arrival, have been in free communication with Carthage by water. This clew, once laid hold of, I followed up in the particular instance.*[4]

In Mahan's view of sea power, two principal meanings emerge: (a) command of the sea through naval superiority; and (b) that combination of maritime commerce, overseas possessions, and privileged access to foreign markets that produces national "wealth and greatness." The two concepts overlap. Mahan wrote of sea power as "that overbearing power on the sea which drives the enemy's flag from it, or allows it to appear only as a fugitive." His second meaning was more succinctly stated: "(a) Production; (b) Shipping; (c) Colonies and Markets—in a word, sea power."[5]

By writing he registered two major achievements. First, he linked maritime policies and events to the national and international processes and in so doing he established naval strategy as a conscious, major element of concern in a nation's overall security policy and strategy. Second, he delineated a series of principles of naval strategy. He was not the only one to do this, but he struck the right note, at the right moment, and firmly established naval history as the basis of his strategic analysis.

Mahan offered six characteristics of Maritime Power:

1. *Geographic position: maritime, colonies.* This refers not only to a state's landmass (whether it is insular or continental), but also to the distance between that home base, potential adversaries, or trade routes.
2. *Physical conformation: coastline borders.* The type and specific features of the permanent base. Large landmasses with small populations and weak naval establishments are a liability for

sea power, whereas heavily populated, long coastlines (like the U.S. East Coast) are a source of strength.

3. *Extent of territory: harbours, lengthy coastlines.* The geostrategic features of the North Atlantic as key determinants of sea power.
4. *Population: large and seagoing.* The number of people in a country obviously influences the "garrisoning" of a given space. But the relationship of population to sea power is not a matter of raw numbers. What might be called the "human resources" of sea power are generally employed in peacetime by the merchant marine and related industries, making for a ready reserve that can be drawn on by the navy. Without the former, the latter rests on weak foundations
5. *National character.* Commercial pursuits must be a distinguishing feature of the nations that have at one time or another been great upon the sea.
6. *Character of government: free, moral.* Consistent support and preparedness are key to the maintenance of Sea Power.

Mahan also identified five geographic key points, the possession of which was crucial to global maritime power:

1. Straits of Dover
2. Gibraltar
3. Singapore/Malacca Strait
4. Cape of Good Hope
5. The Suez Canal [today, we would add the Panama Canal, the Bab el-Mandeb, the Straits of Hormuz, Malacca, and Taiwan, among others].

Mahan used many of Jomini's concepts when he formulated his theory on sea power for example Jomini wrote in *The Art of War* in Article VIII on National Wars:

> *The control of the sea is of much importance in the results of a national invasion. If the people possess a long stretch of coast, and are masters of the sea or in an alliance with a power which controls it, their power of resistance is quintupled, not only on account of the facility of feeding the insurrection and of alarming the enemy on all the points he may occupy, but still more by the difficulties which will be thrown in the way of his procuring supplies by the sea.*[6]

Mahan also believed that the concentration of forces was extremely important and he warned never to split the fleet. He also emphasised the importance of central position, interior lines, and logistics. Mahan, like Jomini, emphasised the importance of defending oceanic lines of communications. Mahan saw warfare at sea much in the way Jomini saw warfare on land in that he analysed past campaigns to devise principles that would allow the US Navy to emulate the glory and successes of earlier maritime empires.

Mahan's ideal of a nation was that a colonial power with overseas naval bases, a strong merchant marine, and a powerful fleet of battle ships, which in the event of war would form up as a single unit, seek out the enemy battle fleet (also helpfully formed up as a single formation), and defeat it in a decisive battle. His theory of maritime power envisioned a climactic battle between fleets.

Mahan drew lessons from the history of the past to the general question of the influence of government upon the sea career of its people. That influence can work in two distinct but closely related ways.

In peace, the government by its policy can favour the natural growth of a people's industries and its tendencies to seek adventure and gain by way of the sea; or it can try to develop such industries and such sea-going bent, when they do not naturally exist; or, on the other hand, the government may by mistaken action check and fetter the progress which the people left to themselves would make. In any one of these ways the influence of the government will be felt, making or marring the sea power of the country in the matter of peaceful commerce; upon which alone, it cannot be too often insisted, a thoroughly strong navy can be based.

In war, the influence of the government will be felt in maintaining an armed navy, of a size commensurate with the growth of its shipping and the importance of the interests connected with it. More important even than the size of the navy is the question of its institutions, favouring a healthful spirit and activity, and providing for rapid development in time of war by an adequate reserve of men and of ships and by measures for drawing out that general reserve power which has before been pointed to, when considering the character and pursuits of the people.

Comments

Mahan considered war to be "simply a political movement, though violent and exceptional in character."[7] Though emphasising on combat, Mahan employs a broader approach and posits that the nature of warfare is fundamentally tied to promoting seaborne commerce, access to overseas markets, and the pursuit of wealth. In *The Influence of Sea Power upon History*, he writes of "the clash of interests, the angry feelings roused by conflicting attempts thus to appropriate the larger share, if not the whole, of the advantages of commerce, and of distant unsettled commercial regions, led to war."[8] In order to protect global commerce and ensure the flow of wealth generating goods, Mahan considers "command of the sea" the supreme objective of maritime warfare.[9] He states plainly that "the use and control of the sea is but one link in the chain of exchange by which wealth accumulates; but it is the central link."[10] Command of the sea, the expression of sea power, in turn, requires strong naval power based around a large blue water fleet. Yet a large coal, oil, or gas burning fleet depends on the same distant stations and overseas bases that the fleet itself was tasked with protecting. Therefore, generating the sea power necessary to create wealth from seaborne commerce is, in Mahan's perspective, also the means to generate sufficient wealth to maintain strong sea power.

Following in the Jominian tradition, Mahan neither offers nor demonstrates the same degree of confidence in the theoretical study of warfare like Clausewitz. Mahan places greater emphasis on drawing principles from historical study than on the utility of abstract theoretical insight. However, his broadly historical work is compatible with Clausewitz's writings on the methods of acquiring military knowledge, with experience, theoretical inquiry, and historical study each providing valuable yet different insights.[11] Nonetheless, Mahan puts forward a comparatively limited theory of sea power and does not demonstrate the same degree of guidance on how to best utilise his theory in general that Clausewitz does.[12]

Mahan believed that the use of navies should not only be fully subordinate to political ends, but also that navies were superior instruments for implementing policy than land forces.[13] Being more mobile and less symbolic of belligerent intentions, navies permit the influence of national policy to "be felt where national armies cannot go."[14] In addition, because Mahan reasons that a navy should be used to secure the safety of maritime commerce, which was vital to national economies, he sees the navy as an instrument of both security policy and economic policy.

Mahan's emphasis on the necessity of achieving total command of the sea and the great efforts of men and materiel needed to achieve this, with the sea being treated as if it were a piece of territory capable of being conquered and ruled, demonstrates a tendency in his writings to see maritime war as tending toward the absolute. He argues that concentration was "the predominant principle" of naval warfare. He reasons that "the maximum offensive power of the fleet... and not the offensive power of the single ship, is the true object of battleship construction." Moreover, Mahan believed that it was only through concentrating in large battle-fleets that one's navy could engage and defeat the enemy's centre of gravity, its fleets, in decisive battles. Beyond this, he argued that the fleet must be most concentrated to strike at decisive points and that, as a general principle, the fleet must never be divided.[15]

Mahan considers the number and character of the seagoing population in a state to be one of the six essential elements of sea power. He specifically emphasises the endurance of the commercial and maritime-focused populace of England compared to the continental and agriculturally-focused French. Mahan also considered the United States to be grossly deficient in this element of sea power in the late 19th century.[16]

Mahan also wrote of "uncertainties peculiar to the sea," including the natural dynamics and vastness of the ocean. Though not discounting the importance of rational calculation, Mahan placed a great deal of emphasis on a talented, courageous, and aggressive commander's capacity to overcome these problems, including the ability to locate the enemy fleet, defeat it, and, consequently, gain command of the sea. In this way, Mahan's solution to the problems of friction and chance is broadly similar to that put forward by Clausewitz.

Mahan also emphasised the power of the offence in war. He argues that, "in naval war...the navy is the offensive," and that the best protection against the enemy's fire is a well-directed fire from our own guns. He reasoned that, unlike soldiers on land, ships at sea cannot prepare ground or remain under cover when attempting to act defensively, which removes much of the advantage of the defence discussed by Clausewitz and Sun Tzu.[17] Mahanian strategy rests on an assumption that the best defence was offense, with the fight carried to a definite issue. This assumption likely contributed to Mahan's belief in the principle of concentration and in seeking decisive battle.

For warlike preparation Mahan advocated the maintenance of suitable naval stations, in those distant parts of the world to which the armed shipping must follow the peaceful vessels of commerce. The protection of such stations must depend either upon direct military force or upon a surrounding friendly population, such as the American colonists once were to England. Such friendly surroundings and backing, joined to a reasonable military provision, are the best of defences, and when combined with decided preponderance at sea, make a scattered and extensive empire, like that of England, secure; for while it is true that an unexpected attack may cause disaster in some one quarter, the actual superiority of naval power prevents such disaster from being general or irremediable. History has sufficiently proved this. England's naval bases have been in all parts if the world; and her fleets have at once protected them, kept open the communications between them, and relied upon them for shelter.

Having no foreign establishments, either colonial or military, the ships of war of the United States, in war, will be like land birds, unable to fly far from their own shores. To provide resting places for them, where they can coal and repair, would be one of the first duties of a government proposing to itself the development of the power of the nation at sea.

The best known competing geopolitical model to Mahan's is Halford Mackinder's 1904 "Heartland" or "World Island" theory: a theoretical and historical argument that control of the landmass of Eurasia underwrote a continental (or land power) that no maritime state could effectively challenge. Mackinder believed that the momentary dominance of European warships and seaborne commerce (from roughly 1500-1900) was largely an accident of technology and not an immutable fact. As new technologies like the railroad knit together states and empires in Central Europe and Asia, the "Columbian Epoch" of European maritime imperialism would soon end and primacy would revert to the historical norm of continental power achieved via control of the Eurasian heartland, such as with Genghis Khan, Tamerlane, and the like. As Mackinder conceived it, the Eurasian heartland is surrounded by an "Inner Crescent" of Western Europe, the Middle East, and South and North East Asia. Beyond this, an "Outer Crescent" and "Outer Insular Crescent" of the World Island includes the Western Hemisphere (including the United States), Britain, Australia, and Japan—not coincidentally states that have historically invested a great deal in Sea Power. Nations in these outer rings were, by Mackinder's definition, peripheral to the "pivot" of history in central Eurasia.

Conclusion

Timeliness contributed no small part to the widespread acceptance of Mahan's theories. Although his history was relatively thin, based as it was on secondary sources, his vigorous style, and clear theory won widespread acceptance of navalists and supporters of the New Imperialism in Africa and Asia.

Given the rapid technological changes underway in propulsion (from coal to oil and from reciprocating engines to turbines), ordnance (with better fire directors, and new high explosives), and armour and the emergence of new craft such as destroyers and submarines, Mahan's emphasis on the capital ship and the command of the sea came at an opportune moment.

Mahan wrote twenty books and hundreds of articles in an effort to educate the American people and their leaders about the importance of history and geography to the study and practice of international relations. His understanding of the anarchical nature of international politics, the importance of geography to the global balance of power, the role of sea power in national security policy, and history's ability to shed light on contemporary world politics remains relevant to the 21st century world.

In his memoirs, *From Sail to Steam*, Mahan credited his reading of Theodore Mommsen's six-volume *History of Rome* for the insight that sea power was the key to global predominance. In *The Influence of Sea Power Upon History*, Mahan reviewed the role of sea power in the emergence and growth of the British Empire. In the book's first chapter, he described the sea as a "great highway" and "wide common" with "well-worn trade routes" over which men pass in all directions. He identified several narrow passages or strategic "chokepoints," the control of which contributed to Great Britain's command of the seas. He famously listed six fundamental elements of sea power: geographical position, physical conformation, extent of territory, size of population, character of the people, and character of government. Based largely on those factors, Mahan envisioned the United States as the geopolitical successor to the British Empire.

In his articles and books, Mahan accurately envisioned the geopolitical struggles of the 20th and 21st centuries. In *The Interest of America in International Conditions* (1910), Mahan foresaw the then-emerging First World War and the underlying geopolitical conditions leading to the Second World War, recognising that Germany's central position in Europe, her unrivalled industrial and military might on the continent, and her quest for sea power posed a threat to Great Britain and ultimately the United States. The rivalry between Germany and Great Britain today," he averred, "is the danger point, not only of European politics but of world politics as well."

Mahan also grasped the fundamental geopolitical realities of the Cold War that emerged from the ashes of the first two world wars. In *The Problem of Asia*, Mahan urged statesmen to "glance at the map" of Asia and note "the vast, uninterrupted mass of the Russian Empire, stretching without a break ... from the meridian of western Asia Minor, until to the eastward it overpasses that of Japan." He envisioned an expansionist Russia needing to be contained by an alliance of the United States, Great Britain, France, Germany, and Japan, which is precisely what happened between 1945 and 1991.

Mahan also recognised the power potential of China and foresaw a time when the United States would need to be concerned with China's rise. In 1893, Mahan wrote a letter to the editor of the *New York Times* in which he recommended U.S. annexation of Hawaii as a necessary first step to exercise control of the North Pacific. If the United States failed to act, Mahan warned, "the vast mass of China ... may yield to one of those impulses which have in past ages buried civilisation under a wave of barbaric invasion." Should China "burst her barriers eastward," he wrote, "it would be impossible to exaggerate the momentous issues dependent upon a firm hold of the [Hawaiian] Islands by a great civilised maritime power."

Similarly, in *The Problem of Asia*, Mahan depicted a future struggle for power in the area of central Asia he called the "debatable and debated ground," and identified the "immense latent force" of China as a potential geopolitical rival. "[I]t is scarcely desirable," Mahan wrote, "that so vast a proportion of mankind as the Chinese constitute should be animated by but one spirit and moved as a single man." Mahan knew that Western science and technology would at some point be globalised and wrote that under such circumstances "it is difficult to contemplate with equanimity such a vast mass as the four hundred millions of China concentrated into one effective political organisation, equipped with modern appliances, and cooped within a territory already narrow for it."

Like Germany before the First World War, China in the 21st century has embraced Mahan.[18] With regard to Mahan's elements of sea power, China is situated in the heart of east-central Asia and has a lengthy sea-coast, a huge population, a growing economy, growing military and naval power, and, at least for now, a stable government. China's political and military leaders have not hidden their desire to supplant the United States as the predominant power in the Asia-Pacific region. The Chinese will support Mahan's theory of sea power as it is at once obsessed with 'economic development' and 'increasingly reliant on seaborne commerce'. This is reason enough to reacquaint with the writings of that great American strategic thinker.

In the 21st century, even as technologies advance, the core insights of Mahan and his method remain fundamental. The main theme in Mahan's writings is the supreme importance of sea power in the shaping of national destinies. No one deny that the possession of sea power is an essential prerequisite for great-power status. No power can be called a great or world power unless it has a significant naval capability.

FURTHER READING

- . Philip A. Crowel, "Alfred Thayer Mahan: The Naval Historian". In *Makers of Modern Strategy: from Machiavelli to the Nuclear Age,* (ed.) Peter Paret (Princeton: Princeton University Press, 1986).
- Alfred Thayer Mahan, *The Influence of Sea Power upon History, 1660-1783* (Boston: Little Brown & Company, 1898).
- Till, Geoffrey. *SEAPOWER: A Guide for the Twenty First Century* (London: Frank Cass Publishers, 2005).
- Kaplan, Robert D., *The Revenge of Geography: What the Maps Tell Us About the Coming Conflicts and the Battle Against Fate* (New York: Random House, 2012).
- Zimmermann, Warren, *First Great Triumph: How Five Americans Made Their Country a World Power* (2002). p. 562. (Chapter on Mahan)
- John Keegan, *The Price of Admiralty: The Evolution of Naval Warfare* (New York: Viking, 1988).

8

Corbett

For whosoever commands the sea commands the trade; whosoever commands the trade of the world commands the riches of the world, and consequently the world itself.[1]

—Sir Walter Raleigh

The Author

Two of the more prominent and respected theorists on naval warfare in the 19th and the 20th century were Sir Julian S. Corbett (1854-1922), and the American Rear Admiral Alfred Thayer Mahan (1840-1914). It is reasonable to state that these two men are the most influential thinkers and theorists in the history of sea power.

Julian Stafford Corbett, a prolific British naval historian, impacted British leaders—naval and civilian—whose works helped shape the Royal Navy's reforms of that era. Corbett became a fixture in British naval circles and became friends with First Sea Lord Admiral Sir John Fisher. Corbett often supported Fisher's efforts to revolutionise the Royal Navy, and he wrote several books and newspaper articles in support. He taught at the Naval College in Greenwich where, after publishing a half dozen significant works of history, he released his highly influential 1911 book on sea power, *Some Principles of Maritime Strategy*. The work is his lasting theoretical contribution to strategic thought which remains a classic among students of naval warfare and international relations theory and continues to be studied in professional military education.

Unlike most military strategists and particularly naval strategists, Corbett was a civilian who never served in the military or the navy. Corbett saw naval warfare as part of a nation's larger policies. He was a meticulous researcher and became a leading maritime strategist to rival Mahan. He complemented Mahan's ideas while presenting a more logical and structured argument of sea power. His development of Maritime Strategy was a necessary complement to Mahan's development of Naval Strategy. Corbett was more pragmatic and therefore, a more effective strategist than Mahan. He had studied Carl von Clausewitz and he adapted the Prussian's military theories to the maritime environment. Corbett's theories eventually became the accepted way of conducting maritime conflicts.

Corbett's primary objective was to fill the void in British naval doctrine by formalising the theories and principles of naval warfare. Corbett focused on the art of naval warfare and defined the differences between land warfare and naval warfare. He set the initial focus towards the employment of manoeuvre type doctrine. Corbett's principles of sea control, focus on the enemy, and manoeuvre for tactical advantage form the foundation of today's naval manoeuvre warfare.

Corbett worked from within the naval community to influence the naval establishment. He believed in studying and developing the theory of war for educational purposes, which he felt established a common vehicle of expression and a common plane of thought ... for the sake of mental solidarity between a chief and his subordinates. Through his lectures at the Naval War College, Corbett conveyed his ideas of limited war and strategic defence which were very different from the accepted norms of naval theory and strategy of the time.

Corbett's arguments were sophisticated and ranged from the highest levels of national policy to naval strategy to officer education to naval doctrine. He followed Clausewitz's notable dictum that "war is the continuation of politics by other means." Effective strategy was the product of national objectives as well as a good understanding of history and solid strategic theory.[2] This meant that at the operational level, navies and armies had to work together to achieve national strategic ends.

While Mahan linked sea power with national power, Corbett

illuminated this relationship and displayed a keen understanding, developed through his own historical study, of the limits of sea power, and war more broadly, as an instrument of national policy. His influential theory on the role of sea power in the geopolitical context of the European balance of power at the turn of the 20th century is a clear reflection of the rapidly changing strategic environment and the equally rapid changes in military technology. Corbett defined maritime strategy, limited war, command of the sea, and, at the height of the British Empire, laid the ground work for understanding a "British way of war."

Corbett was first and foremost a historian and a professional military educator. He tied the study of history to the development of theory with a constant focus on the role of education in developing a leader's critical thinking and judgment. Corbett was one of the earliest and most enduring contributors to fully establish the link between history, theory, and professional military education.

Corbett's Views on War

Corbett offered no general theory of warfare at sea. Instead, he focused his thoughts on the nature of maritime strategy and what naval warfare meant to the power of a nation. While many theorists of naval warfare tried to mechanically adapt land warfare concepts to the maritime environment, Corbett countered that the interests and requirements of naval warfare differed in fundamental ways from those of land warfare.

Corbett felt that protecting lines of communication was much more difficult to enforce at sea than on land. This difficulty was the physical geographical differences of the sea and land. Because of these physical differences, Corbett analysed naval warfare in its own terms, having its own unique characteristics. A maritime strategy must develop an understanding of a maritime perspective, which begins with an understanding of the sea—what Mahan called "The Great Common." One of the fundamental points to understanding the sea is that people are merely visitors. Corbett, commented: "Men live upon the land and not the sea ... you cannot conquer sea because it is not susceptible of ownership, at least outside territorial waters."[3] This remains true, as even modern economic exclusion zones remain governed by the right of innocent passage. This may seem like a very simplistic point, but it has profound implications and gets at the heart of what is different about the sea—human presence on, under, or above the sea is transitory in nature. While only visitors, mankind has had an ancient relationship with the sea, harvesting marine life for food and using waterways as transportation for millennia.

Corbett stated that you cannot conquer the sea because it is not susceptible to ownership. To Corbett, command of the sea was a relative and not an absolute which could be categorised as general or local, temporary or permanent. Corbett defined the two fundamental methods of obtaining control of the lines of communication as the actual physical destruction or capture of enemy warships and merchant ships, and or a naval blockade. Today, this concept is defined as sea control.

Corbett was not infatuated with the search for the decisive battle or with the need for the strategic offensive. In general, he favoured the strategic defensive, with an emphasis on the offensive at the operational level. Corbett's strategic defence advocated such measures as an intense local offensive, the projection of land forces, various types of blockades, and raids on enemy trade routes. Moreover, Corbett recognised that once the enemy has been sufficiently weakened on sea and on land, the shift to the strategic offensive should not be delayed.

Corbett did not believe that the concentration of naval forces at sea was the highest and simplest law of strategy; rather, he observed that the principle of concentration had done more harm than good. The principle of concentration is "a truism—no one would dispute it. As a canon of practical strategy, it is untrue".[4] Corbett felt that superior concentration not only deterred the weaker opponent from seeking battle but presented him with an opportunity to attack his enemy's exposed national lines of communication. He felt that superior concentration of naval forces created yet another serious problem. The greater the concentration of a fleet, the more difficult it was to conceal its whereabouts and movements.

In the process of adapting Clausewitz's theory to the unique circumstances of naval warfare, Corbett developed his own innovative theory of limited war in maritime strategy. The first of his two main points was that in wartime conditions on the continent, as opposed to those in the maritime and imperial environment, wars were fought mostly between adjacent states. Corbett's second point was that in wars between contiguous continental states "there will be no strategical obstacle to his [the enemy's] being able to use his whole force".[5] In other words, the nature of continental war makes it difficult to limit political aims, because one or both states are able to use all of the means at their disposal to protect the inevitably threatened vital interests. This means that the conditions for the ideal limited war exist only in maritime warfare and can only be exploited by the preponderant naval power: "...limited war is only permanently possible to island Powers or between Powers which are separated by sea, and then only when the Power desiring limited war is able to command the sea to such a degree as to be able not only to isolate the distant object, but also to render impossible the invasion of his home territory."[6]

While Corbett shared a belief in the primacy of politics in war and in devising an appropriate strategy to protect the national interests, he was interested in the diplomatic alliance systems and coalitions formed before and during a war, and he was also concerned with the economic and financial dimensions of waging war as well as with the technological and material aspects of war, which were of no interest to Clausewitz.

Corbett's value for today's military professional lies in four of his concepts:

- controlling lines of communications, focus on the enemy, and manoeuvre for tactical advantage;
- the aspects of political, economic and financial dimensions of waging war as well as with the technological and material aspects of war;
- the primacy of politics in war and in devising an appropriate strategy to protect the national interests; and
- the emphasis on efficiency in battle while preserving costly assets.

Corbett's views on the efficacy of commerce protection came face to face with the fact that it was considered of major importance to the policymakers of the 17th century. Corbett explained this by saying:

Thus, although strategists, for the purpose of commending their views to the public and the Treasury, naturally wrote in terms of commerce, we must never forget that what they were really aiming at was command of the sea by the domination of the trade routes and acquisition of focal points as naval stations.[7]

This was written in support of his own view that a trade war was not as important as gaining command of the sea. However, he would slowly come to the conclusion that trade war had its place in maritime strategy. Corbett eventually concluded that command of the sea was for the purpose of protecting trade.

From Clausewitz and his views on Offensive and Defensive War, Corbett advanced his theory of Limited and Unlimited War. His starting point was Clausewitz' description of these types of war and the effort the belligerents would put forth to accomplish their aims. Corbett pointed out that where Clausewitz concentrated on continental aspects of war and their application to European strategy, the problem with Limited War was the usual progression to Unlimited War. However, Corbett went beyond the continental outlook and showed that Limited War is the ideal type of war for a maritime power, especially one that is an island with frontiers not easily assailed and thus serve as a defence against territorial invasion. The object for the island nation in Limited War is to isolate the object of attack and at the same time to retain a home defence that bars an unlimited counter strike.[8] Corbett explained that attack against overseas possessions by the weaker opponent is the ideal Limited War scenario and used the conquest of Canada in the Seven Years War as the best example of the weaker belligerent attaining its end by this form of war.[9] His conclusion was that:

...limited war is only permanently possible to island Powers or between Powers which are separated by sea, and then only when the Power desiring limited war is able to command the sea to such a degree as to be able not only to isolate the distant object, but also to render impossible the invasion of his home territory.[10]

Guerrilla War at Sea: The Submarine

When submarines first went to sea early in the 20th century, they were immediately recognised as an extraordinary threat to surface ships. In World War II they were so effective against warships that they sank nearly as much aircraft carrier tonnage as was sunk by aircraft. Post-war attack submarines, nuclear-powered and armed with missiles and more advanced torpedoes, now pose an even greater threat to surface warships.

In both world wars, submarines were also a serious threat to merchant shipping. In World War II, German U-boats nearly severed the lifelines to Britain. U.S. submarines successfully isolated Japan by nearly wiping out its merchant fleet, and, in the Mediterranean, British and Axis submarines competed in attempts to cut their opponents' communication with North Africa.

Barring a brief period in 1942–43, when U-boats operated successfully in so-called wolf packs, submarines have always been solo performers, relying for successful attack on concealment and surprise rather than concentration of force. These tactics, quite different from fleet actions, are akin to guerrilla war at sea. The submarine stalks its prey while the target—a warship, merchant ship, or convoy—seeks clues as to its presence in order to take evasive action. Simultaneously, anti-submarine forces—destroyers, maritime patrol aircraft, or helicopters—are predators and submarines the prey. The tactical competition between the two is all search and screening, deadly hide-and-seek, for when the submarine closes in, its target can do nothing but try to escape the blow, and when antisubmarine forces localise a submarine, no help will come and it will either have to fight like a cornered beast or go silent and try to slip away.

If submarines were able to protect sea lanes from attack, including air attack, then they would be serious candidates to succeed the aircraft carrier as the capital ship of the missile era. But as soloists their role has remained that of sea denial, not sea control, that of spoilers rather than champions of sea power. They are the latest in a long line of raiders of the deep, carrying on a tradition of isolation and stealth that began in the 16th century, when the English privateers seized treasure ships at sea and raided Caribbean possessions in the teeth of the Spanish navy. Later, in the American Civil War, Confederate raiders harassed Northern shipping despite the overwhelming superiority of the Union navy.

To the modern mind, a convoy has become a group of merchant ships protected against submarines. But, beginning in the age of fighting sail, there was a long tradition of protecting convoys against surface raiders, called "cruisers." In *Some Principles of Maritime Strategy*, Corbett sorted out the separate roles of the battle fleet and the cruisers: the former established control of the seas by its concentrated presence or in a climactic battle; the latter either struck at lines of communication or attempted to fend off other raiders by operating alone or in small detachments. Corbett also traced the influence of long-range radio communication and predicted that this development would allow navies to bring such a swift concentration of superior power that the utility of surface raiders would come to an end. That he was right was proved by the fate of such surface raiders of World War II as the German battleship *Bismarck*, which sank after taking hits from an overwhelming combination of bombs, naval guns, and torpedoes.

Corbett fully appreciated the major role submarines would play against capital ships. Indeed, submarines have become the biggest threat to commerce, ahead of mines and aircraft. In addition, they are effective killers of submarines. Guerrilla war is therefore the apt term for submarine warfare. The battle tactics are dispersion, surprise, strikes where the enemy is weak and unprepared, disappearance into the vastness of the ocean, and a continuing erosion of enemy morale and dilution of his resources.

Sea Power

From his basic precept that Maritime Strategy required both military and naval power, Corbett explained his theories in detail. He first described what he viewed as Command of the Sea. Corbett stated, "The object of naval warfare must always be directly or indirectly either to secure Command of the Sea or to prevent the enemy from securing it."[11] Command of the Sea is not a binary entity; that is, loss of Command of the Sea does not automatically mean that the opponent gains command. As Corbett pointed out, Command of the Sea is usually in dispute with neither party to a conflict in absolute control. It is in the dispute of Command of the Sea that Naval Strategy is primarily concerned while overall Maritime Strategy is tied directly to National Strategy.

Like Mahan, Corbett recognised that battle was important, but he argued that there was more to maritime strategy and naval warfare than just major fleet actions, such as the importance of strategic points that provide navies reach. He even went to great lengths to refute the principle of concentration in naval warfare. According to Corbett, "the current conception of the functions of a fleet is dangerously narrowed and our best minds cramp their strategical view by assuming unconsciously that the sole purpose of a fleet is to win battles at sea."[12] Corbett demonstrated that each nation needs a unique strategic doctrine that is based on history and theory, if it is to meet contemporary strategic needs.

Corbett argued that sea power was a geographically limited, temporary event. It was achieved by applying limited, localised force. Corbett believed the chief mission of the navy was to support land forces and participate in joint operations. Mahan viewed the navy as the country's primary source to providing national security by seeking out and destroying the enemy's fleet and Corbett saw the navy as a supporting arm of the army.[13] These two naval power theorists had different views on how to achieve sea power, however, they did agree on some points, for example, the value of controlling lines of communication, both friend and foe.

Corbett employs a broad approach to warfare, which focuses on the combative nature of war but also diplomatic alliances, coalitions formed before and during a war, and the economic and financial dimensions of warfare. The object of naval warfare, in Corbett's perspective, is to establish control over maritime communications for both military and commercial purposes. Corbett places equal if not greater emphasis on the deceptive nature of warfare. Indeed, he calls for "an appearance of weakness that covers a reality of strength."[14] Corbett's writings reflect a greater respect for Clausewitz's theories of land warfare. As Corbett puts it, "it scarcely needs saying that it is almost impossible that a war can be decided by naval action alone."[15] Also, Corbett shares Clausewitz's belief that theory should play a pre-eminent role in the study of warfare. He also agreed with Clausewitz that, because even the best theory of war is "not... a substitute for judgment and experience," it cannot "systematise strategy into an exactly science."[16]

Corbett argues that naval supremacy is not an end goal in itself; rather, naval supremacy must be pursued to meet political objectives. In accordance with this, Corbett stressed the utilitarian nature of the maritime dimension of war in supporting the primacy of politics. Beyond this, Corbett acknowledges that the military is only one of several options for carrying out state policy and that, even if war is the option chosen, it may itself be "limited by contingent."[17]

Corbett places comparatively little emphasis on the utility of decisive battle. Being fully conscious of the fact that large naval engagements rarely occur and, even when fought, rarely have a decisive influence on the course of a war in the same way that large land battles do, Corbett argues that focusing on decisive naval battle is wasteful.[18] Corbett actually goes so far as to claim that the much-heralded British victory at Trafalgar had little impact on the Napoleonic Wars:

> *Trafalgar is ranked as one of the decisive battles of the world, and yet of all the great victories, there is not one which to all appearance was so barren of immediate result.... It gave England finally the dominion of the seas, but it left Napoleon dictator of the continent. So incomprehensible was its apparent sterility that to fill the void a legend grew up that it saved England from invasion.*[19]

In contrast to decisive battles, Corbett focuses far more attention on blockading, the disruptive threat of a "fleet in being" near enemy shores, and naval support of land operations by transporting, supplying, and landing ground troops in joint operations.[20] Corbett considers these activities to be the core of naval strength.

Corbett does not think that the maximum concentration of forces is the key to winning a decisive battle and defeating the enemy. He calls the principle of concentration "untrue" and "a kind of shibboleth," which is unworthy of its high standing.[21] In contrast, Corbett provides several arguments against the principle of concentration:

- First, superior concentration at sea permits enemy fleets to avoid one's own more easily and, therefore, reduces the probability of decisive battle.[22] As a result, less overt concentration is the way to entice a major engagement.
- Second, concentrating one's fleet reduces the ships available to protect sea lanes and ensure steady seaborne communication.[23]

As these are vital elements of maritime strategy, total concentration at sea is unworkable.

- Third, concentrated fleets are inflexible and comparatively easy to detect.[24] For Corbett, the flexibility to disperse and conceal the true strength and intentions of one's ships, when necessary, are essential to victory.[25]

Corbett believes that any fleet was subject to "peculiar conditions of friction which clog its freedom of disposition," including friction derived from the demands of commerce protection.[26] The need for commerce protection conspires against the desire, in some instances, to concentrate the fleet into one powerful mass. His solution to overcoming the problems of friction and uncertainty, must be granted a certain power over and above successful calculations, Corbett argues that careful calculation and rational strategic creativity were key.

Finally, consistent with his de-emphasis on seeking decisive battle, Corbett favours the strategic defensive, though with an emphasis on the offence at the level of operations. Corbett suggests employing a broadly defensive strategy for the fleet, with some ships tasked with blockade duties and defence of sea lanes, but retaining the flexibility to attack and counter-attack enemy ships through intense local offensives, support amphibious operations, and undertake blockades and commerce raiding when necessary. Corbett reasons that active-defence is the stronger form of warfare.

In the context of war, Command of the Sea means control of passage either over, under or upon the sea. Having possession of the sea is a physical impossibility since to do so would require the stationing of ships in every square mile of ocean throughout the world and no nation can do this. Even today with satellite observation of the whole world, no nation can prevent passage upon every ocean. Only control of choke points or control of specific areas can be accomplished by those in Command of the Sea. This was Corbett's idea and it is still valid today. In war, Command of the Sea can mean control for only some limited period of time or of specific small areas. Only when one opponent or the other is militarily defeated can Command of the Sea be absolute. As Corbett pointed out in *The Campaign of Trafalgar*, though England had Command of the Sea after 1805, France still was able to disrupt sea commerce and Napoleon was able to achieve some of his greatest military victories. Absolute Command of the Sea did not exist and, without a military victory, Sea Power can achieve only limited goals.

The sea also acts as a barrier or defence. Command of the Sea removes that barrier for the belligerent who gains it and also retains that barrier as a defence against invasion. Even when disputed, Command of the Sea can be gained in a specific area or for a critical time. Command of the Sea in the English Channel in 1944 facilitated the virtually unhindered Normandy invasion. Yet at the same time, U-boats were still attacking convoys in the Atlantic thus showing that Command of the Sea was not absolute. Corbett stated: Command of the Sea, therefore means nothing but the control of maritime communications, whether for commercial or military purposes. The object of naval warfare is the control of communications and not as in land warfare the conquest of territory.[27]

Strategic Context and Technology

Corbett postulated that sea power is a combination of naval power and maritime economic power. The former is military in nature and the latter is civilian in nature; therefore, states employ sea power as an instrument of statecraft, not merely a tool of war. This is still the case, but the strategic context has changed in one critical respect since Mahan and Corbett formulated their theories.

Changes in strategic context and advances in technology have changed the effects of sea power. By the second half of the 19th century, the only way for sea power to project itself over vast land areas was through economic power. The advent of the torpedo forced a re-evaluation of even the basics of naval warfare. It was believed that the torpedo boat would overcome large armoured ships in a naval war, and, perhaps more importantly, show no mercy to private commerce or property, which included attacking ports. Thus, torpedoes would attack all enemy maritime commerce which could increase insurance rates, reduce trade, raise unemployment, cause food shortages, trigger economic panic, and perhaps even foment rebellion. However, the major navies of the world retained a doctrine focused on the battle fleet that concentrated on main fleet battles.[28]

The rise of new weapons meant that the effectiveness of sea power itself, and the predominance of British naval mastery was slowly undermined. The rise of professional armies, railroads, and artillery were steadily eroding sea power's ability to impact continental politics. Technological progress however continued to impact naval warfare significantly. The ability of navies to create and adapt to technology was a key determinant of prevailing in naval warfare. Technological advances will continue to affect all forms of warfare, but advances in technology have immense effects on air and sea platforms, along with the cyber and space technology that supports those platforms, as they are especially sensitive to technological improvements. Anti-access/ area denial warfare is a more viable naval strategy today.

Sea power is a means to an end; it is not an end in itself. Sea power works to achieve strategic objectives and ultimately policy goals. A continental power can win a war by securing military command at sea, by achieving sea denial, or even just by disputing command at sea very vigorously. For a sea power, command at sea provides the strategic conditions indispensable for success at war.

Navies are the primary military service that provides sea control, maritime power projection, and ensure maritime communications. Sea control allows friendly use of the sea for naval and maritime purposes as well as denying the enemy the same abilities. Maritime power projection includes conventional strikes against targets ashore, advance force operations, raids, and all forms of amphibious operations, from ship-to-objective manoeuvre and sea-based fire support to forces ashore to missions conducted by Naval Special Warfare and Special Operations Forces. Maritime power projection can determine the outcome of a conflict, open a new front, directly support land forces, force enemy forces to displace, be part of economic warfare, seize or attack naval bases and ports, force an inferior enemy to fight, or serve as political coercion. Finally, navies play a vital role in both attacking and protecting maritime communications.

Corbett's theory for the composition of a fleet required a number of different types of ships which included lightly armed fast 'cruisers' for control of sea communications up to the battleship fleet to gain initial Command of the Sea by destruction of the opposing fleet. In its basic form this theory continues to be valid when the modern fleet is analysed. As previously stated, the submarine can now be considered the 'cruiser' Corbett envisaged as the controlling entity and the modern aircraft carrier fleet as the battle fleet needed to secure Command of the Sea.

What is special about Corbett is his emphasis on the importance of putting naval operations in that broader context which does so much to explain their form and purpose, and which, in his view, was affected so much by their result. In this respect, Corbett emphasised that strategy needs to be consciously related to foreign policy, and naval strategy to land strategy:

> *Naval strategy has to be seen not as a separate entity but simply as part of the art of war. Land power and sea power are not in opposition, but their relationship with one another will be different for worldwide imperial states where the sea becomes a 'direct and vital factor' than it would be for those for whose geography makes the 'German or Continental School of strategy' more appropriate. Britain of course was pre-eminently just such a maritime state and had derived enormous benefit from developing a set of principles governing the conduct of war '... in which the sea is a substantial factor.'*

Of course, Corbett was not confining himself simply to historical analysis. He was advocating a guide for future policy too. The question is whether what he said then has any salience today.

Corbett, in the past few years, has benefited from a renaissance in popularity because so much of what he said, now virtually a century ago, seems almost unerringly apposite to today's world of economic constraint, political uncertainty, small wars and local conflicts.

The Relevance of Sea Power

The ancient Greeks were early practitioners in the use of true sea power. They gave rise to the first state that was sea power in its truest sense, Athens, which they called a "thalassocracy." Thalassocracy comes from the Greek word *thalassa*, meaning sea, and *kratein*, meaning power, resulting in *thalassokratia*, or a sea power. A thalassocracy "requires political and economic systems that can consciously aim at naval control of sea lanes for the transport of useful supplies and armies."[29] Another way of saying "naval control" is command of the sea, which is the ability to get men, equipment, and supplies wherever and whenever required.[30]

Several ancient Mediterranean thalassocracies provide insight into the continuities of sea power and maritime strategy. As Carthage, originally a colony of the seafaring Phoenicians, grew to become another thalassocracy, it naturally led to maritime competition and then naval conflict with Athens and eventually Rome. Sea power proved vital in the long struggle for supremacy between Athens and Sparta, the former a traditional sea power and the latter a traditional land power. Interestingly, Sparta had to build up its naval capabilities in order to finally defeat Athens.

The use of sea power at the strategic level has remained largely unchanged through the ages. Western technological improvements changed the use of sea power at the operational and tactical levels, however. As technology has improved man's ability to use the sea for transportation, communication, and sustenance, it has led to the dominance of Western nations at sea until the 20th century and therefore the focus on these theories. The weapons available to fight at sea similarly changed over time. Galleys armed with cannons altered the nature of naval warfare. The Age of Sail witnessed the waxing and waning of several sea empires, such as the Spanish, Portuguese, Dutch, and French, but the British Empire and the Royal Navy would be dominant after the Napoleonic Wars, through the transition to steam, and would persevere through two world wars. In all these eras, wealth and trade formed the basis of a state's sea power. Much more than war on land, the exercise of sea power requires deep pockets. While society and technology changed and affected the nature of sea power, the nature of naval strategy has remained essentially constant.

Maritime strategy is the effective translation of naval means (force or the threat of force through naval and amphibious capabilities, which can contribute to diplomacy) and civilian means (the use or the threat to use economic and communication maritime capabilities) to political ends (desired policy or political condition). Naval forces do not act for their own purposes; rather, a maritime strategy uses naval and amphibious forces in concert for the pursuit of political goals. This includes the use of shipping during wartime to help achieve the desired ends.

Conclusion

It has been over a century since Sir Julian Corbett published *Some Principles of Maritime Strategy*, yet it continues to be regarded as one of the key foundation texts on maritime strategy. Its ideas and propositions were first tested in the First World War, but the century that followed provided many other opportunities for evaluation across a range of scenarios wherever maritime power was used as an instrument of national policy. The character of sea power, and indeed the maritime domain itself, is constantly evolving and so it is right that the enduring relevance of Corbett's work continues to be regularly debated.

It would be unrealistic to expect every historical strategic theory to remain relevant in perpetuity, but those that do endure tend to do so because they identify fundamental truths that are largely immune to contextual and/or technological change. Thus, there remains much still to be gained from studying 'classic' strategists like Thucydides, Machiavelli, Sun Tzu, or Clausewitz for example. Corbett belongs in the same category.

Corbett's core ideas and concepts on maritime strategy continue to merit its status as an enduring classic work of strategy. His focus on strategic outcomes, not tactical activities, has stood the test of time well, albeit with some modification required along the way.

FURTHER READING

- Jeremy Black, *Naval Power: A History of Warfare and the Sea from 1500* (New York: Palgrave Macmillan, 2009).
- Norman Friedman, *Seapower as Strategy: Navies and National Interests* (Annapolis, MD: Naval Institute Press, 2001).
- Paul M. Kennedy, *The Rise and Fall of British Naval Mastery* (Amherst, NY: Humanity Books, 2006).
- James Stavridis, *Sea Power: The History and Geopolitics of the World's Oceans* (New York: Penguin Books, 2017).
- Geoffrey Till, *Seapower: A Guide for the Twenty-First Century*, 4th edn. (New York: Routledge, 2018).
- Julian S. Corbett, *The Campaign of Trafalgar* (London, UK: Longman, 1910), 408.

9

Douhet

The surest and most effective way of achieving this end is to destroy the enemy air force at its bases, which are found on the surface. This is the principle which governs the situation: it is easier and more effective to destroy the enemy's aerial power by destroying his nests and eggs on the ground than to hunt his flying birds in the air. And every time we ignore this principle we commit an error. Therefore, even if a nation has no other end in view than self-defence, it should be armed with an Independent Air Force capable of launching powerful offensives on land and sea.[1]

—Giulio Douhet

The Author

General Giulio Douhet (1869–1930) was an Italian general and air power theorist. He was a key proponent of strategic bombing in aerial warfare. Born in Caserta, Campania, Italy, he attended the Military Academy of Modena and was commissioned into the artillery of the Italian Army in 1882. Later he attended the Polytechnic Institute in Turin where he studied science and engineering. Assigned to the General Staff, Douhet published lectures on military mechanisation. With the arrival of dirigibles and then fixed-wing aircraft in Italy, he quickly recognised the military potential of the new technology. In a 1910 essay, he predicted, "The skies are about to become a battlefield as important as the land or the sea.... Only by gaining the command of the air shall we be able to derive the fullest benefit" of combat in this realm.

In 1912, Douhet assumed command of the Italian aviation battalion at Turin and wrote *Rules for the Use of Airplanes in War*—one of the first doctrine manuals of its kind. Douhet saw pitfalls in allowing air power to be fettered by ground commanders and advocated the creation of a separate air arm commanded by airmen. He teamed up with a young aircraft engineer, Gianni Caproni, to extol the virtues of air power in the years ahead. However, Douhet's preaching on air power marked him as a radical. After an incident in which he ordered construction of Caproni bombers without authorisation, he was transferred to the infantry.

When World War I began, Douhet began to call for Italy to launch a massive military build-up, particularly in aircraft. "To gain command of the air," he said, was to render an enemy "harmless."[2] When Italy entered the war in 1915 Douhet was shocked by the army's unpreparedness. He proposed a force of 500 bombers that could drop 125 tons of bombs daily to break the bloody stalemate with Austria, but he was ignored. He wrote to his superiors and government officials, criticising the conduct of the war and advocating an air power solution. Douhet was court-martialled and imprisoned for one year for criticising Italian military leaders in a memorandum to the cabinet.

Douhet continued to write about air power from his prison cell, finishing a novel on air power and proposing a massive Allied fleet of aircraft. He was released shortly after the disastrous Battle of Caporetto in 1917 and recalled to service in 1918 to serve as head of the Italian Central Aeronautic Bureau.

He was exonerated in 1920 and promoted to general officer in 1921. The same year, his treatise on strategic bombing, *The Command of the Air* (*Il dominio dell'aria*), was published and he retired from military service soon after. Except for a few months as the head of aviation in Benito Mussolini's government in 1922, Douhet spent much of the rest of his life theorising about the impact of military air power.

Reacting to the horrors he saw in World War I, Douhet became an advocate of airpower. He believed that the airplane could restore decisiveness that ground combat seemed incapable of achieving. Aircraft could fly over the ground battlefield to directly attack the enemy's will. Because of technical problems with detection and interception, stopping an air raid would be impossible. Big bombers with a mix of high explosive, incendiary, and poison gas weapons could target enemy cities. Civilian populations, which were the key to modern warfare, would be unable to stand such bombardment and would soon force their governments to surrender. Although civilian casualties might be high, this would be a more humane method of warfare than prolonged ground combat.

The Theory

The basis of classic airpower theory is *The Command of the Air* by Giulio Douhet, published under the auspices of the Ministry of War. Since the inception of airpower in the early 1920's when Giulio Douhet argued that airpower would transform completely the context of modern warfare, he and other airpower theorists advanced theories of air warfare. The focal point of Douhet's theory rested on what he deemed to be the contrasting situations on land and in the air. From a land warfare perspective, he saw how well the defensive had proved itself during his experiences in World War I and believed it to be vastly superior in intrinsic strength to the offensive:

> *The World War was a long-drawn-out war which almost completely exhausted both victor and vanquished. This was owing to the technical aspects of the conflict more than to anything else that is, to new developments in firearms which strongly favoured the defensive over the offensive; and, to a lesser degree, to a psychology which could not grasp immediately the advantage conferred on the defensive by the improvements in firearms.*[3]

Douhet saw that the advantage would only increase over time rendering ground fronts static in future wars. He believed that strategic bombers possessed the potential to deliver a vast amount of destructive potential and not only on enemy resources like air fields, manufacturing facilities and various other targets necessary for resistance but also on civilian morale which he believed incapable of facing up to bombing attack:

> *For a nation to be equipped with an air force intended for aerial combat alone is not to jeopardise the home front, but also to preclude any possibility of offensive action against enemy objectives a position of profound aerial inferiority. The only really effective aerial defence cannot but be indirect; for it consists in reducing the offensive potentiality of the opponent's air forces by destroying the sources of aerial power at its point of origin.*[4]

It is from this perspective that airpower is labelled as an inherently offensive tool of warfare. Douhet's idea was to eviscerate the enemy's will to resist through strategic bombing, using pre-emptive strikes at the enemy's heartland which included enemy cities, production facilities and airfields. However, he did not see the need for fighter aircraft because he did not believe air-to-air combat would be significant.

The cardinal points for national defence which he proposed, and were accepted and incorporated into the organisation of the armed forces of the nation, were:

1. Coordination of army, navy, and air force under a unified command.
2. The constitution of a Council, then of a Ministry, of Aeronautics.
3. A distinction between an Independent Air force and auxiliary aviation.

Insofar as strategy was concerned, he proposed that:

- A prerequisite for success was command of the air, a theory closely related to command of the sea. Command of the air granted one side the ability to fly where and when it desired while the enemy was unable to do so.
- Because the airplane was an offensive weapon, one gained command of the air by strategic bombardment—ideally catching the enemy's air force on the ground. There was no need for anti-aircraft artillery or interceptors. In fact, resources devoted to air defence or any type of auxiliary aircraft (anything that was not a large bomber) were wasted.[5]

Douhet traced the development of aviation since Italy launched its first dirigible in 1905, and wrote an analysis of Italy's air efforts during the 1911 Ethiopian campaign. In his book, *The Command of the Air,* Douhet described the airplane as the offensive weapon par excellence that made ground forces mostly irrelevant; he indicated that winning future wars would require destroying the enemy air force on the ground at their airfields like eggs in the nest to achieve command of the air.[6]

After achieving command of the air, bombers bypassed ground formations to directly attack the "vital centres" of enemy industry, transportation infrastructure, communications nodes, and government buildings and then destroy the populace will to continue resisting against the threat of unstoppable urban bombing.[7] Douhet's views were heavily couched in the assumptions that enemy government choices of whether to go to war or end a conflict depended upon popular support and the assent of the populace. Additionally, he believed that poison gas would be used as an air weapon, as it had previously in trench warfare, and that no effective air defences could be mounted against offensive air attacks—assumptions which were disproved in the wars to come.[8]

Douhet proposed several axioms for future airpower use, most of which were based on postulated future technological advances as opposed to demonstrated current capabilities. He recognised that aircraft could manoeuvre in three dimensions with increasing speed and extrapolated the idea that airplanes could then fly nearly any distance, height, or speed, "The airplane has complete freedom of action and direction; it can fly to and from any point of the compass in the shortest time—in a straight line—by any route deemed expedient."[9] He proclaimed, "To conquer command of the air means victory; to be beaten in the air means defeat and acceptance of whatever terms the enemy may be pleased to impose."[10]

Douhet followed with two corollaries. First, a nation should always be prepared to gain command of the air by possessing, prior to war, the means to conquer command of the air by building an independent air force of correct and sufficient resources to do the job. Second and more intense, "All that a nation does to assure her own defence should have as its aim procuring for herself those means which, in case of war, are most effective for the conquest of the command of the air."[11] Douhet was not just describing the benefits of airpower but also working to sway the public, civilian policymakers, and military leadership towards a wholly new line of thought regarding war.

Douhet laid a foundation for employment doctrine with several major tenets that while not a guarantee for war, have influenced airpower and warfare ever since. The first tenet included the combination of high explosive, incendiary, and gas bombs with the utility of the latter coming from its ability to prevent emergency responders from assisting after an attack. Targeting has always been an essential element of airpower doctrine and Douhet felt that "in general, aerial offensives will be directed against such targets at peacetime industrial and commercial establishments; important buildings, private and public; transportation arteries and centres; and certain designated areas of civilian population as well."[12] Douhet expanded on the topic of civilian population to convince his audience that the will of the population can be bombed to the point of popular revolt and subsequent government surrender. In effect, the calamity of World War I trenches, properly delivered to the civilian populations and governments, motivates a rapid capitulation. Douhet believed that defence against airpower was a fool's errand, and bombers would easily reach and hit their targets in every mission. As such, he called for the technological capacity of a "unit of bombardment" based on very hopeful calculations, that could destroy all within a 500-metre diameter without the need for a re-attack. While Douhet's ideas were beyond reach at the time and did not advertise much of a downside to airpower, nations have been incorporating them ever since.

Douhet's assertions appear to rest on the assumption that all future wars will be at least as total in their consumption of national resources as World War I. A summary of Douhet's ideas is:

1. An independent air force is necessary for proper use of airpower.
2. To conquer the command of the air for offensive operations equals victory. Ceding command of the air equals certain defeat.
3. Enemy vital centres of industry, transportation, and population are critical targets, with the latter being key to popular uprising and subsequent governmental failure.
4. Battleplanes dropping sufficient units of bombardment including explosive, incendiary, and gas bombs will always penetrate defences rendering air defence worthless.

Douhet called for the means to make ideal war through advanced airpower technology and pioneering doctrine. Even though ideal war through airpower remains out of reach, Douhet's work is the intellectual heritage of much of Air Force doctrine, and therefore much airpower success. Command of the air, now recognisable as air superiority, has become the first operational requirement for air combatant commanders. Targeting methodology has grown more specific, however Douhet introduced analysis of critical target identification. Finally, the evolution of precisely controlled weapon effects demonstrates Douhet's influence on kinetic effects technology. Douhet sought brief, decisive wars through airpower and his ideas have made strides in that direction even if they have not specifically made war ideal.

Douhet captured the imagination of early airmen with his vision of decisiveness through command of the air. Generations of later airpower enthusiasts continue to seek to fulfil his prophecy. Nuclear weapons were supposed to have fixed the technological shortfalls that prevented airpower alone from winning World War II. That they were unusable made little difference. Precision guided munitions are the current mantra of the airpower enthusiast—they have finally made decisive air attack possible. Douhet's assertion of the futility of air defence proved wrong when radar made locating aircraft possible and fighters became capable of catching and shooting down big bombers.

Douhet still has a major influence on airpower doctrine and is the father of all modern airpower theory. He believed that destroying a nation's will to fight was crucial, and thus he advocated the bombing of urban centres. Others believed that destroying an enemy's capability to fight was equally valid. Armies, for example, tended to focus on 'capability' by seeking battle—if the army was destroyed then victory would inevitably follow. Thus airpower was inherently strategic in application and that it was unmatched in its ability to shatter the enemy's will. This belief, combined with the importance of economic dimension, resulted in an airpower theory that advocated attacks on enemy industry designed to break the morale of the factory workers, and by extension, the population as a whole.[13]

The main assumptions of his airpower concept, all contained in *The Command of the Air* and other writings, can be summarised briefly.

- Wars are no longer fought between armies, but between whole peoples, and future wars would be total and unrestrained, with civilians as legitimate targets.
- Wars are won by destroying "the enemy's will to resist"—and only this produces "decisive victory." Defeat of enemy forces is

a poor indirect route. It is far better to strike directly at "vital centres" of power inside an enemy nation.

- World War I was a turning point, showing armies and navies can no longer end wars; the power of the defence—poison gas, machine guns—makes offensive action futile.
- The airplane, though, is revolutionary, "the offensive weapon par excellence," able to bypass surface defences and carry out massive attacks on cities, destroying the enemy's will to resist.
- For national defence, command of the air is necessary and sufficient. The army's job is to mop up after air attacks. The navy is of even less use.

Airpower

Long before the age of powered flight, men dreamed of employing aerial craft as weapons of war. When in the late 18th century the Montgolfier brothers demonstrated free flight by means of a balloon near Paris, others almost immediately speculated about its application in battle. In 1794 the French government established an army balloon unit for the purposes of reconnaissance. Through the 19th century, other military establishments experimented with lighter-than-air ships, not only for observation but for attack. By the time of the Wright brothers' successful flight in 1903, the world was anticipating military aviation. Within a decade, in a war between Italy and Turkey, powered flight for the first time became integral to the conduct of military operations. As instruments of war able to leap over armies and ignore many of the physical barriers of terrain and water, airplanes and dirigibles stirred public imagination and sufficient controversy to force soldiers to ponder the role the airplane would play in future conflict.[14]

Giulio Douhet stands out among military theorists for his prescient insights into how the advent of airpower would change modern warfare. Despite having very little actual flying experience, Douhet formed a theory of airpower that still deserves study today. He recognised that the development of the airplane would make "command of the air" the first objective in any campaign and the ultimate enabler of victory in war. While his insights into the importance of air superiority merit consideration, it is his recognition of how the character of war would change in the airpower age that proved prophetic.

In true Clausewitzian fashion, Douhet acknowledged that the nature of war was a contest of two opposing wills. What Douhet grasped, however, was that airpower had altered the character of war. Since there are no geographical boundaries in the air, airplanes could go everywhere and drop on any surface target. It meant, in his words, that the distinction between soldier and civilian had been removed.

Douhet rightly saw the beginning of total war. Since the population is now a target, his theory relied on leveraging that target to end the war. Bombing the population, he theorised, will cause the citizens to petition their leader to end the war, bringing about peace. There is an element of brilliance in Douhet's ideas as he envisioned how this new target set and airpower could be used to bring about the end of war without the need of a land force. His ideas about population bombing would be tried in World War II with mixed results.

After Douhet wrote the first edition of his book, *The Command of the Air* in 1921, in which he had to be careful not to oppose too strongly certain notions firmly held in high places; he was forced to modify his thought, and confine himself to indispensable fundamentals, and wait for more favourable circumstances before presenting his ideas in full. He felt that, after the first success won by his long and arduous labours to accomplish anything practical and useful for his country, conditions were different after a decade and he could round out his thoughts on the subject of airpower. A second (revised) edition was published in 1927.

Douhet may have been the father of airpower theory, but others followed him quickly. Most of the later airpower theorists worked on one or both of two primary issues that Douhet had first proposed: the most efficient way to organise airpower, a debate generally about an independent air force, or the proper mix of fighters, bombers, and ground-attack aircraft. The debate about separate air forces was important but not a true strategic issue.

Comments

Ever since the first wartime use of air power in the American Civil War between 1861 and 1865, its use has increased substantially in significance and importance in military operations. However, the use and effectiveness of air power has always been subject to an intense debate. Part of the debate is the frequent argument on how to regard air power in relation to other military forces. Questions have also been raised on whether air power really is as effective as it has been argued by air power advocates. Conversely, proponents of air power have hailed it as the future of military intervention. To argue that the use of air power is a highly controversial element of warfare would be an understatement.

Air power is a vast subject that embraces a variety of aspects related to the use of aircrafts as a political and military tool. Providing a survey that covers every single one is thus difficult. Nevertheless, the use of air power has had a major impact on the outcome of some military operations. For almost a century, prominent thinkers on air power have argued that wars can be won through the use of air power. However, though wars are not won solely by the use of air power, they might be lost without its presence.

Douhet in *The Command of the Air* emphasised that the inclusion of air power in a nation's strategy could produce a swift conclusion of a military campaign. This could be achieved in a short manner of time and without the use of ground forces, as "an aerial fleet capable of dumping hundreds of tons of bombs can easily be organised; therefore, the striking force and magnitude of aerial offensives (...) is far more effective than those of any other offensive yet known." The only way to destroy an enemy air force is to strike it on the ground at its own bases is Douhet's constant refrain. An excellent example is the instance when, at 07:45 on 5 June 1967, the Israeli Air Force launched a sudden pre-emptive airstrike that destroyed more than 90 percent of the Egyptian Air Force on the ground. A similar air assault incapacitated the Syrian air force. Without cover from the air, the Egyptian army was left vulnerable to attack. Within three days the Israelis had achieved an overwhelming victory on the ground, capturing the Gaza Strip and all of the Sinai Peninsula up to the east bank of the Suez Canal.

Another useful case study that exemplifies the effectiveness of air power is the air campaign of the 1991 *Operation Desert Storm*, also known as the First Gulf War. In less than forty-eight hours, the strategic bombing had caused severe damage to important military headquarters and strategic positions in Iraq. The air campaign in Kuwait and Iraq resulted in two important achievements. First, as Baghdad had lost its electricity it meant that the Iraqi military forces had to rely on back-up systems, which lacked the standards and reliability of the preferred equipment. Second, the military-political leadership's ability to communicate nationally and internationally was severely damaged and partially absent for the remaining of the war. Thus, the air campaign had a prominent effect and significance on the movement and mobility of Iraqi military forces. In this way, air power established the core preconditions that were needed in order to prevent the operation from becoming a large-scale ground war. Its success and effectiveness in *Operation Desert Storm* clearly indicates that the inclusion of air power in warfare could be decisive if it targeted the vital military, political, and infrastructural headquarters of the hostile opponent. As a matter of fact, the Iraqi ground forces retreated less than one hundred hours after the ground forces moved in following the end of the air campaign.

However, despite the success of the air campaign in achieving air superiority and causing severe damage to the Iraqi military infrastructure, it never became an imminent threat to Saddam's survival. 43 days of bombing against several hundred targets did not bring about the collapse of the regime's command and control system. It was only one part of the final war plan. Even though air power achieved great success in the initial stage of the war, it did not win the war on its own. In order to secure the borders of Kuwait, it was of utmost importance and necessity to be present with military personnel and equipment on the ground. It indicates that although air power alone was not the war winning weapon, it did establish the preconditions for the allied coalition in Iraq and was for that reason an important factor for their success. Without the initial air campaign, the allied forces would have had to embark on a greater large-scale ground invasion which might have been more expensive in terms of blood and treasure. The air campaign of the Gulf War provides a clear example of the powers and abilities of the use of air power in warfare. It also demonstrates that wars are not won merely through the use of air power. Boots on the ground was still inevitable in order to secure Kuwait's border and restore the legitimate government in the country.

Clausewitz averred that the enemy's 'centre of gravity' was key to compelling an opponent in conflict or bending him to your will. This centre of gravity, while traditionally seen as the enemy's forces, can take many forms and many degrees of accessibility. With air power's inception, it became possible to make strategic strikes against the enemy's centre of gravity without the necessity of making contact in a traditional land or sea war. Instead, air power could be used to bypass the enemy's forces and take the fight straight to the enemy's heartland, to his new centres of gravity. Through using strategic bombing, it is possible to undermine the opponent's will and means to continue with a war without the need to engage in traditional battles. While there have been historical issues with land armies being able to navigate enemy terrain, and with naval forces being able to strike deep into enemy territory to obtain objectives without viable waterways, aircraft are unaffected by these factors and can instead, theoretically, attack at any point in the enemy's territory. In addition to an increased level of reach, aircraft are also able to be deployed at a much faster rate than traditional land and naval forces. Due to these innate advantages, air power presents a new aspect of warfare that, if applied correctly, could bring about quick and decisive victories.

In his 1921 book, *The Command of the Air,* Douhet argued that air forces had quickly become the primary means for conducting a war and that wars could be rapidly won through the implementation of a strategic campaign against the enemy's homeland. He believed that in warfare, the enemy's civilian population had developed into being the most important strategic target of all. This is because he believed that a successful aerial bombardment would demoralise civilians to such an extent that they would rise up and force the government to move for peace. This theory was based on the notion that during a war, the civilian population was the enemy's Achilles heel and would therefore provide an excellent target and opportunity for military forces to attack. Through attacking in this way, he believed that a short and relatively concise war could be delivered to avoid the attritional battles that had been seen during World War I. This position did, however, come with some drawbacks, as the German military foresaw, that terror bombing of this kind was likely to cause reciprocation in kind and would prove to be counter-productive, actually increasing civilian resolve.

It is never an easy task to adapt strategy to theory and a few of the problems involved how new technology might be fit into the theory of aircraft vulnerability as Douhet viewed the airplane an almost unstoppable weapon capable of bombing the enemy's air fields, production facilities and even civilian populations into submission. Additionally, new technologies failed to significantly increase the accuracy of bombing targets which would have been necessary to accomplish the type of strategic bombing foreseen by Douhet. Most historians will agree that the air campaigns launched against Germany during World War II were for the most part successful and played a key role in the allied victory, however, the quick and efficient use of strategic bombing foreseen by Douhet never came to pass. Some will ignore Douhet's writings because he incorrectly predicted several aspects of airpower employment. Douhet missed the mark on precision, hypothesising that strategic bombing would never be as precise as artillery, which the precision revolution proved was possible. Furthermore, populations have proved more resilient to bombing campaigns directed at them than Douhet imagined. Yet, Douhet, with little actual airpower experience, did foresee several aspects of airpower employment in existence today.

The need for an independent air arm that could achieve strategic effects still remains a requirement for airpower employment today. Douhet recognised the need to establish "command of the air" as the first objective in any campaign. More importantly, he advocated that airpower should "break the eggs in the nest," which meant attacking the enemy's opposing forces while they are still on the ground. To accomplish this task, Douhet believed that a "battleplane" should be used, a plane capable of offense actions while still able to defend itself from enemy attack.

Finally, a criticism of Douhet's advocacy for the use of chemical weapons, misses the larger picture. What Douhet really saw was the development of combined effects. Bombers, he argued, would break oil storage areas, incendiary munitions would light the spill on fire, and chemical weapons would prevent first responders from putting out the fire. The chain of events proposed by Douhet offered insight into the combined effects airpower would achieve in future conflicts.

Douhet wrote one of the most comprehensive military theories in history. He provided a rationale for the use of force, a mechanism for achieving effects, an organisational construct, and a force structure. Douhet provided not only perceptions into airpower, but also a complete theory. Although written nearly a century ago, The Command of the Air remains a relevant part of today's airpower theory discussions.

Much of what Douhet propounded was not original, but his were perhaps the most coherent, the most systematic, and the most prophetic airpower writings of the era. More than any other thinker, Douhet addressed the basic issues that military theorists have grappled with since the beginning of organised combat. In Douhet's thinking, aircraft altered the fundamental character of warfare, and he argued the case at a level of abstraction and generalisation that elevated argument to principle and the body of thought as a whole to theory. In that theory, airpower became the use of space off the surface of the earth to decide war on the surface of the earth. He discussed the organisation and employment of aircraft in generalities independent of time, place, technology, and even independent of the nature of warfare itself. He believed that the first effort of air forces was "to conquer the command of the air—that is, to put the enemy in a position where he is unable to fly, while preserving for one's self the ability to do so... ." His method of gaining superiority was to attack the enemy air force on the ground. For Douhet, aircraft were only useful as instruments of the offense. By bombing cities and factories instead of military forces (except air forces), the enemy could be defeated through shattering the civilian will to continue resistance. He argued that the character of airplanes—their speed and mobility—and the vastness of air space would prevent the defence from stopping a determined bomber offensive. But in order to mount such an effort, and because air forces had little significance as "auxiliaries" to armies and navies, air forces had to be independent of ground and naval forces, and armed, structured, and deployed for the decisive strategic role.[15]

Douhet certainly possessed the most original mind which addressed itself to a consideration of air power. Considering that it took over two thousand years of warfare on land and sea to produce Jomini, Clausewitz, and Mahan, we should not be overly critical of the airman who began writing a theory of air war scarcely one decade after the invention of the airplane.

FURTHER READING

- Thomas Hippler. *Bombing the People: Giulio Douhet and the Foundations of Air-Power Strategy, 1884-1939* (Cambridge University Press, 2013).
- David MacIsaac, "Voices from the Central Blue: The Air Power Theorists," in *Makers of Modern Strategy from Machiavelli to the Nuclear Age,* ed. P. Paret, G. Craig, and F. Gilbert (Princeton University Press, 1986).
- Robert A. Pape, *Bombing to Win: Air Power and Coercion in War* (Cornell University Press, 1996).

10

Mitchell

Air power may be defined as the ability to do something in the air. It consists of transporting all sorts of things by aircraft from one place to another, and as air covers the whole world there is no place that is immune from influence by aircraft.[1]

—**William Mitchell**

Introduction

Air warfare was anticipated in heroic myths and stories for thousands of years, but for most of human history, use of the air was limited to hurling missiles through it, using birds for carrying messages to and from the battlefield, and using both to start fires in besieged cities. The first use of manned aircraft in warfare began shortly after the first flights of the Montgolfier brothers in 1783, with hot air and hydrogen balloons used for observation and signalling to enhance the performance of traditional military forces.[2] Aviation game changed in 1903 when Orville and Wilbur Wright made the first sustained powered flight in Kitty Hawk, North Carolina.

As with the maritime domain, people are only visitors in the air. But the access that these new air technologies provided—quick, sustained, and precise access to anywhere over the entire surface of the planet—redefined the character of international commerce and warfare, and also maritime warfare, after aircraft were added to ships. It was this new freedom of access to the expanded 'third dimension', rather than the air weapons themselves, that caused a seismic shift in strategic possibilities.[3]

When the speed and reach of airpower was coupled with powerful weapons the nature of warfare changed. Recent developments of highly networked air weapons, with stealthy radar-evading capabilities and precision guidance suggest that the visions of early airpower advocates have finally been validated, changing the nature of warfare itself. It is now believed that the full use of airpower requires new independent air services to realise airpower's tactical, operational, and strategic possibilities.

By 1911, many of the future role's airplanes would play had already been performed experimentally in combat. On 23 October 1911, during a war between the Kingdom of Italy and the Ottoman Empire, an Italian pilot took to the air in a canvas-winged monoplane. He flew at what was considered then an incredibly fast speed of 45 miles per hour, circling over Tripoli, in modern-day Libya. With this new ability to look down upon the Earth, he was able to carry back to his commanders the locations of enemy positions. But the effect of this new technology was not just better reconnaissance.

A week later, the same pilot decided to bring up into the air with him four hand grenades, which he dropped over the side of his plane upon the Ottomans below. This first ad-hoc bombing certainly didn't affect the outcome of the war, but the era of air warfare had begun and there was no turning back.

The outbreak of World War I in 1914 became the true spark igniting the full development of airpower theory, driven by the need to develop alternatives to static trench warfare. While aircraft were mostly used as an auxiliary force for observation, reconnaissance, and signalling, World War I also saw the birth of air-to-air combat and strategic bombing. The first large combined air and ground operations with 1,481 coalition aircraft supporting the St. Mihiel offensive occurred in September 1918, forcing a reconsideration of all prior assumptions about the likely character of future wars.

Brigadier General William 'Billy' Mitchell (1879-1936) was a man who saw the future of air power. A determined and intelligent soldier, he pushed authorities to the limits in order to prove his point. His 'radical' ideas included using fighter planes, instead of battle ships, and soldiers transported by air and not just through land.

Mitchell: A Prophet of Airpower

William 'Billy' Mitchell was born on 29 December 1879, in Nice, France. Son of a wealthy Wisconsin senator he came from a distinguished family. He learned German, Italian and Spanish and also spoke French as fluently as English.

A contemporary of Douhet, Mitchell began his U.S. Army career in May 1898, when he enlisted at age of 18 in the Army as a private in the 1st Wisconsin Infantry Regiment when the Spanish-American War broke out. He was commissioned and served in the Army Signal Corps in Cuba, the Philippines and Alaska before becoming interested in aviation. In March 1912, as a captain, he was the only Signal Corps Officer on the Army General Staff and the youngest out of the 21 officers selected to serve the General Staff.

In 1913, Mitchell was sent to the Army Staff College. As aviation was assigned to the Signal Corps, Mitchell was well placed to further develop his interest. He was chosen as temporary head of the Aviation Section, U.S. Signal Corps, predecessor of the modern United States (US) Air Force.

On 6 April 1917, the US declared war on Germany and Mitchell, by then a Lieutenant Colonel, went to France as an observer. In Paris, he learned how to develop aerial combat strategies and planned large-scale air operations when working closely with the Royal Flying Corps' General Sir Hugh Trenchard. He became the first American officer to fly over enemy lines and quickly earned a reputation as a daring and tireless leader. He was promoted to Brigadier General and given command of all American air units in General John J. Pershing's American Expeditionary Force.

On Sunday, 14 April 1918, America put its first squadron into combat. Mitchell's flair for combat leadership was proven at the Battle of Saint-Mihiel when he coordinated a force of British, French and Italian planes, to support American ground forces. For his performance in World War One I, Mitchell received several awards including the Distinguished Service Cross. Mitchell proved a highly effective commander, but his aggressive approach and unwillingness to operate in the chain of command made him numerous enemies.

Mitchell returned to the US as a hero in 1919 and was appointed Assistant Chief of the US Army Air Service but the organisation he had helped to build in war disintegrated in peacetime.[4]

Mitchell's experiences in World War I gave him a deep conviction to the belief that the nation needed an "air force," not an "air service" and the notion that he was the only one capable of accomplishing that change. Behind that strong belief was a commitment to the idea that an air force could do much more than just fight alongside ground and naval forces. He saw war as three-dimensional, not two, and believed that only experienced airmen understood how to operate successfully in that third dimension.

Mitchell came to aviation late in his career, but like Douhet, quickly recognised not only its potential, but also its inefficient use by ground commanders. Mitchell also wrote and spoke prolifically about the need for an independent air force. A relentless advocate for aviation, he encouraged US Army Air Force pilots to challenge records, as well as promoted races, and ordered aircraft to aid in fighting forest fires. Convinced that air power would become the driving force of war in the future, he pressed for the creation of an independent Air Force.

Mitchell's vocal support of air power brought him into conflict with the US Navy as he felt that the importance of an Air Force would make the Navies' battleships increasingly obsolete. He tried to prove that airplanes could actually accomplish the things he had said and proposed a number of daring innovations for the Air Service that stunned the non-flying Army generals—a special corps of mechanics, troop-carrying aircraft, a civilian pilot pool for wartime availability, long-range bombers capable of flying the Atlantic and armour-piercing bombs. Convinced that bombers could sink battleships, he argued that aviation should be the US's first line of defence. He encouraged the development of the bombsight, ski-equipped aircraft, engine superchargers, aerial torpedoes and the concept of Airborne, an idea that allowed troops to parachute from airplanes to land in the amidst of a battlefield.

With each success, Mitchell stepped on the egos of Army generals and Navy admirals with his fiery way of words and boasted that Army planes could sink any battleship afloat under any conditions of war.

Dynamic and impulsive, Mitchell sought out the American press and announced that if he were given permission to bomb captured German battleships, he would be able to prove his assertions.

In February 1921, Mitchell was anxious to test his theories of destruction of ships by aerial bombing, in a series of joint Army-Navy exercises to be held that summer in which captured ships could be used as targets. In the early tests, Mitchell's aircraft sank a captured German destroyer and light cruiser. In July 1921, they attacked the German battleship *Ostfriesland*. However, Mitchell violated the rules of engagement by sinking the battleship. All the target vessels were stationary and effectively defenceless at that point of time.

Mitchell continued to criticise his superiors regarding aviation policy. In 1924, Mitchell was sent on a tour of Asia and the Far East. During this tour, Mitchell foresaw a future war with Japan and predicted an aerial attack on Pearl Harbour. When his term of Assistant Chief ended, he was sent to San Antonio, Texas with the rank of Colonel, to oversee air operations.

Later that year, following the loss of the US Navy airship *USS Shenandoah*, Mitchell issued a statement accusing the military's senior leadership of 'almost treasonable administration of the national defence' and incompetence. As a result of these statements, he was brought up on court-martial charges for insubordination at the direction of President Calvin Coolidge. Beginning that November, the court-martial saw Mitchell receive broad public support and notable aviation officers testifying on his behalf. However, on 17 December 1925, Mitchell was found guilty and sentenced to a five-year suspension from active duty and loss of pay. Rather than accept the punishment, Mitchell resigned from service on 1 February 1926.

Mitchell wrote more than 60 articles, several newspaper series and five books, never deviating from his appeal for public understanding of the promise and the potential of air power. Mitchell not only foresaw that an Air Force was essential for national survival, he also educated the public and its leaders on the role that air power would eventually play in national defence. For his foresight and willingness to sacrifice his career for his beliefs, the US owes this visionary man a debt of gratitude it can never repay.

Air Power Theory

Mitchell built on Douhet's ideas in offering durable tenets of air doctrine. His most resounding call was for an independent air force, since "so many erroneous doctrines have been enunciated about aviation by the older services that see in the development of air power the curtailment of their ancient prerogatives, privileges and authority, that we consider it time to challenge these proceedings and to make our views known."[5] Throughout his writings, Mitchell added other indictments of Army and Navy control over airpower including comparisons to other modern air forces, examples of employment efficiency stemming from centralised airpower control, and lengthy descriptions of the singular and superior nature of "the most highly organised individual fighting men that the world has ever seen."[6]

Mitchell did not believe that bombers would be invincible, just unvanquishable to ground attack. "The air is so vast and extends so far that the shooting of airplanes out of the sky, with cannon from the ground, is almost impossible of achievement, especially when planes are almost always protected by the clouds, by the glaring sun or the darkness."[7] He deduced that an air force of two-thirds pursuit aircraft and one-third bombardment aircraft could achieve victory.[8]

Mitchell took multiple conflicting positions on the future shape of airpower depending on what constituency he was addressing. The reality was that he was trying to devalue future contributions of the Army and Navy while convincing the public, Congress, and other national leaders of airpower's promise. His recommended ratio of pursuit to bombardment aircraft is an acknowledgement that strategic bombardment of vital centres is necessary but he saw a need for aerial battle too since, "it was proved in the European war that the only effective defence against aerial attack is to whip the enemy's air forces in air battles."[9]

Mitchell's final major tenet was in alignment with Douhet's plan for targeting. "The air forces will strike immediately at the enemy's manufacturing and food centres, railways, bridges, canals and harbours. The saving of lives, manpower and expenditures will be tremendous to the winning side. The losing side will have to accept without question the dominating conditions of its adversary, as he will stop entirely the manufacture of aircraft by the vanquished."[10]

He later expands to say, "...the hostile nation's power to make war must be destroyed—this means the manufactories, the means of communication, the food products, even the farms, the fuel and oil and the place where people live and carry on their daily lives."[11] So, while Mitchell does not dwell on the unpalatable notion that killing civilians will make other civilians overthrow their government, he does allow that making it risky and unpleasant to be a civilian in a hostile country will lead to degraded war-making capacity.

Mitchell did not focus on the specifics of technology such as units of bombardment or battleplanes in his major work as Douhet did, but his most important concepts are:

1. An independent air force, run by airmen, is a necessary component of airpower.
2. Strategic bombardment of vital industrial and population centres will eliminate the enemy's ability to make war.
3. Defence against aircraft comes only from other aircraft, which enable air superiority, which in turn enables strategic bombardment.

Like Douhet, Mitchell did not foresee certain developments that would dampen airpower's effects. Anti-aircraft artillery and surface-to-air missiles can wreak havoc on aircraft. In other areas however, Mitchell's foresight might have saved many Allied lives. His view that pursuit or fighter aircraft would be a vital component of air superiority not only endures today, but seems all but proven by the Allied success in the latter months of World War II in Europe.

Prior to his resignation, General Mitchell synthesised various thoughts of air power of his time to establish fundamentals, which would later be defined as "tenets of air power." Mitchell used these fundamentals in his campaign to establish a separate US Air Force. Notable among his arguments was the requirement to establish unity of command of the air effort by an air-minded commander, as well as centralised command/de-centralised execution.

Flexibility, synergy, persistence, and concentration of purpose for air power would only be gained through establishing an Air Force, separate from the Army or the Navy. Mitchell argued for the autonomy of the air power commander, to be given reign to employ these "tenets" to accomplish appropriate objectives, without subservience to a ground commander. He did believe in collaboration between air and surface forces, and was supportive of joint structure.[12] Mitchell's argument of reasons why there needed to be a separate Air Force, would later become doctrinal "truths" institutionalised as USAF Tenets of Air power:

1. Requires Centralised Control and Decentralised Execution.
2. Is Flexible and Versatile.
3. Produces Synergistic Effects.
4. Uniquely Suited to Persistent Operations.
5. Operations Must Achieve Concentration of Purpose.
6. Operations Must Be Balanced

The Tenets of Air power are congruent to Principles of War, but require an airman's expert understanding to be applied correctly, to achieve the desired end-state of the air power effort; as such, they are the accepted basis of organising and employing elements of the US Air Force.

Often regarded as the "father" of the U.S. Air Force, Mitchell's ideas remain prevalent alongside Douhet's in modern doctrine. While he did not have the solution for ideal war, he contributed many ideas that carried airpower towards its critical roles in future wars.

Leveraging Airpower for Strategic Effect

"Military power at all times and in all kinds is united in its function and dynamics.... It is important to recognise that each geographically specialised form of military power is vitally important, both in itself and as a contributor to strategic effect, and as an enabling factor for other contributing agents."[13]

Douhet captured the core of airpower's contribution to strategy when he wrote: "A nation's naval forces, like all armed forces, influence international politics by their potentialities."[14] The airpower community traditionally focused on "more narrow perspectives of flying, aircraft, tactical air combat and technology."[15] This is as much a cultural shortcoming as a conceptual one, as one can never generate and sustain new and better ideas if an organisation's internal incentive structures and norms do not incentivise development of new and improved airpower theories, and sustain the careers of those who develop them.

Airpower will continue to provide vital and unique tactical capabilities to joint and coalition forces, but it can only achieve strategic efficacy if its place in the general theory of strategy is embraced and understood. Paralyzing one's enemies—and dislocating or defeating their fielded forces—will continue to be tactically necessary, but the ability to attack targets or hold them at risk from a distance is only the price of entry to the strategy game. Strategists use military force and threats of force to remove barriers to cooperation between otherwise warring societies, ideally using a portfolio of options to enlist former adversaries in new complementary patterns of political interaction. Making that connection between tactical actions and strategic outcomes requires a general theory of strategy, not a narrow domain-focused strategy done in isolation from the wider process of social context creation that airpower—like all forms of military power—serves when strategy is done well.

Comments

Mitchell's theory on the decisiveness of airpower was simultaneously right and wrong. This theory's dichotomy lends itself to perpetual and more thorough examination. Mitchell was correct in stating that the decimation of an enemy's air force would enable its adversary to fly uncontested over the enemy's territory and strike freely at its centres of production and infrastructure. This notion was in sync with other contemporary air theorists who posited the need to aggressively incapacitate an enemy's air force. However, Mitchell's subsequent assumption that air superiority would be the pivotal factor in a conflict and quickly compel the enemy to capitulate proved mostly inaccurate.

Mitchell did not anticipate the possibility of a country's ability to endure continuous bombing, maintain its military-industrial complex, and continue production. Additionally, he did not account for the evolution of warfare away from conventional force-on-force conflicts to limited wars with countries that possessed little to no industrial base.

Mitchell, however, was far ahead of his time when he articulated his vision for the employment of airpower during conflicts. He made the United States and its military aware of how vital aircraft could be in determining the outcome of wars, thus laying the foundation for the formation of the United States Air Force. However, Mitchell's ability to forecast the evolution of airpower was stunted and focused on the aerial tactics, techniques, and procedures utilised during World War I. He did not anticipate how advancements in technology would mitigate or counterbalance airpower's effectiveness and decisiveness. Mitchell also could not predict changes in warfare tactics from the conventional battles he participated in to guerrilla and irregular campaigns that limited the efficacy of aircraft. Mitchell was instrumental in conceiving the modern-day understanding of airpower, but his concepts and theories lasted only as long as the technology of his day.

Mitchell never deviating from his appeal for public understanding of the promise and potential of air power. He made his last public appearance on 11 February 1935, when he addressed the US House Military Affairs Committee.

Mitchell did not live to see his ideas come to fruition. Weakened by his struggle, he died in a New York hospital on 19 February 1936, at the age of 56. He had elected to be buried in Milwaukee, his hometown, where he enlisted in 1898, rather than at Arlington National Cemetery.

In 1955, the Air Force Association passed a resolution to void Billy Mitchell's court-martial. Although the conviction was not removed, Billy Mitchell had already received a measure of official recognition from a grateful nation when President Harry S. Truman signed legislation in 1946 bestowing a special medal posthumously on Mitchell 'in recognition of his outstanding pioneer service and foresight in the field of American military aviation.'

Should Billy Mitchell be remembered today? The answer is a definite and strong affirmative. He not only foresaw that an air force was essential for national survival but also educated the public and its leaders on the role that the airplane would eventually play in national life. For his foresight and willingness to sacrifice his career for his beliefs, history owes to this unorthodox visionary a debt of gratitude it can never repay.

World War II brought vindication for Mitchell. In 1939, the Army Air Corps began using a bomber—the B-25 Mitchell—named in his honour. The navy used almost 700 of these planes during World War II. Mitchell believed that Japan was the dominant nation in Asia and was preparing to do battle with the United States. He predicted the air attacks would be made by the Japanese on Pearl Harbour and the Philippines and described how they would be conducted.

Mitchell's predictions came true in World War II. On 26 July 1947, President Harry S. Truman signed the National Security Act of 1947 creating a National Military Establishment including a Department of the Army, a Department of the Navy, and a Department of the Air Force. Billy Mitchell's legacy, the U.S. Air Force, came into being on 18 September 1947.

Mitchell should be remembered for two important qualities: his ability to intelligently forecast the future, and his willingness to sacrifice his career for his beliefs. He firmly believed that "the influence of air power on the ability of one nation to impress its will on another in armed contest will be decisive."[16]

FURTHER READING

- Tami Davis Biddle, *Rhetoric and Reality in Air Warfare: The Evolution of British and American Ideas About Strategic Bombing, 1914–1945* (Princeton, NJ: Princeton University Press, 2002).
- Stephen Budiansky, *Air Power: The Men, Machines, and Ideas that Revolutionized War, From Kitty Hawk to Gulf War II* (New York: Penguin Group, 2004).
- Colin S. Gray, *Airpower for Strategic Effect* (Maxwell Air Force Base, AL: Air University Press, 2012).
- Phillip S. Meilinger, ed., *The Paths of Heaven: The Evolution of Air-power Theory* (Maxwell Air Force Base, AL: Air University Press, 1997).
- John Andreas Olsen, *A History of Air Warfare* (Washington, DC: Potomac Books, 2010).
- Alfred Hurley, *Billy Mitchell, Crusader for Air Power* (Bloomington IN: Indiana University Press, 1964).

11

Liddell Hart

People have killed only when they could not achieve their aim in other ways.... There is a broadened strategy, with intellectual weapons.... Why should I demoralize the enemy by military means if I can do so better and more cheaply in other ways? Our strategy is to destroy the enemy from within, to conquer him through himself.'[1]

—**B.H. Liddell Hart**

Introduction

Sir Basil Henry Liddell Hart (1895–1970) was a British soldier, military historian, and military theorist. He wrote a series of military histories that proved influential among strategists. Arguing that frontal assault was bound to fail at great cost in lives, as proven in World War I, he advocated the "indirect approach" and reliance on fast-moving armoured formations. His pre-war publications are known to have influenced German World War II strategy.

Liddell Hart was born in Paris, the son of a Methodist minister. He had his education at Willington School in Putney, St Paul's School in London and at Corpus Christi College, Cambridge. On the outbreak of World War I, in August 1914, Liddell Hart volunteered for the British Army, where he became an officer in the King's Own Yorkshire Light Infantry and served with the regiment on the Western Front. Liddell Hart's war experience was brief, confined to two short spells in the autumn and winter of 1915, being sent home from the front after suffering concussive injuries from a shell burst. In the rank of captain, he returned to the front for a third time in 1916, in time to participate in the Battle of the Somme. He was hit three times without serious injury before being badly gassed and sent out of the line on 19 July 1916. His battalion was nearly wiped out on the first day of the offensive on 1 July, a part of the 60,000 casualties suffered in the heaviest single day's loss in British war history. His personal experience led him to conclude that war was horrible and battles like Somme and Passchendaele should not be repeated. Hence, he originally developed the "Indirect Approach" as a Grand Strategy to persuade the British Government not to participate in another war on continental Europe.

After the war, Liddell Hart transferred to the Royal Army Educational Corps, where he prepared a new edition of the Infantry Training Manual. He was placed on half-pay from 1924 and retired from the Army in 1927. He spent the rest of his career as a theorist and writer. He worked as the military correspondent of *The Daily Telegraph* from 1925 to 1935 and of *The Times* from 1935 to 1939.

In his early writings on mechanised warfare, Liddell Hart had proposed that infantry be carried along with the fast-moving armoured formations in their own tracked vehicles and dismount to help take better-defended positions that otherwise would hold up the armoured units. Liddell Hart foresaw the need for a combined arms force with mobile infantry and artillery, which was similar but not identical to the make-up of the panzer divisions that Heinz Guderian developed in Germany.

In 1954, Liddell Hart published his most influential work, *Strategy*. It was followed by a second expanded edition, in 1967, largely devoted to a historical study of the indirect approach in which he analysed various battles and campaigns using that concept. His early writings on 'indirect approach' could be found in *'The Decisive Wars of History: A Study in Strategy'* published before World War II. It was later revised and titled *'Strategy: The Indirect Approach'*.

Liddell Hart's reputation as a military thinker stood very high at his death on 29 January 1970 at the age of 74. Contemporary assessments, however, are more unsettled.

The Theory

Military strategy, as defined by Liddell Hart, is "the art of distributing and applying military means to fulfil the ends of policy."[2] By this definition, strategy, firstly, becomes applicable both to peace and war, and, secondly, clearly subordinates strategy to a larger purpose, i.e., politics. This led to the development of another term to differentiate military strategy from the overarching strategy applicable at the highest levels incorporating all the ingredients of national power to achieve national policy—grand strategy. The purely military aspect of strategy was given a subordinate term, *operational art*.

Liddell Hart saw that the indirect approach that he recommended in military strategy was in fact part of a much broader indirect approach that could be applied elsewhere in human affairs. In further explanation he stated that there are two great forces in warfare, the physical and the moral. These two forces employed at the strategic level suggest two distinct approaches to warfare. A *direct approach*—attacking the opponent's physical forces; and the other—an *indirect approach*—focusing on his moral forces. When two states oppose each other, they bring to bear both physical and moral attributes of force in a contest not only of physical capabilities but of will. War is in large part a violent clash between two opposing wills. Thus, the object of war is to impose our will on our enemy. The means to that end is the organised application or threat of violence by military force. However, we quickly put aside the moral context and concentrate on the physical elements for our objectives.

War is characterised by the interaction of both moral and physical forces. The physical characteristics of war are generally easily seen, understood, and measured: hardware, technology, physical objectives seized, force ratios, losses of material or life, terrain lost or gained, prisoners or material captured. The moral characteristics are less tangible. (The term *moral* as used here is not restricted to ethics—although ethics are certainly included—but pertains to those forces of psychological rather than tangible nature, to include the mental aspects of war.) Moral forces are difficult to grasp and impossible to quantify. We cannot easily gauge forces like national and military resolve, national or individual conscience, emotion, fear, courage, morale, leadership, or esprit. Yet moral forces exert a greater influence on the nature and outcome of warfare than do physical.

In warfare we must either destroy the enemy's *ability* to resist or destroy his *will* to resist. The distinction between the two approaches is that attacking hostile ability is the *direct approach* aimed at physical forces and attacking hostile will is the *indirect approach* aimed at moral forces. Thus, it is not the object or effect of the attack that matters but how one *moves* (avenue of approach) to the attack. For example, a frontal assault is direct; attacking from the flank or rear is an indirect approach. One could take this definition further by qualifying it to the defences of the opponent, i.e. attacking other than into his defensive strength or orientation is an indirect approach. Any military action has two perspectives, the *object* (what) and *effect* (result) of the attack to distinguish the type of approach being applied.

***Object* of an Attack.** This orientation focuses on the *'what'* of the attack, i.e., the *object* being targeted. If the object of the attack is the opponent's military force, this is a direct approach. The aim of such an attack is to destroy the enemy's military forces and their ability to resist. When, on the other hand, the object of the attack is something other than an opponent's military forces, it comprises an indirect attack. Those other forces can include, by major category, leadership, industry, population, transportation, communications, and alliances. In sum, an approach aimed at military forces is *direct* and an approach at other (than armed forces) targets is *indirect.*

***Effect* of the Attack.** The focus in this orientation is not so much the what (object) of the attack but the *result* or *effect* of the attack. From this orientation there are multiple results related to targeting, all expressed as effects: material, systemic, and psychological. The purpose of targeting for a *material effect* is physical destruction; the desire is to kill or damage to incapacitate; the realm of these effects is predominantly in the physical dimension and hence measurable. This might in part explain our preoccupation with material effects.

The purpose of targeting for a *systemic effect* is to disrupt or dislocate a system. The desire is to induce a cascading effect by attacking a critical node of the system and in turn cause its degradation or collapse. The realm of these effects is in the physical and mental-moral dimensions.

These effects are more difficult to measure; the effectiveness is indicated not by physical destruction so much as by the overall result of the effects to the system function as a whole. The effectiveness of the attack should be considered in more than the physical destruction (material effect) of the target.

The purpose of a *psychological effect* is moral destruction, the desire is to demoralise, create fear, doubt, and uncertainty, to erode the will of the opponent, the realm of these effects is in the moral-mental dimensions. These effects are the hardest to measure, and are usually not the main purpose of the attack. It has been said that attacks from the air have a large component of "shock" and are, therefore, inherently psychological. Nonetheless, shock aside, if an indirect approach is to succeed, not only must targets be chosen with moral degradation in mind, but the attendant psychological effects need to be measurable as well. Thus, an attack with the main purpose to affect materially (physical destruction) is direct and an attack with the purpose to affect systemically or psychologically is indirect.

The Indirect Approach

The Indirect Approach was a strategy described and chronicled by Liddell Hart as an attempt to find a solution to the problem of high casualty rates in conflict zones with high force to space ratios, such as the Western Front in Europe, during World War I, on which he served. The strategy calls for armies to advance along the line of least resistance. There were two fundamental principles which governed the "Indirect Approach":

1. Direct attacks on firm defensive positions almost never work, and should never be attempted.
2. To defeat the enemy, one must first disrupt his equilibrium. This cannot be an effect of the main attack; it must take place before the main attack is commenced.

Explaining how this strategy applies to other aspects of life, Liddell Hart said:

> *The direct assault of new ideas provokes a stubborn resistance, thus intensifying the difficulty of producing a change of outlook. Conversion*

> *is achieved more easily and rapidly by unsuspected infiltration of a different idea or by an argument that turns the flank of instinctive opposition ... In commerce, the suggestion that there is a bargain to be secured is far more potent than any direct appeal to buy. And in any sphere it is proverbial that the surest way of gaining a superior's acceptance of a new idea is to persuade him that it is his idea! As in war, the aim is to weaken resistance before attempting to overcome it; and the effect is best attained by drawing the other party out of his defences.*[3]

In the military realm, Liddell Hart's theories about mechanised warfare, mobility, surprise attack and air warfare, developed during the 1920s and 1930s, were put into practice in World War II initially, and with great effectiveness, by the Germans with their *blitzkrieg* (i.e. lightning war) offensives. His enemies acknowledged their debt. General Heinz Guderian, who established the panzer units in the German army, and Field Marshal Erwin Rommel opined that the British would have been able to prevent the greatest part of their defeats if they had paid attention to the modern theories expounded by Liddell Hart before the war.

The idea of the Indirect Approach is to discover the enemy's Achilles heel and strike it quickly in order to secure a swift and decisive victory. He espoused the theory of striking at the enemy's 'moral objective', such as static civil centres, which would overcome the enemy's will to resist rather than confronting the enemy's armed forces.

Benefits of an Indirect Approach. There is value in an indirect approach, in understanding an enemy's moral forces better. If it is the nature of war, that the moral is to the physical as 'three to one', then we need to exploit that potential leverage. However, the direct approach should not be abandoned while developing the indirect approach. The requirement to attack an enemy's physical force is well established. However, both approaches have benefits; both serve to weaken and coerce an opponent. We should do both, but do the indirect better by:

1. Recognising it (acknowledging need and benefit);
2. Developing channels for available analysis on psychological aspects of an opponent;

3. Develop an ability to translate an assessment of an adversary's moral forces and psychological aspects into targets for attack, as a means to defeat an opponent's hostile will; and
4. Think more in terms of influence than destruction.

There is good reason for many war theorists and force application thinkers to have not attempted to describe in detail the moral forces of an opponent and name targets that can be directly associated to these moral forces. The reason is that the task is very difficult, because moral forces are largely within the province of the non-physical realm being mostly things of the mind, notions, thoughts and feelings (behaviour).

This statement may be disputed by those who conceive the destruction of the enemy's armed force as the only sound aim in war, who hold that the only goal of strategy is battle, and who are obsessed with the Clausewitzian saying that 'blood is the price of victory'. Yet if one should concede this point and meet its advocates on their own ground, the statement would remain unshaken. For even if a decisive battle be the only goal, the object of strategy is to bring about this battle under the most advantageous circumstances. And the more advantageous the circumstances, the less proportionately will be the fighting.

Aim of Strategy

A perfect strategy would be to produce a decision without any serious fighting. History, as we have seen, provides examples where strategy, helped by favourable conditions, has practically produced such a result. While there are cases where the destruction of the enemy's armed forces was economically achieved through their disarming by surrender, such 'destruction' may not be essential for a decision, and for the fulfilment of the war aim. In the case of a State that is seeking, not conquest, but the maintenance of its security, the aim is fulfilled if the threat be removed—if the enemy is led to abandon his purpose.

While bloodless victories have been exceptional, their rarity should enhance rather than detract from their value—as an indication of latent potentialities, in strategy and grand strategy. Despite many centuries' experience of war, we have hardly begun to explore the field of psychological warfare. From deep study of war, Clausewitz was led to the conclusion that 'all military action is permeated by intelligent forces and their effects.' Nevertheless, nations at war have always striven, or been driven by their passions, to disregard the implications of such a conclusion. Instead of applying intelligence, they have chosen to batter their heads against the nearest wall.

It rests normally with the government, responsible for the grand strategy of a war, to decide whether strategy should make its contribution by achieving a military decision or otherwise. And just as the military is but one of the means to the end of grand strategy, so battle is but one of the means to the end of strategy. If the conditions are suitable, it is usually the quickest in effect, but if the conditions are unfavourable it is folly to use it. Let us assume that a strategist is empowered to seek a military decision. His responsibility is to seek it under the most advantageous circumstances in order to produce the most profitable result. Hence his true aim is not so much to seek battle as to seek a strategic situation so advantageous that if it does not of itself produce the decision, its continuation by a battle is sure to achieve this. In other words, dislocation is the aim of strategy; its sequel may be either the enemy's dissolution or his disruption in battle. Dissolution may involve some partial measure of fighting, but this has not the character of a battle.

Action of Strategy

How is strategic dislocation produced? In the physical, or 'logistical', sphere it is the result of a move which:

1. upsets the enemy's dispositions and, by compelling a sudden change of front, dislocates the distribution and organisation of his forces;
2. separates his forces;
3. endangers his supplies;
4. menaces the route or routes by which he could retreat in case of need and re-establish himself in his base or homeland.

A dislocation may be produced by one of these effects, but is more often the consequence of several. Differentiation is difficult because a move directed towards the enemy's rear tends to combine these effects. Their respective influence, however, has varied throughout history according to the size of armies and the complexity of their organisation. With armies which 'live on the country', drawing their supplies locally by plunder or requisition, the line of communication has negligible importance. Even in a higher stage of military development, the smaller a force is, the less dependent it is on the line of communication for supplies. A large army, and the more complex its organisation, the quicker and serious in effect is a menace to its line of communication.

Where armies have not been so dependent, strategy has been correspondingly handicapped, and the tactical issue of battle has played a greater part. Nevertheless, even thus handicapped, strategic artists have frequently gained a decisive advantage previous to battle by menacing the enemy's line of retreat, the equilibrium of his dispositions, or his local supplies. To be effective, such a menace must usually be applied at a point closer, in time and space, to the enemy's army than a menace to his communications; and thus, in early warfare it is often difficult to distinguish between the strategical and tactical manoeuvre.

In the psychological sphere, dislocation is the result of the impression on the commander's mind of the physical effects. His impression is strongly accentuated if his realisation of being at a disadvantage is sudden, and if he feels that he is unable to counter the enemy's move. In fact, psychological dislocation fundamentally springs from this sense of being trapped. This is the reason why it has most frequently followed a physical move on to the enemy's rear. An army, like a man, cannot properly defend its back from a blow without turning around to use its arms in the new direction. Turning temporarily unbalances an army as it does a man, and with the former the period of instability is inevitably much longer. In consequence, the brain is much more sensitive to a menace to its back. In contrast, to move directly on an opponent is to consolidate his equilibrium, physical and psychological, and by consolidating it to augment his resisting power. In the case of an army it rolls the enemy back towards their reserves, supplies, and reinforcements, so that as the original front is worn thin, new layers are added to the back. And, at best, it imposes a strain rather than producing a shock.

Thus, a move round the enemy's front against his rear has the aim not only of avoiding resistance on its way but in its issue. In the profoundest sense, it takes the line of least resistance. The equivalent in the psychological sphere is the line of least expectation. They are the two faces of the same coin, and to appreciate this is to widen the understanding of strategy. For if we merely take what obviously appears the line of least resistance, its obviousness will appeal to the opponent also: and this line may no longer be that of least resistance. In studying the physical aspect, we must never lose sight of the psychological, and only when both are combined is the strategy truly an indirect approach, calculated to dislocate the opponent's equilibrium.

Thus, we see that the mere fact of marching indirectly towards the enemy and on to the rear of his dispositions does not constitute a strategic indirect approach. Strategic art is not so simple. Such an approach may start by being indirect in relation to the enemy's front, but the very directness of its progress towards his rear may allow him to change his dispositions so that it soon becomes a direct approach to his new front.

Because of the risk that the enemy may achieve such a change of front, it is usually necessary, for the dislocating move to be preceded by a move, or moves, which can perhaps best be classified under the term 'distract' in its literal sense of 'to draw asunder'. The purpose of this 'distraction' is to deprive the enemy of his freedom of action, and it should operate in both the physical and psychological spheres. In the physical, by causing a distension of his forces or their diversion to unprofitable ends, so that they are too widely distributed, and too committed elsewhere, to have the power of interfering with one's own decisively intended move. In the psychological sphere, the same effect is sought by playing upon the fears of, and by deceiving, the opposing command. To mystify and to mislead constitutes 'distraction,' while surprise is the essential cause of 'dislocation'. And it is through the 'distraction' of the commander's mind that the distraction of his forces follows. The loss of his freedom of action is the sequel to the loss of his freedom of conception.

A more profound appreciation of how the psychological permeates and dominates the physical sphere has an indirect value. For it warns us of the fallacy and shallowness of attempting to analyse and theorise about strategy in terms of mathematics. To treat it quantitatively, as if the issue turned merely on a superior concentration of force at a selected place, is as faulty as to treat it geometrically: as a question of lines and angles. Even more remote from truth—because in practice it usually leads to a dead end—is the 'grooved' tendency to treat war as mainly a matter of concentrating superior force. It is the art of pouring out all one's resources at a given moment on one spot; of making use there of all troops, and, to make such a thing possible, of making those troops permanently communicate with each other, instead of dividing them and attaching to each fraction some fixed and invariable function; its second part, a result having been attained, is the art of again so disposing the troops as to converge upon, and act against, a new single objective.

It is perhaps more lucid, to say that an army should always be so distributed that its parts can aid each other and combine to produce the maximum possible concentration of force at one place, while the minimum force necessary is used elsewhere to prepare the success of the concentration. To concentrate all is an unrealisable ideal. And dangerous even as a hyperbole. Moreover, in practice the 'minimum necessary' may form a far larger proportion of the total than the 'maximum possible'. It would even be true to say that the larger the force that is effectively used for distraction of the enemy, the greater is the chance of the concentration succeeding in its aim. For otherwise it may strike an object too solid to be shattered. Superior weight at the intended decisive point does not suffice unless that point cannot be reinforced in time by the opponent. It rarely suffices unless that point is not merely weaker numerically but has been weakened morally.

The Concentrated Essence of Strategy and Tactics

According to Liddell Hart, the concentrated essence of strategy and tactics can be expressed in eight maxims—six are positive and two are negative. These are:

Positive

1. ***Adjust your end to your means***. Clear sight and cool calculation should prevail. Do not bite off more than you can chew. Keep a clear sense of what is possible. Face facts while preserving faith. Confidence will be of no avail if the troops are run down.

2. ***Keep your object always in mind, while adapting your plan to circumstances.*** Recognise that alternatives exist but make sure they all bear on the object. Weigh the feasibility of attaining an objective against its contribution to the attainment of the end in mind.
3. ***Choose the line (or course) of least expectation.*** Put yourself in your opposition's shoes and try to see what course of action he will see as least probable and thus not try to forestall.
4. ***Exploit the line of least resistance—so long as it can lead you to any objective that would contribute to your underlying object.*** Seize on opportunity—but not any opportunity. Tactically, this refers to following up on success; strategically, it refers to the management and deployment of your reserves.
5. ***Take a line of operation which offers alternative objectives.*** Choose a single course of action that could have several objectives; do not let your actions reveal your objectives. This puts your opponent on the horns of a dilemma. It introduces uncertainty regarding that which is to be guarded against.
6. ***Ensure that both plans and dispositions are flexible—adaptable to circumstances.*** Include contingencies or next steps—for success as well as failure. Organise and deploy your resources in ways that facilitate adaptation to either.

Negative

7. ***Do not throw your weight into a stroke whilst your opponent is on guard—whilst he is well placed to parry or evade it.*** Unless your opponent is much inferior, do not attack until he has been disorganised and demoralised. cedes physical warfare. Similarly, physical warfare can be psycho-logical in nature.
8. ***Do not renew an attack along the same line (or in the same form) after it has once failed.*** If at first you don't succeed, give up. Your reinforcements will likely be matched by the enemy. Moreover, successfully repulsing you the first time will morally strengthen him for the second time.

The essential truth underlying these maxims is that, for success, two major problems must be solved—*dislocation* and *exploitation*. One precedes and one follows the actual blow, which in comparison is a simple act. You cannot hit the enemy with effect unless you have first created the opportunity; you cannot make that effect decisive unless you exploit the second opportunity that comes before he can recover.

The importance of these two problems has never been adequately recognised—a fact which goes far to explain the common indecisiveness of warfare. The training of armies is primarily devoted to developing efficiency in the detailed execution of the attack. This concentration on tactical technique tends to obscure the psychological element. It fosters a cult of soundness, rather than of surprise. It breeds commanders who are so intent not to do anything wrong, according to 'the book', that they forget the necessity of making the enemy do something wrong. The result is that their plans have no result. For, in war, it is by compelling mistakes that the scales are most often turned.

Here and there a commander has eschewed the obvious, and has found in the unexpected the key to a decision—unless fortune has proved foul. For luck can never be divorced from war, since war is part of life. Hence the unexpected cannot guarantee success. But it guarantees the best chance of success.

Comments

Liddell Hart averred that Clausewitz incited generals "to seek battle at the first opportunity, instead of creating an advantageous opportunity," resulting in mutual mass slaughter resulting from blind adherence to the direct approach."[4] Liddell Hart eschewed Clausewitz's direct approach for an indirect approach and built his theory of strategy around it. Central to his theory was the psychological dislocation made up on the mind of the enemy. Liddell Hart advocated defeating the enemy through dislocation and the breaking of his cohesion. "Man in war is not beaten, and cannot be beaten, until he owns himself beaten."[5]

Seeking strategic enlightenment, Liddell Hart conducted an "extensive study of hundreds of military campaigns, during which:

> *"...One impression became increasingly strong—that, throughout the ages, effective results in war have rarely been attained unless the approach has had such indirectness as to ensure the opponent's unreadiness to meet it. The indirectness has usually been physical, and always psychological."*[6]

In striking at weakness, Liddell Hart explained:

> *It is thus more potent, as well as more economical, to disarm the enemy than to attempt his destruction by hard fighting. For the 'mauling' method entails not only a dangerous cost in exhaustion but the risk that chance may determine the issue. A strategist should think in terms of paralyzing, not of killing. Even on the lower plane of warfare, a man killed is merely one man less, whereas a man unnerved is a highly infectious carrier of fear, capable of spreading an epidemic of panic. On a higher plane of warfare, the impression made on the mind of the opposing commander can nullify the whole fighting power that his troops possess. And on a still higher plane, psychological pressure on the government of a country may suffice to cancel all the resources at its command—so that the sword drops from a paralyzed hand.*[7]

Liddell Hart argued that there were three levels of strategy; grand strategy, strategy and tactics, distinguished by their level of analysis. Grand strategy connected policy—the political object of war—with the means of achieving it through the coordination and direction of all of a nation's resources. Its scope extended beyond war to include the way to achieve and maintain peace in its aftermath. Liddell Hart described the range of national resources to be employed through grand strategy as follows:

> *Grand strategy should calculate and develop the resources and man-power of nations in order to sustain the fighting services. Also, the moral resources—for to foster the people's willing spirit is often as important as to possess the more concrete forms of power. Grand strategy, too, should regulate the distribution of power between the several services, and between the services and industry. Moreover, fighting power is but one of the instruments of grand strategy—which should take account of and apply the power of financial pressure, of diplomatic pressure, of commercial pressure, and, not the least of ethical pressure, to weaken the opponent's will. A good cause is a sword as well as armour. Likewise, chivalry in war can be a most weapon in weakening the opponent's will to resist, as well as augmenting moral strength.*[8]

Liddell Hart described strategy (which he also called pure, or military strategy) as the "art of the general."[9] Successful strategy employed the calculation and coordination of the ends and the means through a measured economy of force. In other words, a balance had to be struck between the value of the objective and the means employed to achieve it. Calculation of this economy was easier at the level of strategy than at the lower level of tactics, because the human will, which was the chief incalculable, which manifested itself as resistance and was more operative at the lower level of war.

Liddell Hart eschewed Clausewitz' dictum that the aim of strategy was the destruction of the enemy's armed forces, instead describing it as the establishment of advantageous circumstances for the ensuing battle. Instances in history whereby commanders had established such circumstances that resulted in relatively bloodless disarming, surrender or abandonment of the military objective by the opposing forces illustrated that the perfection of strategy was to" produce a decision without any serious fighting". In this sense, dislocation was the true aim of strategy, with its sequel "either the enemy's dissolution or his easier disruption in battle."[10]

Liddell Hart's concept of dislocation provided an alternative, volition-focused approach to the strategy of annihilation. Rather than achieving victory in decisive battle through local military superiority over an enemy, Liddell Hart averred that a decisive victory could also be achieved through psychological dislocation, springing from surprise. Liddell Hart's alternative approach to the strategy of annihilation was through the psychological sphere and breaking the enemy's resolve rather than through a contest of numbers. If the explanation provided by Liddell Hart sounded strangely reminiscent of Sun Tzu, it was not by accident. Liddell Hart was greatly influenced by Sun Tzu's ideas on war.[11] Like Sun Tzu, Liddell Hart inculcated psychological factors into his theory of war.

Liddell Hart and his indirect approach has won a wide following among strategists. However, the issue of 'direct' versus 'indirect' is actually a smoke screen. The indirect approach is a tactical concept elevated to the strategic level, and it loses some of its validity in the transition. Strategically, it is sometimes (if not often) advantageous to take a direct approach. This is particularly true in cases when the contending parties have disproportionate power—that is, when one side possesses overwhelming force. In such cases, the stronger side invariably benefits from direct action.

Surprise, which Liddell Hart acknowledges is how an indirect approach produces mental dislocation, is a tremendous advantage; however, designing strategies purely or even primarily to achieve surprise overlooks the rest of the equation—surprise to do what? Surprise for what purpose? If a strategist can accomplish his purpose in a direct manner, it might be more desirable than contending with the disadvantages inherent in achieving surprise. Nevertheless, the indirect approach is a recognised strategic tool that has tremendous utility if not elevated to a dogma.

There are seven key themes of the indirect approach. They are all expressions of a characteristic Liddell Hart paradox: 'In strategy, the longest way round is often the shortest way there'.[12]

- First, the dislocation of the enemy's psychological and physical balance should be the 'vital prelude' to his overthrow; not his utter destruction.
- Second, always negotiate an end to unprofitable wars. The method should remain the same as he advocated in the 1930s: 'a shrewd calculation of the military economic factor' based on hard-headed business-like methods. The danger of nuclear war gave these an added urgency.
- Third, the methods of the indirect approach were 'better suited to the psychology of a democracy'. Strategists should be 'attuned...to the popular ear'. Democracies, he warned, were less tolerant of the prodigious cost of modern war.
- Fourth, military power rests on economic endurance; a decision should be gained by 'sapping the opponent's strength and will'. He placed great weight therefore on the significance of blockades. The latter represent an effective indirect approach 'which incurred no risk except in its slowness of effect'.
- Fifth, and implicit in the foregoing, his concept rested on an assumption that war was an activity between states. Its fundamental object, Liddell Hart held, ensured the maintenance of state policy 'in face of the determination of the opposing state to pursue its contrary policy'. He adds, 'For a state to gain its object in war it has to change this adverse will into compliance with its own policy'.

- Sixth, he urged the adoption of what he called in the 1930s, 'Rational pacifism'. This standpoint was expressed in a maxim of his own devising, that his post-war disciples took to heart, 'if you wish for peace, understand war'. But Liddell Hart remained adamantly opposed to unwise one-sided disarmament, as it would render the disarmer 'impotent either to check war or to control its cause'.
- Seventh, and finally, Liddell Hart's study of history revealed that victory often emerged as the result of self-defeating action by the enemy. In 1945 'Germany went far to defeat herself'. But he feared that the exhaustion of 1945 would 'incubate the germs of another war': the spectre of the World War III that preoccupied a generation.[13]

FURTHER READING

- John J. Mearsheimer, *Liddell Hart and the Weight of History* (Ithaca, N.Y.: Cornell University Press, 1988).
- Brian Bond, *Liddell Hart. A Study of his Military Thought* (London: Cassel 1977).
- B.H. Liddell Hart, *The Memoirs of Captain Liddell Hart* two volumes (London: Cassel, 1965).
- B.H. Liddell Hart, *Why Don't We Learn From History?* (London: George Allen and Unwin, 1944).

12

Boyd

"Machines don't fight wars. Terrain doesn't fight wars. Humans fight wars. You must get into the minds of humans. That's where the battles are won.

—John Boyd, *"Patterns of Conflict"*

Introduction

Colonel John Richard Boyd (1927–1997) was a United States Air Force officer and Pentagon consultant during the second half of the 20th century. His theories have been highly influential in military, business, and litigation strategies and planning. He was a fighter pilot by trade, who some regard as the most important strategist of the 20th century.[1] He is widely known for developing the decision cycle known as the OODA (Observation-Orientation-Decision-Action) Loop, the process by which an entity reacts to an event. Boyd, together with Thomas Christie, created the Energy–Manoeuvrability theory of aerial combat, which became the world standard for the design of fighter aircraft.

Boyd was born on 23 January 1927, in Erie, Pennsylvania. He enlisted in the Army Air Forces on 30 October 1944, while he was still a junior in high school. After graduation, he completed his basic training and skill training as an aircraft turret mechanic during the waning months of World War II. He attained the rank of sergeant, and served in the Air Force Reserve until he graduated from the University of Iowa in 1951 with a bachelor's degree in economics and later earned a second bachelor's degree in industrial engineering from the Georgia Institute of Technology.

Boyd was commissioned as a second lieutenant in the Air Force following completion of the ROTC programme at the University of Iowa. On 27 March 1953, Boyd arrived in Korea as an F-86 pilot. In the two months until the armistice on 27 July, Boyd flew a short tour (22 missions) in F-86 Sabres during the Korean War in which he served as a wingman and never fired his guns or claimed an aerial kill. After his service in Korea, he attended the Fighter Weapons School (FWS) where he rose to the top of his class. Upon graduation, he was invited to stay at the FWS as an instructor. He became head of the Academic Section and wrote the tactics manual for the school.

During the 1950s, John Boyd dominated fighter aviation in the U.S. Air Force. His fame came on the wings of the quirky and treacherous F-100 aircraft; the infamous "Hun." Boyd was known throughout the Air Force as "Forty-Second Boyd," because he had a standing offer to all pilots that, beginning from a position of disadvantage, he could defeat them in simulated air-to-air combat in under 40 seconds; if not he would pay them $40. Like any gunslinger with a name and a reputation, he was called out many times. As an instructor at the FWS at Nellis AFB, he fought students, cadre pilots, Marine and Navy pilots, and pilots from a dozen countries, who were attending the FWS as part of the Mutual Defence Assistance Pact. He never lost.

Boyd was famous for a manoeuvre he called "flat-plating the bird." He would be in a defensive position with a challenger tight on his tail, both pulling heavy G's, when he would suddenly pull the stick full aft, brace his elbows on either side of the cockpit, so the stick would not move laterally, and stomp the rudder. It was as if a manhole cover were sailing through the air and then suddenly flipped 90 degrees. The underside of the fuselage, wings, and horizontal stabiliser became a speed brake that slowed the Hun from 400 knots to 150 knots in seconds. The pursuing pilot was thrown forward and now Boyd was on his tail radioing "Guns. Guns. Guns." The myth of "Forty-Second Boyd" still rankles fighter pilots. They say there is no "best" pilot; that everyone has a bad day. But if they went through Nellis in the late 1950s, they know Boyd had no bad days. And they cannot come up with the name of anyone who ever defeated him.

Boyd was equally famous in the classroom where he developed

the "*Aerial Attack Study*." Until Boyd came along, fighter pilots thought that air combat was an art rather than a science; that it could never be codified. Boyd proved them wrong when he demonstrated that for every manoeuvre there are a series of counter manoeuvres. And there is a counter to every counter. Afterwards, when fighter pilots attacked (or were attacked), they knew every option open to their adversary and how to respond. After the study was declassified, foreign pilots passing through Nellis AFB took it home where it changed the way every air force in the world flies and fights. Even today, nothing substantial has been added to the *Aerial Attack Study*.

After a six-year assignment at Nellis AFB, Boyd returned to college for another undergraduate degree. He went to the Georgia Institute of Technology where, one night while studying for an exam in thermodynamics, he had the epiphany that became his famous *Energy-Manoeuvrability Theory*, or E-M Theory, as it came to be known, together with Thomas Christie, a civilian mathematician,. The E-M Theory changed everything that everyone thought they knew about fighter combat. It enabled fighter pilots to evaluate their energy potential at any altitude and at any manoeuvre. And, perhaps more importantly, the energy potential of their adversary. It changed forever the way aircraft are fought in combat.

Boyd then used E-M as a design tool. Until E-M came along, fighter aircraft had been designed to fly fast in a straight line or fly high to reach enemy bombers. The F-X, which became the F-15, was the first Air Force fighter ever designed with manoeuvring specifications. Boyd was the father of the F-15, the F-16, and the F-18.

During the Vietnam War, Boyd served as Vice Commander of Task Force Alpha and as Commander of the 56th Combat Support Group, in Thailand, from April 1972 to April 1973.

Boyd is credited for largely developing the strategy for the invasion of Iraq in the Gulf War of 1991. In 1981, Boyd had presented his briefing, *Patterns of Conflict*, to US Representative Richard "Dick" Cheney. By 1990, Boyd had moved to Florida because of declining health, but Cheney, now Defence Secretary in the George H.W. Bush administration, called Boyd back to work on the plans for Operation Desert Storm.[2] Boyd had substantial influence on the ultimate "left hook" design of the offensive plan.[3] He was an architect of that victory as surely as if he had commanded a fighter wing or a manoeuvre division in the desert.[4]

Military Theories

The E-M theory. In the early 1960s, the E-M theory, of aerial combat became the world standard for the design of fighter aircraft. The Air Force's FX project (subsequently the F-15) was then floundering. Boyd's deployment orders to Vietnam were cancelled, and he was brought to the Pentagon to redo the trade-off studies according to E-M theory. His work helped save the project from being a costly dud even though its final product was larger and heavier than he had desired.

The OODA Loop. Boyd's key concept was that of the Observe-Orient-Decide-Act decision cycle or OODA Loop, the process by which an entity (either an individual or an organisation) reacts to an event. The OODA loop has since been used as the core for a theory of litigation strategy that unifies the use of cognitive science and game theory to shape the actions of witnesses and opposing counsel. It has also been proposed as a tool for work-based learning and management education.

Just what is the OODA Loop and why is it important? It is the basis for everything in Boyd's thinking and a metaphor for life itself. It is an extended biological metaphor for stimulus and response and a diagram for the way the mind works. It is an organic model, not a mechanistic one. Observation is really "sensing" but the acronym thus produced—SODA—didn't pass the giggle test so Boyd used observation instead. And, for fighter pilots in early air-to-air engagements, "first sight wins the fight" was gospel. But successful use of the OODA Loop is a complex process. Observation entails the sensing of external information and the unfolding of circumstances. It is an assessment of our environment, our place in it, and the interaction of the two. It begins a process of scanning for danger, an adversary, and threats to us. It provides a base from which to proceed and feeds forward into the second part of the process, orientation.

Orientation, what Boyd called "the big "O," is the central part of the process. It is an amalgam of genetic heritage, culture, education, experiences, and analysis and synthesis—literally how and why we think as we do. This informs our action, which is a test of our hypothesis (decision). It may be correct or it may fail. But because of the series of forward and backward feedback loops, and the implicit guidance and control we can exert, we are able to revise and repeat the process continuously. Our insights condition our actions or reactions to the environment and events in it. These also are critical to understanding an opponent. It is a complex set of filters and inputs that leads us toward decisions. Orientation involves trade-off thinking to make selective judgments and projection into some future state of affairs and its consequences.

Based on this, we make a decision—a choice about how best to proceed to interact effectively with our environment. This choice, our decision, is the hypothesis to be tested. The test is the action we have selected and its implementation. We constantly monitor the success or failure of the action taken in an effort to comprehend, shape, adapt to and in turn, be shaped by the environment. As Boyd described it, it is a circular process with constant feedback and feed-forward channels and implicit guidance and control to help us cope with a constantly evolving, open-ended, far from equilibrium process of self-organisation, emergence and natural selection.

The OODA Loop is thus an analytical and synthetic tool to deal with our environment and a strategic theory of how to do so. It is simple, elegant and comprehensive, able to describe, explain and predict. It is in essence, a depiction of life itself. Regrettably, its reduction and misunderstanding by many have demeaned the significance and utility of the concept. Perhaps future versions of the OODA Loop chart will emphasise its original insights.

Aerial Attack Study. Boyd also served to revolutionise air-to-air combat in that he was the author of the *Aerial Attack Study*, which became the official tactics manual for fighter aircraft. Boyd changed how pilots thought; prior to his tactics manual, pilots had thought that air-to-air combat was far too complex to ever be fully understood. With the release of the *Aerial Attack Study*, pilots realised that the high-stakes death dance of aerial combat was solved. Boyd said that a pilot going into aerial combat must know two things: the position of the enemy and the velocity of the enemy. Given the velocity of an enemy, a pilot can decide what the enemy can do. When a pilot knows what manoeuvres the enemy can perform, he can then decide how to counter any of the other pilot's actions.[5]

Using stolen computer time in dummy accounts, Boyd diverted several hundred thousand dollars of computer time to studying the comparative flight performance envelopes at different speeds, altitudes and G-forces for every American fighter aircraft and plotted them against every Soviet fighter aircraft. He discovered that every Soviet fighter airplane had greater manoeuvrability when compared to its American counterpart. He was nearly court martialled for theft before being presented two Air Force awards for his work.

Patterns of Conflict. In January 1980 Boyd gave his briefing *Patterns of Conflict* at the US Marines Amphibious Warfare School, which led to the changing of the curriculum.

Boyd published his theory of strategy as a five-part briefing entitled, *A Discourse on Winning and Losing*,[6] rather than a book. The briefing was terse and abbreviated, with much of the material demanding familiarity with some of the major battles of military history and strategy theory by theorists such as Sun Tzu, Clausewitz, Jomini and Liddell Hart. As a result, a mystique surrounds Boyd's theory, similar in respects to Clausewitz's unfinished manuscript, *On War*. Nonetheless, Boyd's thoughts on strategy had great influence up on the U.S. Marine Corps fighting doctrine, forming the basis for "manoeuvre warfare."

Comments

Considered brilliant, Boyd was also outspoken, arrogant and profane. He was a polarising figure in the Air Force, with his fellow servicemen either loving or hating him. His irreverence and intensity were often anathema to his seniors. In spite of Boyd's colossal contributions to air combat with his OODA Loop and Energy Manoeuvrability theories that dramatically changed U.S. Air Force fighter design, he was treated as a pariah by the Air Force. The U.S. Marine Corps thought different, adopting Boyd as an honorary Marine for his contributions to strategy theory.[7] On Boyd's passing in March 1997, the Commandant of the Marine Corps, General C.C. Krulak, paid homage to him in an open letter, noting "He was a towering intellect who made unsurpassed contributions to the American Art of War."[8]

John Boyd challenged Air Force orthodoxy continuously. He challenged fighter tactics in his *Aerial Attack Study*, redesigned fighter aircraft in Energy Manoeuvrability Theory and developed the aircraft themselves in his design work on the F-15 and F-16. And he challenged the theory of how wars were to be fought and won in his 15-hour briefing, a *"Discourse on Winning and Losing."*

In the abstract of the document, Boyd described the major section of his briefing, *"Patterns of Conflict,"* as "a compendium of ideas and actions for winning and losing in a highly competitive world." In the same vein as Sun Tzu and Liddell Hart, Boyd viewed psychological disruption as the key to triumph. Like Liddell Hart before him, Boyd analysed the great battles of military history to discern the essence of victory. He also read the great strategists and developed an eclectic form of manoeuvre warfare that synthesised aspects of previous theory and warfare styles designed to "destroy the adversary's moral-mental-physical harmony, produce paralysis, and collapse his will to resist."[9] Lethal effort, in the form of attrition, was utilised to "tie-up, divert, or drain away an adversary's attention and strength, as well as (or thereby) overload his critical vulnerabilities and generate weaknesses." Manoeuvre-type warfare was used to "subvert, disorient, disrupt overload, or seize those vulnerable yet critical connections, centres, and activities as basis to penetrate, splinter, and isolate remnants of adversary organism for mop-up or absorption." Moral warfare was used to "create an atmosphere of fear, anxiety, and alienation to sever human bonds that permit an organic whole to exist." In the aggregate, this resulted in a synthesised warfare style that, in Boyd's words, would:

> *"Penetrate [an] adversary's moral-mental-physical being to dissolve his moral fibre, disorient his mental images, disrupt his operations, and overload his system, as well as subvert, shatter, seize, or otherwise subdue those moral-mental-physical bastions, connections, or activities that he depends up on, in order to destroy internal harmony, produce paralysis, and collapse [an] adversary's will to resist."*[10]

Boyd addressed the course of military history and what it could teach us. He introduced the theory of manoeuvre warfare, and included briefings entitled *"The Conceptual Spiral," "The Strategic Game of ? and ?,"* and *"An Organic Design for Command and Control."* He also explained and expanded his famous concept of the "OODA Loop." Combined into the *"Discourse,"* this is the main body of Boyd's thinking. His courage to state his views—and defend them regardless of consequence—his integrity and willingness to challenge and persevere were what were admired and respected by his supporters. "The OODA Loop may appear too humble to merit categorisation as grand theory, but that is what it is. It has an elegant simplicity, an extensive domain of applicability, and contains a high quality of insight about strategic essentials, such that its author well merits honourable mention as an outstanding general theorist of strategy."[11]

Boyd's focus was clearly on defeating the enemy mentally, destroying his will to resist rather than his means of resistance. The physical instruments used in war were most important in the effects they imparted on the mind, though diminishing the physical body also worked against the mind as well. He borrowed heavily from previous theorists such as Sun Tzu, Clausewitz, Marx, Engels and Lenin, J.F.C. Fuller, Heinz Guderian, and Mao Tse Tung to develop a monolithic, concepts-based theory of strategy.

Boyd realised that the subversive strategy employed by the Communists was effective in destabilising an opponent through agitation of the masses, division of the workers from the elites, focusing hatred on leaders, and creating indecision in government.[12] Nurturing insurrection was but one element of Boyd's strategy, however. He also borrowed infiltration and isolation from *blitzkrieg* and guerrilla warfare. Infiltration was used to shatter the enemy society through propaganda exploiting the internal frictions, contradictions, and differences of opinion in order to foment distrust and discord. Propaganda was also used to isolate the enemy from potential allies.

Three of the central concepts of Boyd's strategy were surprise, speed and tempo, also borrowed from his reading of German World War II operational thought. Attacks were to be carried out with surprise and speed in order to confuse and disorient the enemy, with high tempo, follow-up operations preventing the enemy from recovering. In this way, the enemy's will to resist was shattered through both destruction and disruption. This necessitated decentralised command, with lower-level commanders given more freedom to carry out mission orders, using their initiative to exploit opportunities once the battle devolved away from the opening moves of a battle plan. These high tempo operations, in which one's own OODA Loop was decidedly quicker than the opponents, translated into always being one step ahead of a confused and demoralised enemy.[13]

Boyd's theories have formed the foundation of U.S. Marine Corps fighting doctrine. Institutionalised as the Marine Corps way of war since 1997, Boyd's theory of "manoeuvre warfare" has guided Marine Corps fighting philosophy through its seminal doctrinal manual, *Warfighting*.[14] The Marines define manoeuvre warfare as:

> *... a warfighting philosophy that seeks to shatter the enemy's cohesion through a variety of rapid, focused, and unexpected actions which create a turbulent and rapidly deteriorating situation with which the enemy cannot cope.*[15]

For the Marines, the "manoeuvre" in "manoeuvre warfare" refers to both time and space. Manoeuvre was described in *Warfighting* as a multi-dimensional construct:

> *The traditional understanding of manoeuvre is a spatial one; that is, we manoeuvre in space to gain a positional advantage. However, in order to maximise the usefulness of manoeuvre, we must consider manoeuvre in other dimensions as well. The essence of manoeuvre is taking action to generate and exploit some kind of advantage over the enemy as a means of accomplishing our objectives as effectively as possible. That advantage may be psychological, technological, or temp oral as well as spatial. Especially important is manoeuvre in time—we generate a faster operating tempo than the enemy to gain a temporal advantage. It is through manoeuvre in all dimensions that an inferior force can achieve decisive superiority at the necessary time and place.*[16]

It should be noted that the concept of manoeuvre in strategy is still evolving, with many practitioners claiming that cyberspace represents another of its dimensions. Boyd's thoughts on strategy exist only in his briefing book, in books on Boyd written by his disciples, and Marine Corps doctrine. Nonetheless, although his legacy as a strategist may suffer as a result, his ideas should live on. Boyd is often known exclusively for the so-called 'OODA' loop model he developed which refers to a decision-making process and to the idea that military victory goes to the side that can complete the cycle from observation to action the fastest.

John Boyd's original contribution to strategic theory is undiminished. His work is much more comprehensive, richer and deeper than is generally thought. With his ideas featuring in the literature on Network Centric Warfare, a key element of the US and NATO's 'military transformation' programmes, as well as in the debate on Fourth Generation Warfare, Boyd continues to exert a strong influence on military thinking. His work can help us to understand the new strategic threats in the present-day world, and establishes that John Boyd should be regarded as one of the most important (post)modern strategic theorists. America has dominated the skies because of John Boyd.

FURTHER READING

- John Richard Boyd (3 September 1976), *"Destruction and Creation"*, US Army Command and General Staff College.
- Robert Coram, *Boyd: The Fighter Pilot Who Changed the Art of War* (New York: Little, Brown, 2002).
- Daniel Ford (2010), *A Vision So Noble: John Boyd, The OODA Loop, and America's War on Terror* (Greenwich, London: Daniel Ford, 2010).
- Grant T Hammond, *The Mind of War: John Boyd and American Security* (Washington, D.C.: Smithsonian Institution Press, 2001).
- William S. Lind, *Maneuver Warfare Handbook* (Boulder, Colorado: Westview Press, 1985).
- Frans P.B. Osinga, *Science, Strategy and War: The Strategic Theory of John Boyd* (London: Routledge, 2007).

13

Mao

The process of knowing a situation goes on not only before the formulation of a military plan but also after. In carrying out the plan from the moment it is put into effect to the end of the operation, there is another process of knowing the situation, namely, the process of practice. In the course of this process, it is necessary to examine anew whether the plan worked out in the preceding process corresponds with reality. If it does not correspond with reality, or if it does not fully do so, then in light of our knowledge, it becomes necessary to form new judgments, make new decisions and change the original plans so as to meet the new situation....[1]

—**Mao Tse-tung, *"Strategy in China's Revolutionary War"***

Introduction

Mao Tse-Tung (Mao Zedong) (1893-1976) was a soldier, statesman and Chinese Marxist theorist who led his country's communist revolution. Mao was the leader of the Chinese Communist Party (CCP) from 1935 until his death, and he was chairman (chief of state) of the People's Republic of China from 1949 to 1959 and chairman of the party also until his death. He developed the most famous theory of insurgency warfare. His concepts, designed initially for the Chinese campaign against the Japanese in World War II, were expanded and adapted by him and others to become a general theory of revolutionary warfare.

Mao emphasises the political nature of war and the reliance of the army on the civilian population, especially the Chinese peasant population. He advocated a protracted war against the Japanese; victory would come in time through attrition. He believed in avoiding large battles except in the rare instances when they had the advantage. Guerrillas should normally operate dispersed across the countryside and concentrate only to attack. Because the Chinese had a regular army contending with the Japanese, Mao had to pay particular attention to how guerrilla and regular operations complemented each other. He postulated a progressive campaign that would move slowly and deliberately from a stage when the Chinese were on the strategic defensive through a period of strategic stalemate to the final stage when Chinese forces assumed the strategic offensive. The ratio of forces and their tactical activities in each stage reflected the strategic realities of the environment. Thus, guerrilla forces and tactics dominated the phase of the strategic defensive. During the strategic stalemate, mobile and guerrilla warfare would complement each other, and guerrilla and regular forces would reach approximate equilibrium (largely by guerrilla forces combining and training into progressively larger regular units). Mobile warfare conducted by regular units would dominate the period of strategic offensive. Although guerrilla units would never completely disappear, the regular forces would achieve the final victory.[2]

Mao has had an enormous impact on the field of revolutionary warfare theory. Mao's military thought and his unified politico-military approach—is important as it became a model for people's wars or Chinese-style insurgencies in several countries in Asia, Africa, and Latin America. It is also relevant in that the same approach applies to the handling of China's affairs on the world stage.

The Origins

Mao Tse Tung was born into a peasant family in the rural region of Hunan province in 1893.[3] Notwithstanding, Mao would receive a good education by the standards of the day. He had a voracious reading appetite that he maintained throughout his life and was self-schooled in the writings of the masters of war, to include Sun Tzu and Clausewitz, both of whom he quoted often.[4] He was also a student of military history, analysing military operations in past wars for what made them successful and what did not.

Mao wrote *On Guerrilla Warfare* (also known as *Yu Chi Chan*) in

1937, followed by *Problems of Strategy in Guerrilla War Against Japan* and *On Protracted War* in 1938, in which he articulated the strategy the Chinese should employ against the Japanese in the Second Sino-Japanese War. The three-stage strategy he developed would apply equally well to his war against the Kuomintang, fought later, and other communist revolutionary struggles with similar conditions around the world.

The origins of the people's war may be traced back to the period of the first and second revolutionary wars in China (1927-35). There are two main elements: social revolution and nationalist resistance, in that order.

Early on, before the war with Japan, Mao realised that the communist revolutionary strategy as laid out by the Russian Revolution would not work in China. The industrial workers in China were not the oppressed class; rather, it was the 400 million peasants, many of who were landless and barely able to eke out an existence. Mao championed the peasant, rather than the worker, as the engine of communist revolution in China:

> *All talk directed against the peasant movement must be speedily set right. All the wrong measures taken by the revolutionary authorities concerning the peasant movement must be speedily changed. Only thus can the future of the revolution be benefited. In a very short time, in China's central, southern and northern provinces, several hundred million peasants will rise like a mighty storm, like a hurricane, a force so swift and violent that no power, however great, will be able to hold it back. They will smash all the trammels' that bind them and rush forward along the road to liberation. They will sweep all the imperialists, warlords, corrupt officials, local tyrants and evil gentry into their graves. Every revolutionary party and every revolutionary comrade will be put to the test, to be accepted or rejected as they decide.*[5]

Mao's faith in the peasantry would ultimately prove well-founded. Mao realised that the peasants were ripe for political exploitation. After some initial, sporadic successes and failures with guerrilla warfare, the Communist revolution in China was put on hold when the Japanese invaded in July 1937.

Mao's appraisal of China's war-making capacity against the Japanese was more circumspect. His overall assessment was as unflattering as it was accurate. While the peasants would again play an important role in his strategy, he was well aware of the asymmetric disadvantage China faced in fighting the more advanced Japanese. He assessed China's prospects relative to their Japanese aggressor thus:

> *China is a country half colonial and half feudal; it is a country that is politically, militarily, and economically backward. This is an inescapable conclusion. It is a vast country with great resources and tremendous population, a country in which the terrain is complicated and the facilities for communication are poor. All these factors favour a protracted war; they all favour the application of mobile warfare and guerrilla operations.*[6]

Opinions of Chinese leaders on how to fight the Japanese invaders were divided, with many opting for a regular war of army vs. army. Based on his strategic assessment of the situation, Mao advocated a hybrid strategy that included guerrilla warfare. In an effort to convince others to adopt this strategy, Mao wrote extensively and convincingly on the mechanics and merits of his strategy. Well-versed in the teachings of previous masters of war, Mao began with the political objective, which he described as "the basic political principle of China's War of Resistance Against Japan, i.e., its political aim, is to drive out Japanese imperialism and build an independent, free and happy new China".[7] In order to achieve this aim, the one basic, guiding principle, from which all others were derived, was "to strive to the utmost to preserve one's own strength and destroy that of the enemy".[8]

Six supplemental principles supported his basic principle:

1. The use of initiative, flexibility and planning in conducting offensives within the defensive, battles of quick decision within protracted war, and exterior-line operations within interior-line operations;
2. Co-ordination with regular warfare;
3. Establishment of base areas;
4. The strategic defensive and the strategic offensive;
5. The development of guerrilla warfare into mobile warfare; and
6. Correct relationship of command.[9]

In describing the relationship between the defensive and the offensive, between protractedness and quick decision, and between the interior and exterior lines, Mao explained the virtues of his hybrid strategy:

> *The enemy forces, though strong (in arms, in certain qualities of their men, and certain other factors), are numerically small, whereas our forces, though weak ... are numerically very large. Added to the fact that the enemy is an alien nation invading our country while we are resisting his invasion on our own soil, this determines the following strategy. It is possible and necessary to use tactical offensives within the strategic defensive, to fight campaigns and battles of quick decision within a strategically protracted war and to fight campaigns and battles on exterior lines within strategically interior lines. Such is the strategy to be adopted in the War of Resistance as a whole. It holds true both for regular and for guerrilla warfare. Guerrilla warfare is different only in degree and form.*
>
> *Offensives in guerrilla warfare generally take the form of surprise attacks. Although surprise attacks can and should be employed in regular warfare too, the degree of surprise is less. In guerrilla warfare, the need to bring operations to a quick decision is very great, and our exterior-line ring of encirclement of the enemy in campaigns and battles is very small. All these distinguish it from regular warfare.*[10]

Protracted War

In his essay *"On Protracted War"* Mao divided his overarching strategy of protracted war against the Japanese and Kuomintang into three overlapping stages: the strategic defensive, strategic stalemate (preparation for the counter-offensive); and the counter-offensive. These stages were specifically designed to counter the enemy stages of strategic offensive, consolidation and strategic retreat, respectively.

The first stage of Mao's protracted war strategy, the strategic defensive, consisted of political and military mobilisation of the people through subversion and limited fighting in the form of mobile warfare, supplemented by guerrilla and positional warfare. It is not just an operational defensive. It is designed to lure the enemy past its culminating point of attack, at which point, small insurgent bands can overwhelm over-extended and isolated enemy units. These small offensives within the larger strategic defence are an important source of arms and ammunition. They are also designed to push the population toward more active support of the revolutionary movement. Mao considered mobilisation the key feature of the first stage of protracted war:

> *This move is crucial; it is indeed of primary importance, while our inferiority in weapons and other things is only secondary. The mobilisation of the common people throughout the country will create a vast sea in which to drown the enemy, create the conditions that will make up for our inferiority in arms and other things, and create the prerequisites for overcoming every difficulty in the war. To win victory, we must persevere in the War of Resistance, in the united front and in the protracted war. But all these are inseparable from the mobilisation of the common people. To wish for victory and yet neglect political mobilisation is like wishing to "go south by driving the chariot north", and the result would inevitably be to forfeit victory.*[11]

To Mao, political mobilisation had to be total, not just in terms of reaching the entire population but also in the scope of the political indoctrination and the means by which it was to be spread. In Mao's words:

> *What does political mobilisation mean? First, it means telling the army and the people about the political aim of the war. It is necessary for every soldier and civilian to see why the war must be fought and how it concerns him. The political aim of the war is "to drive out Japanese imperialism and build a new China of freedom and equality"; we must proclaim this aim to everybody, to all soldiers and civilians, before we can create an anti-Japanese up surge and unite hundreds of millions as one man to contribute their all to the war.*
>
> *Secondly, it is not enough merely to exp lain the aim to them; the step s and policies for its attainment must also be given, that is, there must be a political programme. We already have the Ten-Point Programme for Resisting Japan and Saving the Nation and also the Program of Armed Resistance and National Reconstruction; we should popularise both of them in the army and among the people and mobilise everyone to carry them out. Without a clear-cut, concrete political programme it is impossible to mobilise all the armed forces and the whole people to carry the war against Japan through to the end.*
>
> *Thirdly, how should we mobilise them? By word of mouth, by leaflets and bulletins, by newspapers, books and pamphlets, through plays and films, through schools, through the mass organisations and through our cadres. What has been done so far in the Kuomintang areas is only*

a drop in the ocean, and moreover it has been done in a manner ill-suited to the people's tastes and in a spirit uncongenial to them; this must be drastically changed.

Fourthly, to mobilise once is not enough; political mobilisation for the War of Resistance must be continuous. Our job is not to recite our political programme to the people, for nobody will listen to such recitations; we must link the political mobilisation for the war with developments in the war and with the life of the soldiers and the people, and make it a continuous movement. This is a matter of immense importance on which our victory in the war primarily depends.[12]

In the second phase, strategic stalemate, the enemy has essentially ceded large swathes of territory, and the insurgency moves from relying on the generosity of the population to building a government to lead the population. At the same time, the army is gaining in competence and continuing to capture supplies and weapons.

Ideally, the third phase, strategic counteroffensive, is the shortest phase of a protracted war. The guerrillas have the manpower, materiel, and training necessary to meet the enemy in a conventional campaign. Ultimately, the conventional defeat of the counter-revolutionary army in the field compounds the internal weaknesses of the now-hollow regime and convinces its allies to abandon it. This phase is appealing in theory, but it is a challenge to implement in practice. A premature leap into a strategic counteroffensive may actually play to the strengths of the incumbent regime. Mao was aware of this problem, and his answer was for the rebels to fall back on a robust second phase, or even the first phase.

"*On Protracted War*" actually relates to two distinct struggles: the war of national liberation against the Japanese and the revolutionary war against Chiang Kai-shek's Nationalist Party. This is particularly relevant to the third phase, because the scale of the final counteroffensive will vary depending on whether the rebels are dealing with a foreign occupier or an indigenous government.

Mao's strategy involved "the imposition of a political party organised in accordance with Leninist principles and animated by faith in basic tenets of Marxism-Leninism onto a purely peasant mass base."[13] Mao was able to meld communist ideology with the wants of the people through the use of propaganda, by carefully integrating the grievances expressed in the exoteric appeals of the intelligentsia and masses with the ideological fixes promised in the esoteric appeals of the communists.[14] As Mao would later go on to state:

> *In all the practical work of our Party, all correct leadership is necessarily "from the masses, to the masses". This means: take the ideas of the masses (scattered and unsystematic ideas) and concentrate them (through study turn them into concentrated and systematic ideas), then go to the masses and prop agate and explain these ideas until the masses embrace them as their own, hold fast to them and translate them into action, and test the correctness of these ideas in such action. Then once again concentrate ideas from the masses and once again go to the masses so that the ideas are persevered in and carried through. And so on, over and over again in an endless spiral, with the ideas becoming more correct, more vital and richer each time. Such is the Marxist theory of knowledge.*[15]

Through political indoctrination and the cultivation of support through more humane treatment of non-combatants, Mao extended political mobilisation to transform his overarching strategy of "protracted war" into "protracted popular war." By building a common ideological foundation and a harmonious relationship between military troops and the people, mutual support was gained with the people providing logistical and intelligence support to the troops with the troops doing the fighting.

In order to establish and maintain "unity of spirit" between troops and local inhabitants, Mao established "The Three Rules and the Eight Remarks" for the conduct of troops with civilians:[16]

Rules

1. All actions are subject to command.
2. Do not steal from the people.
3. Be neither selfish nor unjust.

Remarks

1. Replace the door when you leave the house.
2. Roll up the bedding on which you slept.
3. Be courteous.
4. Be honest in your transactions.

5. Return what you borrow.
6. Replace what you break.
7. Do not bathe in the presence of women.
8. Do not without authority search the pocketbooks of those you arrest.

The comprehensiveness of the political indoctrination and civilian-military cooperation effort was such that it not only moved the people to support the war, but to also buy further into the communist ideology and the political end game. Whatever allegiance the people held for their government was completely subverted.

Political mobilisation was also the foundation up on which guerrilla warfare was built. While Mao included mobile and positional warfare with guerrilla warfare in the first stage, its primary aim was the building of a guerrilla warfare capability. Mao described guerrilla warfare as "a weapon that a nation inferior in arms and military equipment may employ against a more powerful aggressor nation."[17] In guerrilla warfare, terrain, climate, and society in general, were used as obstacles in resisting and defeating an enemy. In terms of execution:

> *In guerrilla warfare, select the tactic of seeming to come from the east and attacking from the west; avoid the solid, attack the hollow; attack; withdraw; deliver a lightning blow, seek a lightning decision. When guerrillas engage a stronger enemy, they withdraw when he advances; harass him when he stops; strike him when he is weary; pursue him when he withdraws.*[18]

Mao summed up the lessons of early defeats in his famous 16-character formula, in a work he wrote in 1930.

> *Ours are guerrilla tactics. They consist mainly of the following points:*
>
> *'Divide our forces to arouse the masses, concentrate our forces to deal with the enemy.'*
>
> *'The enemy advances, we retreat; the enemy camps, we harass; the enemy tires, we attack; the enemy retreats, we pursue.'*
>
> *'To extend stable base areas, employ the policy of advancing in waves; when pursued by a powerful enemy, employ the policy of circling around.'*
>
> *'Arouse the largest numbers of the masses in the shortest possible time and by the best possible methods.'*

> *These tactics are just like casting a net; at any moment we should be able to cast it or draw it in. We cast it wide to win over the masses and draw it in to deal with the enemy.*[19]

Surprise was an essential principle in guerrilla operations, more so than in regular warfare. Only through surprise could operations be brought to a quick decision, given the thin margins of local superiority that the guerrillas could generally muster over the Japanese.

Mao also advocated twin principles of dispersal and concentration in the conduct of guerrilla operations:

> *Because of its dispersed character, guerrilla warfare can spread everywhere, and in many of its tasks, as in harassing, containing and disrupting the enemy and in mass work, its principle is dispersal of forces; but a guerrilla unit, or a guerrilla formation, must concentrate its main forces when it is engaged in destroying the enemy, and especially when it is striving to smash an enemy attack. "Concentrate a big force to strike at a small section of the enemy force" remains a principle of field operations in guerrilla warfare.*[20]

Mobile warfare was also a key feature in the first stage of protracted war. Mao described mobile warfare as:

> *quick-decision offensive warfare on exterior lines in campaigns and battles within the framework of the strategy of interior lines, protracted war and defence. Mobile warfare is the form in which regular armies wage quick-decision offensive campaigns and battles on exterior lines along extensive fronts and over big areas of operation. At the same time, it includes "mobile defence", which is conducted when necessary to facilitate such offensive battles; it also includes positional attack and positional defence in a supplementary role. Its characteristics are regular armies, superiority of forces in campaigns and battles, the offensive, and fluidity.*[21]

In the first stage of protracted war, in both guerrilla and mobile operations, battle was only to be sought when the Chinese had a numerical superiority, with conditions suitable for a surprise attack, and the anticipated outcome was estimated to yield a quick decision. In Mao's words:

> *[W]e should not only employ large forces against small and operate from exterior against interior lines, but also follow the policy of seeking quick decisions. In general, to achieve quick decision, we should attack*

> *a moving and not a stationary enemy. We should concentrate a big force under cover beforehand alongside the route which the enemy is sure to take, and while he is on the move, advance suddenly to encircle and attack him before he knows what is happening, and thus quickly conclude the battle. If we fight well, we may destroy the entire enemy force or the greater part or some part of it, and even if we do not fight so well, we may still inflict heavy casualties. This applies to any and every one of our battles. If each month we could win one sizable victory like that at Pinghsingkuan or Taierhchuang, not to speak of more, it would greatly demoralise the enemy, stimulate the morale of our own forces and evoke international support. Thus, our strategically protracted war is translated in the field into battles of quick decision. The enemy's war of strategic quick decision is bound to change into protracted war after he is defeated in many campaigns and battles.*[22]

Mao also considered positional warfare as necessary in the first stage, but strategically auxiliary and secondary to guerrilla and mobile warfare. Mao described positional warfare in terms of the attack and defence of fixed positions and strategic points, to include "defence works with deep trenches, high fortresses and successive rows of defensive positions."[23] Positional warfare was the work of armies, requiring more sophisticated munitions than could be fielded by relatively untrained guerrilla forces until later in the war, when more training and experience, greater numbers, more hierarchical organisation, and better weapons provided through external support, increased their fighting capacity.

The growth of a politically mobilised population in the first stage of protracted war resulted in the capacity of guerrilla warfare to emerge as the preeminent form in the second stage of strategic stalemate, supplemented by mobile and positional warfare. Mao described his vision of how guerrilla warfare would unfold in the second stage of protracted war as follows:

> *Except for the troops engaged in frontal defence against the enemy, our forces will be switched in large numbers to the enemy's rear in comparatively dispersed dispositions, and, basing themselves on all the areas not actually occupied by the enemy and coordinating with the people's local armed forces, they will launch extensive, fierce guerrilla warfare against enemy-occupied areas, keeping the enemy on*

the move as far as possible in order to destroy him in mobile warfare.... The fighting in the second stage will be ruthless, and the country will suffer serious devastation. But the guerrilla warfare will be successful, and if it is well conducted the enemy may be able to retain only about one-third of his occupied territory, with the remaining two-thirds in our hands, and this will constitute a great defeat for the enemy.... In the second stage, we will have to call up on the whole country resolutely to maintain a united government, we will have to oppose splits and systematically imp rove fighting techniques, reform the armed forces, mobilise the entire people and p rep are for the counter-offensive.... [24]

In the third and final stage of the strategic offensive, Mao saw China shifting from primarily guerrilla warfare to mobile warfare to recover lost territories. However, Mao realised that China was too weak to fight Japan alone, and would need allies to overcome them. He foresaw that a shift from fighting defensively along strategically interior lines to an offensive fight along strategically exterior lines would be required. Guerrilla warfare would shift to provide a strategic support function, supplementing both mobile and positional warfare.

In terms of strategy, Mao had devised a mixed strategy that by the third stage, simultaneously incorporated the strategies of subversion, exhaustion and annihilation. In describing political mobilisation, Mao effectively laid out the mechanics of a strategy of subversion, although he never used the term. Mao was quite clear in his explanation of the strategies of exhaustion and annihilation, explaining their relationship as follows:

To begin with, we may say that the anti-Japanese war is at once a war of [exhaustion] and a war of annihilation. Why? Because the enemy is still exploiting his strength and retains strategic superiority and strategic initiative, and therefore, unless we fight campaigns and battles of annihilation, we cannot effectively and speedily reduce his strength and break his superiority and initiative. We still have our weakness and have not yet rid ourselves of strategic inferiority and passivity; therefore, unless we fight campaigns and battles of annihilation, we cannot win time to improve our internal and international situation and alter our unfavourable position. Hence campaigns of annihilation are the means of attaining the objective of strategic [exhaustion]. In this sense war of annihilation is war of [exhaustion]. It is chiefly by using the method of [exhaustion] through annihilation that China can wage protracted war.[25]

People's War

Mao's ideas on Revolution rested on three essential principles: the decisive role of military forces; the importance of rural base areas; and the protracted character of the struggle. Guerrilla warfare was an important element in Mao's scheme which is employed by a nation inferior in arms and equipment. But it is only one aspect of the revolutionary struggle and by itself cannot achieve total success. It is not an end in itself and, therefore, cannot be divorced from the operations of regular forces. While guerrilla operations may temporarily become 'paramount' in the whole context of the war, regular forces are 'of primary importance.' For, only the latter are capable of 'producing the decision.' Guerrilla warfare can, of course, assist regular forces in producing this favourable decision. Thus, while it must be promoted as "a necessary strategical auxiliary to orthodox operations," guerrilla warfare must not be assigned the primary position in the overall military strategy. Nor must it be substituted for "mobile and positional warfare as conducted by orthodox forces." But Mao tied his analysis with the caveat that under specific conditions, guerrilla warfare can "develop and assume orthodox characteristics."[26]

Guerrilla warfare in the Maoist conceptualisation was only one in a series of merging phases of the revolutionary struggle. Phase one was the preparatory stage, when regional bases are organised and consolidated.[27] Guerrilla attacks, limited to small actions in the first phase, were stepped up in the next. At the same time, political activities were expanded to peripheral districts to absorb them within the 'liberated' zone. Phase three was the decisive stage when the enemy is destroyed through orthodox military operations. A significant percentage of the guerrilla force must be transformed into a regular army at this stage. Though guerrilla operations were not altogether precluded at this stage, they would play only a subsidiary role.[28]

Guerrilla operations must flow from a clearly defined political goal, which, in turn, must coincide with the aspirations of the people. If people's support and assistance are not gained, guerrilla warfare will fail. Guerrilla warfare also cannot contribute to victory if it is unorganised. The importance of the political factor led Mao to articulate the concept of the three unities, namely, political activities as applied first to the troops, next to the people, and lastly to the enemy. What these got translated into were three fundamental actions: 'spiritual unification' of officers and men within the Red Army, 'spiritual unification' of the Red Army and the people, and 'destruction of the unity of the enemy.'

The first of these could be achieved by ensuring that officers and common soldiers lived and fought under the same conditions. Bringing about 'spiritual unification' of the Communist Army and the people is essentially a question of convincing the populace to identify itself with the revolutionary forces. For this purpose, Mao laid down detailed rules on troop behaviour towards the people. It is in this context that he likened people to water and guerrillas to 'the fish who inhabit it'. The third unity was to be attained by 'propagandising' enemy troops and by treating captured enemy soldiers with consideration. Failure in this regard would only strengthen the enemy's solidarity.[29]

Legacy

Mao's victory in China made him an icon among communists in the developing world. By the 1950s, insurgent leaders were following Mao's writings, and China was sending aid and advisors to movements around the globe. But Mao's legacy goes far beyond the Cold War. His prescriptions for revolution have maintained their appeal and their apparent effectiveness. It was a strategy that was also exportable to many other communist revolutionary movements.[30] Not only did Mao devise a brilliant hybrid strategy integrating the three strategies of subversion, exhaustion and annihilation into protracted popular war, he also illustrated how strategies could be nested across levels of analysis.

Mao's writings synthesised his own experience of revolutionary struggle with his vision of how the revolution should be carried forward. The principles of operation Mao espoused are:

1. Attack dispersed, isolated enemy forces first; attack concentrated, strong enemy forces later.

2. Take small and medium cities and extensive rural areas first; take big cities later.
3. Make wiping out the enemy's effective strength our main objective; do not make holding or seizing a city or place our main objective. Holding or seizing a city or place is the outcome of wiping out the enemy's effective strength, and often a city or place can be held or seized for good only after it has changed hands a number of times.
4. In every battle, concentrate an absolutely superior force (two, three, four and sometimes even five or six times the enemy's strength), encircle the enemy forces completely, strive to wipe them out thoroughly and do not let any escape from the net. In special circumstances, use the method of dealing the enemy crushing blows, that is, concentrate all our strength to make a frontal attack and an attack on one or both of his flanks, with the aim of wiping out one part and routing another so that our army can swiftly move its troops to smash other enemy forces. Strive to avoid battles of attrition in which we lose more than we gain or only break even. In this way, although inferior as a whole (in terms of numbers), we shall be absolutely superior in every part and every specific campaign, and this ensures victory in the campaign. As time goes on, we shall become superior as a whole and eventually wipe out all the enemy.
5. Fight no battle unprepared, fight no battle you are not sure of winning; make every effort to be well prepared for each battle, make every effort to ensure victory in the given set of conditions as between the enemy and ourselves.
6. Give full play to our style of fighting—courage in battle, no fear of sacrifice, no fear of fatigue, and continuous fighting (that is, fighting successive battles in a short time without rest).
7. Strive to wipe out the enemy when he is on the move. At the same time, pay attention to the tactics of positional attack and capture enemy fortified points and cities.
8. With regard to attacking cities, resolutely seize all enemy fortified points and cities which are weakly defended. At opportune moments, seize all enemy fortified points and cities

defended with moderate strength, provided circumstances permit. As for all strongly defended enemy fortified points and cities, wait till conditions are ripe and then take them.

9. Replenish our strength with all the arms and most of the personnel captured from the enemy. Our army's main sources of manpower and materiel are at the front.
10. Make good use of the intervals between campaigns to rest, train and consolidate our troops. Periods of rest, training and consolidation should not in general be very long, and the enemy should so far as possible be permitted no breathing space.

Regardless of Mao's failings as a political leader, Mao was a master strategist, arguably, the best of the 20th century.

FURTHER READING

- Mao Tse-tung, *On Guerrilla Warfare*, trans. Samuel B. Griffith (New York: Praeger Publishers, 1961).
- Mao Tse-tung, "On Protracted War," in *Selected Works of Mao Tse-Tung*, Vol. II (Peking: Foreign Language Press, 1965).
- Edgar Snow, *Red Star Over China* (New York: Grove Press, 1968).
- Robert Tabor, *War of the Flea* (New York: L. Stuart, 1965).
- Delia Davin, *Mao: A Very Short Introduction* (Oxford: Oxford University Press, 2013).

14

Summation

We know from the study of military history how fallible man is in matters concerning war and how difficult it has been to adjust to new weapons. Almost always in the past there was time even after hostilities began for the significance of technological changes to be learned and appreciated. Such time will not again be available in any unrestricted war of the future.[1]

—**Bernard Brodie**

War and violence to achieve personal or political aims has been a constant throughout recorded history. Men have also studied war for almost as long as they have been making it. 'War does not belong in the realm of art and science; rather it is a part of man's social existence', wrote Carl von Clausewitz.[2] Alfred Mahan concurred: 'Conflict is the condition of all life.'[3] Giulio Douhet added: 'Whenever two men meet, conflict is inevitable.[4]

At the beginning of the 19th century Clausewitz defined strategy as the use of the battle for the purposes of the war. For him, strategy was the art of the commander. Today strategy is too often employed simply as a synonym for policy. A strategy needs a clear geographical focus. Wars are defined by the hostility which underpins them: the participants need to know who the enemy is, not least in order to be able to construct a strategy with which to direct the war.

Strategy is a profoundly pragmatic business: it is about doing things, about applying means to ends. It is an attempt to make concrete a set of objectives through the application of military force to a particular case. In other words strategy lies at the interface between operational capabilities and political objectives: it is the glue which binds each to the other and gives both sense. But it is even more than that: it is based on a recognition of the nature of war itself.

War is an unpredictable business, and because of this soldiers and scholars throughout history have searched for a magic solution to the business of war; some list of golden rules that, if satisfied, will guarantee victory. Past battles and campaigns have been closely studied and compared, the reasons for defeat or victory examined and principles of war evolved. Battle changes for the soldier from war to war and often during them. However, at the operational and strategic levels these principles dominate the teachings of modern military institutions because they are a summary of great historical experience and provide guidelines for studying and thinking about war. But it is not knowledge of the principles alone that is important, rather the degree of intelligent use made of them.

Strategy has to deal in the first instance not with policy, but with the nature of war. Strategy should serve the ends of policy, but it cannot do that if it is not based on a proper appreciation of war. War is distinct from policy. Carl von Clausewitz's statement that 'war is nothing but the continuation of policy with other means'[5] is a statement about how governments might use war; it is not a statement about the nature of war. Clausewitz says little about the relationship between war and policy, and even less about policy itself. Policy is a statement to tackle problems. They may be adapted and refined in the light of circumstances. (In this respect, war shapes policy, not the other way round.) A policy remains a statement of a government's intent.

War on the other hand is bilateral or even multilateral. Governments have policies which lead them into wars, but once they are engaged in conflict those policies are shaped by the actions of the adversary. War is, therefore, not the unilateral application of policy any longer but the product of reciprocal exchanges between diverging policies. Moreover, that interaction itself creates an independent dynamic, that is both incremental and unpredictable. More often wars themselves have shaped the policies of the belligerents, so that the governments' policies at the outset of a war have not proved consistent over its course. The actual outcomes of the war, even if still desirable from the point of view of at least one of the belligerents, are likely to have been very different from the objectives entertained at its outset. Strategy, therefore, has to rest on an understanding of war and war's nature because it will shape policy. Strategy is no longer an intellectual concept.

Machiavelli, Clausewitz, Jomini, Sun Tzu and Basil Liddell Hart are the doyens of the continental school, which is concerned with ground warfare between armies and has historically been the major instrument of military strategy. It has also been the main influence on the contemporary shape of warfare. Machiavelli, Jomini and Clausewitz are described as the strategists of 'offensive war' whereas Liddell Hart and Sun Tzu are the theorists of 'limited or defensive war'. There is also a considerable amount of common basic military theory in Jomini's *Summary of the Art of War* (1838) and Clausewitz's *On War* (1831).

Kautilya's writings come in the realm of realpolitik. He was the first political thinker to grasp the competitive nature of the global system. He saw politics and wars as natural and necessary. He believed that political institutions must be organised in such a way as to create favourable preconditions for the functioning of the military.

Liddell Hart is famous for his 'strategy of the indirect approach', and as the prophet of mechanised warfare or *blitzkrieg*. In the strategy of the indirect approach his objective was to consider how war could be fought more cleanly, more decisively, more intelligently and, above all, as humanely as possible. His main conclusion was that the strength of the enemy is dependent upon stability or "equilibrium" of control, morale and supply. He stressed that, in all the decisive campaigns, the dislocation of the enemy's psychological and physical balance has been the vital prelude to a successful attempt at his overthrow. This dislocation has been produced by the indirect approach.

Liddell Hart was not the first strategist to consider the indirect approach. Many of the maxims developed in his writings had also been expounded by Sun Tzu in about 500 BC. Indeed Sun Tzu was the first to advocate an indirect approach. He contended that 'in all fighting ... indirect methods will be needed in order to ensure victory'.[6] Sun Tzu's military ideas contained many of the tenets of the indirect approach:

deception, speed, avoidance of attrition, striking what is weak and vulnerable, emphasis on manoeuvre and, more importantly, attacking the enemy's will to fight. Sun Tzu's *Art of War*, is the oldest military work in existence. It deals with principles and fundamentals that are as relevant today as they were centuries ago. It teaches how to win with a minimum of fighting by knowing the enemy, deceiving the enemy and exploiting the enemy's weaknesses.

Clausewitz said nothing about sea power, and one challenge that classical strategy had to confront in 1918, therefore, was that posed by maritime strategy, particularly if the allied victory in World War I was indeed brought about by sea power, as thinkers like Liddell Hart argued. Although the application of British sea power had pointed the way to its importance, there was a tendency to see maritime strategy as belonging in a separate compartment from strategy itself.

Alfred Thayer Mahan held that control of the seas will ultimately determine decisions ashore. He believed that domination of critical sea lanes and choke points enables forces afloat to exert indirect pressure on forces ashore by means of naval blockades, interdiction missions and so on. Maritime theory thus consists of control of the sea and the exploitation of this control to help establish control on the land. It does not necessarily focus directly on the destruction of enemy forces, but rather on strangling trade and limiting manoeuvrability. 'No other single person has so directly and profoundly influenced the theory of sea and naval strategy as Mahan'.[7]

The idea of decisive battle also links Mahan with Clausewitz. The subordination of strategy to policy was as central to his scheme of thought as it was to that of Clausewitz. 'War,' wrote Mahan in 1896, 'is simply a political movement, though violent and exceptional in character ... the military arm awaits upon and is subservient to the political interests and civil power of the state.'[8] Clausewitz also stressed that war is subordinate to politics.

Julian Corbett, who had read Clausewitz, argued that naval strategy was not a thing by itself. He distinguished between minor strategy and major strategy by keeping in view constantly the politico-diplomatic position of the country (on which depends the effective action of the instrument), and its commercial and financial position (by which the energy for working the instrument is maintained).'[9] He stated that 'our peace strategy must formulate our war strategy, by which .... there cannot be two forms of strategy, one for peace and one for war'.[10]

The early advocates of air power were those involved in promoting the importance of air power prior to World War I. Unlike the continental and maritime strategists, the early air power theorists were unable to base their theories on the lessons of history. They essentially argued that air power was, or had the potential to be, a weapon of immense capability. Therefore the war of attrition experienced in World War I, which led to significant loss of life, could become a thing of the past. Much like Liddell Hart, their ideas were influenced by the conduct of World War I. They believed that the outcome of future conflict would be decided not on the ground in trench warfare, but up in the air. They were convinced that strategic bombing or the use of offensive air power could shatter the morale of the civilian population and destroy the enemy's defence-industrial infrastructure and thereby end the war very quickly.

By air power, we mean the use of aircraft for military purposes. Air power has redrawn traditional battle lines and introduced a third dimension into warfare. Douhet expressed air power in its purest form, unhindered by a counter-force. In his view there is no other weapon, be it machine gun or tank, capable of changing the face of warfare like air power. In Douhet's thinking, air power was the ultimate strategic weapon because he defined strategy only in terms of the imagined destructive potential of air power. For Douhet there was only one strategy, and that was total war.

Mitchell did not advocate air power at the expense of ground forces. He did not think, as Douhet did, that the enemy's surface forces could be ignored. Nor was he convinced of the ability of air power alone to achieve victory. He appreciated the importance of concerted action between land, sea and air forces. There were, however, some similarities in the strategic thinking of Mitchell and Douhet. Mitchell was convinced that in an age of aerial warfare, ground and naval campaigns were subsidiary to the main air effort, if not totally unnecessary. Like Douhet, Mitchell believed that strategic bombing could have a greater influence on the ultimate decision of war than any other arm, and in the long run would provide a more humane outcome to war. Mitchell's advocacy of a mixed air force structure shows his preference for a tactical aviation role. This could be interpreted to mean that, for Mitchell, air power was not the ultimate strategic weapon in the sense it was for Douhet.

However, it is worth remembering one important fact: throughout history, weapons have appeared that have been referred to as 'the ultimate strategic weapon', or a weapon for which there is no answer. Just as frequently, weapons have been developed to counter them.

Boyd described his "*Patterns of Conflict*," as a compendium of ideas and actions for winning and losing in a highly competitive world. In the same vein as Sun Tzu and Liddell Hart, he viewed psychological disruption as the key to triumph. Like Liddell Hart, he analysed the great battles of military history to discern the essence of victory.

Boyd's focus was clearly on defeating the enemy mentally, destroying his will to resist rather than his means of resistance. The physical instruments used in war were most important in the effects they imparted on the mind, though diminishing the physical body also worked against the mind as well. Three of the central concepts of Boyd's strategy were surprise, speed and tempo. Attacks were to be carried out with surprise and speed in order to confuse and disorient the enemy, with high tempo, follow-up operations preventing the enemy from recovering whereby the enemy's will to resist was shattered through both destruction and disruption. This necessitated decentralised command, with lower-level commanders given more freedom to carry out mission orders, using their initiative to exploit opportunities once the battle devolved away from the opening moves of a battle plan. These high tempo operations, in which one's own OODA loop was decidedly quicker than the opponents, translated into always being one step ahead of a confused and demoralised enemy.

Revolutionary warfare differs from conventional interstate or international conflicts in the sense that revolutionary wars are intra-state wars; they occur within states. The chief objective of revolutionary war is 'the seizure of political power by the use of armed force, destruction of an existing society and its institutions and their replacement with new state structure'.[11] Mao Tse-tung, Ho Chi Minh and Che Guevara were the leading proponents and practitioners of this type of warfare. Widespread popular discontent is the primary cause of revolutionary war. 'The revolutionary war is a war of the masses; it can be waged only by mobilising the masses and by relying on them', said Mao Tse-tung. Moreover 'a revolutionary war is never confined within the bounds of military action'.[12] Revolutionary warfare can assume different forms: wars of national liberation, rebellions against or violent efforts to overthrow an established socio-political system, civil war or people's war, secessionist movements, guerrilla war, insurgency and small wars.

Many of Sun Tzu's strategic ideas were adopted by the practitioners of guerrilla warfare—avoid costly pitched battles, attack weakness and avoid strength, use hit and run tactics, elude enemy pursuit by hiding in the hills, in forests or among the populace, and forage off of the enemy. In a sense, Sun Tzu laid the foundations of revolutionary warfare. Mao Tse-tung was a great admirer of Sun Tzu and his military writings. All of Sun Tzu's reasons for taking a country intact were pertinent to Mao as a revolutionary. It provided his logistical support. Destroying it would have been quite counterproductive and costly to rebuild. His was a battle for the hearts and minds of the people. Mao's military ideas have the same ring of simplicity as those of Sun Tzu. When the enemy advances, retreat. When the enemy halts, advance. When the enemy seeks to avoid battle, attack; when the enemy retreats, pursue.

Small bands of revolutionaries armed with small arms and the tactics of revolutionary warfare have succeeded in forcing large occupying armies to withdraw. Revolutionary war is by and large the tool of the weak against the strong. That revolutionaries resort to guerrilla warfare reflects their recognition of the fact that their opponents are stronger militarily. There have been instances when the growing costs of waging a conventional war have forced traditional rivals to turn to unconventional means to achieve their strategic objectives.

As in the past, revolutionary warfare will remain the predominant form of conflict in the future. Revolutionary warfare is manifesting itself in two types of low-intensity conflict: ethnic conflict and urban warfare.

In the 1980s there was the discovery of operational thought, which expostulated how militaries all over the world now think about war, calling it the 'operational art', although at one level it was no more than a reiteration of classical strategy. Its obvious product is now referred to as 'manoeuvre warfare' and there is an increasing dominance of operational thought in military doctrine. Be that as it may, there is also an increasing tendency to ignore the true nature of war, its reciprocity, its unpredictability and its friction.

The nature of war (war in general) is violence. The character of a war or a category of wars is determined by how that violence is applied by the parties to the conflict in question. Those who know the hazards, confusion and complexity of war first-hand are more likely to effectively visualise, describe and direct their units towards mission success. However, leaders must place their experiences within the context of a broad understanding of war and warfare. Doing so will prevent them from assuming that experience in one conflict will necessarily translate into success in the next.

> *"War is more than a mere chameleon that slightly adapts its characteristics to the given case. As a total phenomenon its dominant tendencies always make war a paradoxical trinity – composed of primordial violence, hatred, and enmity... ; of the play of chance and probability... ; and of its element of subordination, as an instrument of policy, which makes it subject to reason alone."*[13]

Strategy, in the contemporary era appears to have lost its identity: part of it subsumed by policy and part by operational thought. However, without a clear grasp of strategy, it is difficult to see what has changed in war as opposed to what merely seems to have changed. By confusing strategy with policy, governments have denied themselves the intellectual tool to manage war for political purposes, and so have allowed themselves to project their daily political concerns back into strategy.

Terrorism is the case in point. It is a means to wage war not an objective of war: this is why the 'global war on terror' is so strategically illiterate. But what is new is the exaggeration of its effects through the media and in turn through the reactions of political leaders. Strategy, because it is in dialogue with policy, is affected accordingly. Its ability to put terrorism in context and in perspective is undermined. The novelty of terrorism lies not in its own actions but in the responses to the governments trying to oppose it, which paradoxically themselves accord it the very effects that they seek to deny it.

Terrorism is not the only facet of contemporary conflict that is not new. Non-state actors, many of them in the business of war for personal profit, were features of medieval and early modern warfare: indeed the effort by 17th century European states to establish a monopoly on the use of armed force was in part a direct response to the advent of mercenaries and private military companies. Moreover, outside Europe many of the native populations which resisted colonialism in the 19th century did so not as representatives of states or to further political objectives, but to defend their religious beliefs, their ways of life or their control of resources: their motivations were existential rather than utilitarian. The methods that they used against their European opponents were (in today's jargon) asymmetric. Knowing that, if they directly confronted an organised and disciplined military force, they would lose, they reacted pragmatically and avoided battle. Their strengths in war rested on their local knowledge and their links to the population, and their methods were those of guerrilla warfare and even terrorism.

The identification of 'asymmetric warfare' as a fresh phenomenon reveals how naïve strategic thought has become. As any military commander knows, even when two armies with comparable organisations and similar weapons systems confront each other, they will not fight 'symmetrically'. Instead they seek to exploit each other's weaknesses, often looking for the line of least expectation to maximise their own relative advantage. Even the application of overwhelming military force by one side against another is 'asymmetric'. The popular belief that 'asymmetric war' is new is a reflection of the way in which peacetime norms have shaped the understanding of strategy. Strategic studies, during the Cold War, flourished on the back of the idea that their purpose was to avoid war bereft of the understanding of the consequences of using war. If war is an instrument of policy, strategy is the tool that enables us to understand it and give us our best chance of managing it.

War has an enduring nature that demonstrates four continuities: a political dimension, a human dimension, the existence of uncertainty and that it is a contest of wills.

War is the clash of two competing wills. An attacker needs to be resisted for fighting to occur. War begins with defence. As a result, the directions which war takes are unpredictable, because its nature is defined by the competition between two opposing elements, with each side doing its best to prevent the other achieving its objectives. Those objectives will themselves be adapted in the light of the war's conduct and course. The more protracted the conflict, the more other factors extraneous to the war itself and those intrinsic to it including 'chance', 'friction' and the 'fog of war' will shape it.

The nature of strategy is eternal. Regardless of time or place, those using military force for the purposes of policy will face the same complex phenomena. Strategy has always been, and will remain, a complex, non-linear, multi-dimensional, violent, and competitive activity. Thus, although every case of strategy in action displays unique features, each has something to teach us about dealing with the universal challenges.

The capacity for strategic thinking—and its ongoing development—is especially compelling given that the complex problem of running military operations is liable to occupy the skills and minds of senior commanders so completely that it is easy to forget what it is being run for.[14] The capacity for effective strategic thought is even more important than tactical or operational competence. The importance of getting strategy right, and its underpinning strategic education, is more important to make correct decisions at the political and strategic level than it is at the operational or tactical level. Mistakes in operations and tactics can be corrected, but political and strategic mistakes live forever.[15]

There is also apparent acceleration in military endeavours. The accelerated speed of war ensures the ability to recover from early missteps is greatly reduced. The accelerating pace of change has already impacted societies across the world, as older linear models of change are challenged. Changes in technology have enabled the rapid economic growth in many nations. It is an environment where potential frictions can emerge with little notice, and the pace of change can lead to multiple, interacting challenges and conflicts. Strategy comes into play where there is actual or potential conflict, when interests collide, and forms of resolution are required. Strategy is required when others might frustrate one's plans because they have different and possibly opposing interests. More than ever, this is an environment where strategy is essential to anticipate, stave off, minimise, or conclude conflict.

Four elements will underpin the future of strategy:

- Strategy is still needed to underpin national approaches to evolving geopolitical, technological, and demographic challenges.
- There is a need for continued integration in all elements of power in national security strategies.
- We need to evolve education and talent management systems to build more creative and adaptive strategists.
- Future strategy development and execution will no longer just be produced via biological intelligence; there will be an increasing application of artificial intelligence in developing, testing, implementing, and adapting strategy.

Since war has remained a constant feature in man's existence, history books are replete with accounts of conflict. An integral part of these historical accounts of war is the role played by great commanders. The likes of Hannibal and Napoleon are credited with displaying an unusually harmonious combination of the qualities required to excel in strategy. In order to understand best practice in strategy we must look to history, for 'the only empirical data we have about how people conduct war and behave under its stresses is our experience with it in the past'.[16] Since the core principles of strategy are eternal, the study and analysis of any historical example, however ancient, has value to the modern theorist and practitioner. Indeed, it was Clausewitz who wrote that 'all wars are things of the same nature'.[17] 'Because war and strategy are unchanged and unchanging in their natures, it has to follow that we should allow ourselves to seek education from historical experience.[18]

National security practitioners, and military leaders, must remain at the forefront of understanding the various elements of change and continuity in their environment. Strategy in the future must also be founded on engagement between like-minded military institutions and continue to evolve and embrace a greater sharing of ideas. There is a wide array of ideas in the realm of military endeavours and in strategy.

If wars are to be waged in the 21st century, those waging them will need a firm grasp of strategy. Strategy will not flourish if the armed services are silent on the issue, or feel themselves to be constrained by norms in relation to the proper and 'politically correct' conduct of civil-military relations. Just as politicians will never read *On War*, and so – by extension – will fail fully to understand war's true nature, so it is beholden on servicemen to embrace a sense of strategy that is at once both classical and unfettered by its proper links to policy. The first step in this process is a clear articulation of what strategy is; the second is its application in the machinery of state.

"The function of strategy is management of potentially lethal dangers."[19] In the past decade, the full spectrum of accelerating changes across the fields of technology, geopolitics, demographics, and military endeavours—and the impact of their convergence—has become more evident across government, academia, business, and the wider community. What distinguishes the current era from its predecessors is the pace of change. Artificial intelligence and robotics have the potential to increase the pace of technological change beyond any past experience, and may be outpacing the ability of economies, societies, and individuals to adapt. The world has shifted into an era of rapid and often disorienting change.

Technological advances are driving changes in the nature of warfare. Few would argue that the tools and methods used to wage war change with the times. However, war's nature does not change—only its character. The way we use these words today can seem to render such a distinction meaningless, but careful attention to semantics can reveal real problems in how we think about war, society, and the future. The nature of war describes its unchanging essence: i.e., those things that differentiate war from other things. War's nature is violent, interactive, and fundamentally political. Absent any of these elements the phenomena is not war but something else.

The character of war describes the changing way that war as a phenomenon manifests in the real world. As war is a political act that takes place in and among societies, its specific character will be shaped by those politics and those societies. War's conduct is undoubtedly influenced by technology, law, ethics, culture, methods of social, political, and military organisation, and other factors that change across time and place. War will continue to be a human endeavour, albeit continually evolving due to the impacts of new technologies, different warfighting ideas, and geopolitics. Strategy will still matter in the future.

Military officers who can think strategically have an important contribution to make to the development of strategy. The development of future strategists not only rounds out the intellectual capacity of an individual, but also provides an institutional and national asset: someone who can develop better approaches to the strategic challenges faced by military organisations and nation states in the coming decades.

A significant part of the technological revolution is the omnipresence of social media. The battle to shape domestic, enemy, and global opinion is emerging as a significant element of modern war. The growing role of social media also is a double-edged sword. Not only does it allow immediate reporting of events, but it also opens the door for sophisticated propaganda that can sway populations. The potential to manipulate an adversary's population will be balanced by how savvy—or how distrusting—those populations are, as well as government efforts to counter enemy information campaigns.

In this environment, spending the way out of a strategic problem is not possible. While seeking an edge in size, geographic position, and technology still remain highly desirable, an edge in superior thinking will be essential. History provides a guide for strategists. But ideas such as containment and end states are unlikely to provide an intellectual foundation for the next several decades of competition.[20] Future strategies where we seek success not just survival, therefore, will depend on more creative, lateral thinking by strategic planners and leaders. This will demand enhancements in education and talent management.

Given the proliferation of cyber activities and political warfare, the strategic space below the threshold of war is as strategically consequential as that above the threshold. In developing strategy that spans the competition and conflict spectrum, notions of separate peace and war constructs—which have dominated the last three decades—are no longer relevant.

General Douglas MacArthur once said, "New conditions require, for solution ... new and imaginative methods. Wars are never won in the past." The pace of technological change is quickening, resulting in constant changes to the character of war. In the end, what must guide the actions of the strategist is the attainment of the policy objective; it is that which should dictate how to use force. Organisations and people who can rapidly and effectively adapt are more likely to prevail.

> *We know from the study of military history how fallible man is in matters concerning war and how difficult it has been to adjust to new weapons. Almost always in the past there was time even after hostilities began for the significance of technological changes to be learned and appreciated. Such time will not again be available in any unrestricted war of the future.*[21]
>
> —**Bernard Brodie**

FURTHER READING

- Bernard Brodie, *Strategy in the Missile Age* (Princeton, NJ: Princeton University Press, 1959).
- Eliot Cohen, *The Big Stick: The Limits of Soft Power and the Necessity of Military Force* (New York: Basic Books, 2016).
- P.W. Singer and Emerson T. Brooking, *Like War: The Weaponization of Social Media* (Boston: Houghton Mifflin Harcourt, 2018).
- Barry D. Watts, *Friction in Future War* (Washington, DC: National Defense University Press, 1996).
- Williamson Murray, MacGregor Knox, and Alvin Bernstein, *The Making of Strategy: Rulers, States and War* (Cambridge: Cambridge University Press, 1994).

Notes

CHAPTER 1
INTRODUCTION

1 Colonel (later General) Sir William F. Butler, *Charles George Gordon* (London: MacMillan and Co. 1889) p. 85

2 Bernard Brodie, 'The Continuing Relevance of Clausewitz', in Carl von Clausewitz, *On War* trans. Michael Howard and Peter Paret (London: David Campbell Publishers Ltd, 1993), p. 62.

3 Colin S. Gray, *Modern Strategy* (Oxford: Oxford University Press, 1999), p. 1.

4 Colin S. Gray, *The Strategy Bridge: Theory for Practice* (Oxford: Oxford University Press, 2010), p. 4.

5 Lawrence Freedman, *Strategy: A History* (New York: Oxford University Press, 2013), p. 73.

6 Basil H. Liddell Hart, *Strategy* (New York: Meridian, 1991), p. 321.

7 Colin S. Gray, *The Strategy Bridge: Theory for Practice* (Oxford: Oxford University Press, 2010), pp. 17–19.

8 *Ibid.*, p. 18.

9 H. Richard Yarger, "Toward a Theory of Strategy: Art Lykke and the U.S. Army War College Strategy Model," in *The U.S. Army War College Guide to National Security Issues*, vol. 1, ed. J. Boone Bartholomees Jr., 5th edn. (Carlisle Barracks, PA: Strategic Studies Institute, US Army War College, 2012), p. 45.

10 J. Boone Bartholomees Jr., "A Survey of the Theory of Strategy," in Bartholomees, *The U.S. Army War College Guide to National Security Issues*, pp. 18–19.

11 For the "unequal dialogue," see Eliot Cohen, *Supreme Command: Soldiers, Statesmen, and Leadership in Wartime* (New York: Anchor Books, 2003).

12 Harry G. Summers Jr., *On Strategy: A Critical Analysis of the Vietnam War* (Novato, CA: Presidio Press, 1982). The author notes that the North Vietnamese never defeated the United States on the battlefield—a perspective that a Vietnamese counterpart noted was irrelevant.

13 Everett Carl Dolman, *Pure Strategy: Power and Principle in the Space and Information Age* (London: Frank Cass, 2005), pp. 4–5.

14 J.R. Russell, *Strifeblog*. 'With rifle and bibliography: General Mattis on professional reading', May 7, 2013. See http://www.strifeblog.org/2013/05/07/with-rifle-and-bibliography-general-mattis-on-professional-reading/.

CHAPTER 2
SUN TZU

1 Sun Tzu, *The Art of War*, trans. and introduced by S. B. Griffith (Oxford, 1963), p. 66
2 See Sun Tzu, *The Art of War*, trans. and introduced by S. B. Griffith (Oxford: Oxford University, 1963).
3 T.R. Phillips (ed.) *Sun Tzu: The Art of War* (Harrisburg, PA, 1944), p. 12.

CHAPTER 3
KAUTILYA

1 Kautilya *Arthaśāstra*, Book 10, Chapter 6, Paragraph 51. (All references are for Book; Chapter; Sutra.)
2 Johannes Bronkhorst, "Thinking about Peace in Ancient India," in *Peace in the Ancient World: Concepts and Theories*, (ed.) Kurt A. Raaflaub (John Wiley & Sons, 2016), pp. 87–88.
3 R.P. Kangle, note 2, pp. 5-10, [1.2.1-1.4.16].
4 Some scholars challenge the date of Kautilya's work but none place it later than 150 A.D. See also I. W Mabbett, "The Date of the *Arthaśāstra*," *Journal of the American Oriental Society*, 84:2 (April 1965), 162-169.
5 Roger Boesche, "Kautilya's *Arthaśāstra* on War and Diplomacy in Ancient India," *The Journal of Military History*, 67:1 (January 2003), pp. 9-37.
6 L. N. Rangarajan, *Arthaśāstra* (New Delhi: Penguin Books, 1987), p. 543; also 6.2.30-34; 7.1.20-22; 7.1.2-19.
7 Some Indian scholars trace the origins of the Mahabharata as far back as 1,500 years ago; authorship is usually attributed to "Vyasa," a possibly mythical or historically composite sage.
8 Roger Boesche, "*Kautilya's Arthaśāstra*," p. 19.
9 George J. Gilboy and Eric Heginbotham, *Chinese and Indian Strategic Behavior: Growing Power and Alarm* (Cambridge: Cambridge University Press, 2012), p. 31.
10 Kautilya *Arthaśāstra*, 6.2.13-14; 6.2.30-38; 7.1.2-37; 7.2.1-5.
11 Kautilya *Arthaśāstra*, 7.2.1-2; 7.5.13-20.
12 Kautilya *Arthaśāstra*, 2.1.16; 7.5.27.
13 Kautilya *Arthaśāstra*, 7.30-37; 17-22; 3.18.5; 3.19.4; 4.8.11; 9.4.26.
14 Kautilya *Arthaśāstra*, 7.3.12; 7.5.16-18; 7.13.11-12; 7.16.17-28.
15 Kanti Bajpai, Saira Basit and V. Krishnappa, *India's Grand Strategy: History, Theory, Cases* (New Delhi: Routledge, 2014), p. 204.
16 Kautilya: *The Arthaśāstra*. L.N. Rangarajan (Ed.) (New Delhi: Penguin Classics, 1992).
17 Kautilya *Arthaśāstra*, 7.6.17.
18 *Ibid*.
19 Kautilya *Arthaśāstra*, 7.6. 40-41.
20 Kautilya *Arthaśāstra*, 12.1.17.
21 *Ibid*.
22 Kautilya *Arthaśāstra*, 10.5.

23 Kautilya *Arthaśāstra*, 7.7.1-31.
24 Kautilya *Arthaśāstra*, 7.1.
25 Kautilya *Arthaśāstra*, 7.13.
26 Kautilya *Arthaśāstra*, 1.15.
27 Kautilya *Arthaśāstra*, 1.12.
28 Kautilya *Arthaśāstra*, 7.1.
29 Kautilya *Arthaśāstra*, 7.2.
30 Kautilya *Arthaśāstra*, 9.4.
31 See Adda Bozeman, *Politics and Culture in International History: From the Ancient Near East to the Opening of the Modern Age* (Princeton: Princeton University Press, 1960).
32 Rangarajan, *The Arthaśāstra*, 160.

CHAPTER 4
MACHIAVELLI

1 Rule 1 from Lord Fabrizio. (Book 7)
2 F. Gilbert, 'Machiavelli: The Renaissance of the Art of War', in Paret, *Makers of Modern Strategy*, pp. 23-6.
3 *Ibid.*, p. 31
4 Christopher S. Celenza, *Machiavelli: A Portrait* (Cambridge, MA: Harvard University Press, 2015), p. 66.
5 *Art of War* 1.11.
6 *Art of War* 1.75-6.
7 Niccolò Machiavelli, *The Art of War*, trans. Ellis Farneworth, with a foreword by Neal Wood (New York: De Capo Press, Inc., 1965), p. xlvi.
8 Leo Strauss, *Thoughts on Machiavelli* (Chicago: The University of Chicago Press, 1984), pp. 54-55.
9 *Ibid.*, pp. 83-84.
10 *Art of War* 1.33.
11 *Art of War* 1.13, 15.
12 *Art of War* 3.134.
13 Karl von Clausewitz, *War, Politics, and Power: Selections from On War and I Believe and Profess*, trans. and ed. Edward M. Collins (Washington, DC: Regnery Publishing, 1997), p. 176.
14 *The Prince* 12.
15 *The Prince* 17.
16 *The Prince* (1513), Ch. 6; translated by W. K. Marriott.
17 Book 7.
18 Chapter 14, pp. 53-54.
19 Chapter 12, p. 46.

CHAPTER 5
CLAUSEWITZ

1 C. von Clausewitz, *On War*, trans. and ed. M. Howard and P. Paret (Princeton: Princeton University Press, 1976). p.54

2 B. Brodie, 'Clausewitz: A Passion for War', *World Politics* 25/2 (1973), pp. 228-308.
3 A.J. Echevarria II, *Clausewitz and Contemporary War* (Oxford: Oxford University Press, 2007), p. 3.
4 *On War*, p. 149. Air power theorist Giulio Douhet added: 'Whenever two men meet, conflict is inevitable.' G. Douhet, The Command of the Air (Rome, 1921, trans. D. Ferrari, Washington, DC, 1983), p. 3.
5 *On War*, p. 9.
6 *On War*, p. 4.
7 Michael Howard, *Clausewitz* (New York: Oxford University Press, 1983), p. 8.
8 James King, "On Clausewitz: Master Theorist of War," *Naval War College Review* 30 (Fall 1977), p. 9.
9 *On War*, p. 63.
10 Hew Strachan, *European Armies and the Conduct of War* (Boston: George Allen & Unwin, 1983), p. 94.
11 *On War*, p. 75.
12 *Ibid.*, p. 77.
13 *Ibid.*, pp. 69, 77, 91.
14 *Ibid.*, p. 91.
15 *Ibid.*, p. 81.
16 *Ibid.*, p. 87.
17 *Ibid.*, p. 89.
18 *Ibid.*, p. 85.
19 Raymond Aron, "Clausewitz' Conceptual System," *Armed Forces and Society* 1, no. 1 (Fall 1974), p. 56.
20 *On War*, p. 62.
21 *Ibid.*, pp. 87, 605.
22 *Ibid.*, pp. 87-88.
23 *Ibid.*, pp. 87-88, 605.
24 *Ibid.*, p. 75.
25 *Ibid.*, p. 85.
26 *Ibid.*, p. 86.
27 Echevarria, *Clausewitz and Contemporary War*, p. 66.
28 *On War*, p. 606.
29 Gray, *War, Peace and International Relations*, p. 23.
30 *On War*, p. 89.
31 *On War*, p. 104.
32 *Ibid.*, p. 119.
33 *On War*, p. 97.
34 *On War*, p. 70.
35 *On War*, p. 89.
36 Michael I Handel, *Masters of War* (Great Britain: Frank Cass Publishers, 2001), p. 103.
37 *On War*, p. 89.
38 See Edward J. Villacres and Christopher Bassford, "Reclaiming the Clausewitzian Trinity," *Parameters* (Autumn 1995), pp. 9-19.
39 *On War*, pp. 595-6.

40 *On War*, p. 258.
41 *On War*, p. 596.
42 *On War*, p. 54.
43 *On War*, trans. and ed. Michael Howard and Peter Paret (Princeton, NJ: Princeton University Press, 1976), pp. 605–610.
44 Geoffrey Blainey, *The Causes of War* (New York: The Free Press, 1973), p. 114.
45 *On War*, p. 483.
46 *Ibid.*
47 *On War*, pp. 85–86.
48 *On War*, p. 17.
49 *On War*, p. 121.
50 B. Brodie, 'The Continuing Relevance of On War', in Carl von Clausewitz, *On War*, trans. and ed. M. Howard and P. Paret (Princeton: Princeton University Press, 1993) 48; Clausewitz, *On War*, 76.
51 *On War*, 119.
52 *Ibid.*
53 *On War*, p. 177.
54 *On War*, p. 101.
55 *Ibid.*, p. 146.
56 *Ibid.*, p. 147.
57 *Ibid.*, p. 146.
58 *Ibid.*
59 *On War*, p. 136.
60 *On War*, p. 104.
61 *Ibid.*, 77.
62 Carl von Clausewitz, *On War*, trans. Colonel J.J Graham (New York: Barns & Noble, Inc., 2004), p. 666.

CHAPTER 6
JOMINI

1 John Shy, "Jomini." In *Makers of Modern Strategy*, edited by Peter Paret (Princeton, N.J., 1986), p. 144.
2 Jomini 2005, p. 9.
3 Jomini 2005, p. 10.
4 Jomini was very vague in his definitions of the types of war.
5 Jomini 2005, p. 20.
6 Jomini 2005, p. 21.
7 Jomini 2005, p. 21.
8 Jomini 2005, p. 30.
9 Jomini 2005, p. 9.
10 Jomini 2005, p. 54. Similarly, he also defined it as "the art of bringing the greatest part of the forces of an army up on the important point of the theatre of war or of the zone of operations," p. 259.
11 Jomini 2005, p. 53.
12 Jomini 2005, p. 54.
13 Jomini 2005, p. 55.

14 Jomini 2005, p. 68.
15 Jomini 2005, p. 59.
16 Alger 1982, p. 21.
17 Jomini 2005, pp. 22-23.
18 Alger 1982, 206.
19 Shy, 'Jomini', op. cit., p. 158.
20 *Ibid.*, p. 161.
21 *Ibid.*, p. 30.
22 *Ibid.*, p. 29.
23 United States Military Academy, *Jomini, Clausewitz, Schlieffen* (New York, 1967), p. 23.
24 M. Howard, *Clausewitz* (Oxford, 1983), p. 41.
25 Clausewitz, *On War*, op. cit., p. 204.

CHAPTER 7
MAHAN

1 Alfred Thayer Mahan, "*Works of Alfred Thayer Mahan*", Version 12.1.
2 Alfred Thayer Mahan, *The Influence of Sea Power Upon History 1660-1783* (New York: Dover Publications, Inc., 1987) pp. 11-12.
3 Jon Robb-Webb, "Corbett and *The Campaign of Trafalgar*: Naval Operations in their Strategic Context," *Defense Studies*, Vol. 8, No. 2 (June 2008), p. 157.
4 Alfred Thayer Mahan, *From Sail to Steam: Recollections of Naval Life* (New York: Harper Bros. Press, 1907; repr., New York: Da Capo Press, 1968), p. 277.
5 *Ibid.*, p. 451.
6 Baron De Jomini, *Excerpts from The Art of War, by de Jomini, Baron*. pp. 13-14, 25-177 (Greenwood Publishing Group, Inc., Rightsholder Public Domain, 1971), p. 7.
7 Alfred Mahan, *Interest of America in Sea Power, Present and Future* (Boston, MA: Little-Brown, 1897), pp. 177-180.
8 Mahan, *The Influence of Seapower upon History*, p. 1.
9 William Livezey, *Mahan on Seapower* (Oklahoma City, OK: University of Oklahoma Press, 1981), p. 52.
10 Mahan, *The Influence of Seapower upon History*, pp. 225-26.
11 Clausewitz, 164.
12 Colin Gray, *Modern Strategy* (New York, NY: Oxford University Press, 1999), p. 80 and Mahan, pp. 1-77.
13 Philip Crowl, "Alfred Thayer Mahan: The Naval Historian," in *Makers of Modern Strategy: From Machiavelli to the Nuclear Age*, (ed.) Peter Paret (Princeton, NJ: Princeton University Press, 1986), p. 462.
14 Crowl, 462 and Alfred Mahan, *Armaments and Arbitration, or the Place of Force in the International Relations of States* (New York, NY: Harper and Brothers, 1912), 66-67
15 Mahan, *The Influence of Seapower upon History*, pp. 8-9 and 82-83.
16 *Ibid.*, pp. 39-43.
17 Alfred Mahan, *Naval Strategy Compared and Contrasted with the Principles and Practice of Military Operations on Land* (Westport, CT: Greenwood Press, 1975), pp. 150, 153, and 143.
18 See James R. Holmes and Toshi Yoshihara, *Chinese Naval Strategy in the Twenty First Century: The Turn to Mahan* (London: Routledge, 2008).

CHAPTER 8
CORBETT

1 Sir Walter Raleigh, "A Discourse of the Invention of Ships, Anchors, Compass, &c.," in *The Works of Sir Walter Raleigh*, vol. 8 (Oxford: Oxford University Press, 1829), p. 325

2 Andrew D. Lambert, ed., *21st Century Corbett: Maritime Strategy and Naval Policy for the Modern Era* (Annapolis, MD: Naval Institute Press, 2017), pp. 1-2.

3 Julian S. Corbett, *Some Principles of Maritime Strategy* (Annapolis, MD: Naval Institute Press, 1988), pp. 16 and 93.

4 Corbett, 1918, p. 144.

5 Corbett, 1918, pp. 45-46.

6 Corbett, 1918), p. 48.

7 Julian S. Corbett, *England in the Mediterranean*, quoted in D.M. Schurman, *The Education of a Navy*, 163.

8 Corbett, *Some Principles*, 54.

9 *Ibid.*, 53.

10 *Ibid.*, pp. 54-55.

11 Corbett, *Some Principles*, p. 87.

12 Julian S. Corbett, *England in the Seven Years' War: A Study in Combined Strategy*, vol. 1 (London: Forgotten Books, 2015), 3–4; and quoted in Donald M. Schurman, The *Education of a Navy: The Development of British Naval Strategic Thought, 1867–1914* (Malabar, FL: Robert E. Krieger, 1984), p. 165.

13 Cole, "Maritime Strategy", 13.

14 Corbett, *Some Principles*, pp. 152 and 206.

15 Corbett, *Some Principles*, p. 12.

16 Corbett, *Some Principles*, p. 10.

17 Corbett, *Some Principles*, Chapter 5.

18 Corbett, *Some Principles*, 16.

19 Julian S. Corbett, *The Campaign of Trafalgar* (London, UK: Longman, 1910), p. 408.

20 Corbett, *Some Principles*.

21 Corbett, *Some Principles*, p. 134 and 160.

22 Corbett, *Some Principles*, p. 138.

23 Corbett, *Some Principles*, p. 132.

24 Corbett, *Some Principles*, pp. 131 and 138.

25 Corbett, *Some Principles*, pp. 134, 152, and 206.

26 Corbett, *Some Principles*, pp. 160 and 134.

27 *Ibid.*, 90.

28 John F. Beeler, *British Naval Policy in the Gladstone-Disraeli Era, 1866–1880* (Palo Alto, CA: Stanford University Press, 1997), pp. 14–18.

29 Chester G. Starr, *The Influence of Sea Power on Ancient History* (New York: Oxford University Press, 1998), p. 5.

30 Lawrence Freedman, *Strategy: A History* (New York: Oxford University Press, 2013), p. 115.

CHAPTER 9
DOUHET

1 Giulio Douhet, *The Command of the Air*, Sheila Fischer, trans. (Rome: Rivista Aeronautica, 1958), p. 54.
2 *Ibid.*, p. 4.
3 Giulio Douhet, The Command of the Air (Washington, D.C.: Office of Air Force History, 1983), p. 141.
4 *Ibid.*, p. 53.
5 *Ibid.*
6 *Ibid.*, p. 23.
7 Phillip S. Meilinger, *The Paths of Heaven: The Evolution of Airpower Theory* (Maxwell AFB, AL: Air University Press, 1997, pp. 10–11.
8 See Thomas Hippler, "Democracy and War in the Strategic Thought of Giulio Douhet," in *The Changing Character of War,* (ed.) Hew Strachan and Sibylle Scheipers (Oxford: Oxford University Press, 2011).
9 Giulio Douhet, "The Command of the Air," in *Roots of Strategy Book 4*, (ed.) David Jablonski (Mechanicsburg, PA: Stackpole Books, 1999), p. 283.
10 *Ibid.*, pp. 300-01.
11 *Ibid.*, p. 300.
12 *Ibid.*, p. 294.
13 *Ibid.*, p. 10.
14 Lee Kennett, *A History of Strategic Bombing* (New York: Scribner, 1982), pp. 1–9.
15 For studies of Douhet's life and thinking, consult Edward Warner, "Douhet, Mitchell, Seversky: Theories of Air Warfare," in *Makers of Modern Strategy: Military Thought from Machiavelli to Hitler*, (ed.) Edward Mead Earle (Princeton, NJ: Princeton University Press, 1943) pp. 485–97; Bernard Brodie, "The Heritage of Douhet," Air *University Quarterly Review* VI, no. 2 (Summer 1953), 64–69, 120–26; and Kennett, *A History of Strategic Bombing*, pp. 54–57.

CHAPTER 10
MITCHELL

1 William Mitchell, *Winged Defense* (New York: G.P. Putnam's Sons, 1925), p. xii.
2 See Donald Dale Jackson and the Time-Life Editors, *The Epic of Flight: The Aeronauts* (Alexandria, VA: Time-Life Books, 1980).
3 Air Vice-Marshal E.J. Kingston-McCloughry, *War in Three Dimensions: The Impact of Air Power upon the Classical Principles of War* (Oxford: Alden Press, 1949), p. 21.
4 Colonel Phillip S. Meilinger, USAF. Maxwell AFB. *American Airpower Biography: Billy Mitchell*. http://www.au.af.mil/ au/404.asp.
5 William Mitchell, "Winged Defence: The Development and Possibilities of Modern Air Power—Economic and Military," in *Roots of Strategy Book 4*, (ed.) David Jablonsky (Mechanicsburg, PA: Stackpole Books, 1999), p. 422.
6 *Ibid.*, p. 499.
7 *Ibid.*, p. 502.
8 *Ibid.*, p. 511

9 *Ibid.*, p. 502
10 *Ibid.*, pp. 427-28.
11 *Ibid.*, p. 489.
12 Earle, Edward Meade, *Makers of Modern Strategy, Military Thought from Machiavelli to Hitler* (Princeton NJ: Princeton University Press, 1943), p. 498.
13 Colin S. Gray, *The Future of Strategy* (Cambridge: Polity Press, 2015), pp. 94–95.
14 Giulio Douhet, *The Command of the Air* (Tuscaloosa, AL: University of Alabama Press, 1998), p. 287.
15 Colin S. Gray, *The Airpower Advantage in Future Warfare: The Need for Strategy* (Maxwell Air Force Base, AL: Air University Press, 2007), p. vii.
16 Harold R Winton, *A Black Hole in the Wild Blue Yonder: The Need for a comprehensive Theory of Airpower* (Winter 1992), pp. 32-42. Virginia Military Institute: Air Force Historical Foundation, 1992, p. 35.

CHAPTER 11
LIDDELL HART

1 B.H. Liddell Hart, *Strategy.* 2nd Revised (New York: Meridian [1954] 1991), p. 209.
2 *Ibid.*, p. 321.
3 *Ibid.*, p. 18.
4 B.H. Liddell Hart, *Strategy.* 2nd Revised Edition (New York: Meridian [1954] 1991), p. 209.
5 See B.H. Liddell Hart, *Thoughts on War* (London: Faber & Faber, 1944). This text is a treatise on the nature, conduct and operations of war; from minor tactics to grand strategy
6 B. H Liddell Hart, *Strategy.* 2nd Revised (New York: Meridian [1954] 1991), p. 6.
7 *Ibid.* pp. 212-13.
8 *Ibid.*, p. 322.
9 *Ibid.*
10 *Ibid.*, p. 325.
11 See B.H. Liddell Hart's foreword to Samuel B. Griffith's translation of Sun Tzu's *The Art of War* for the high esteem for which he held it.
12 Liddell Hart, *Strategy*, p. 25.
13 Also see B.H. Liddell Hart, *The British Way in Warfare* (London: Faber and Faber, 1932), p. 8.

CHAPTER 12
BOYD

1 Robert Coram, *Boyd: The Fighter Pilot Who Changed the Art of War* (New York: Little, Brown; 2002), p. 3.
2 Coram 2002, pp. 422–24.
3 Wheeler and Korb 2007, p. 87.
4 Hammond 2001, p. 3.
5 Coram 2002, p. 115.

6 John R Boyd, *A Discourse on Winning and Losing*, 1987.
7 Grant T. Hammond, *The Mind of War* (Washington D.C.: Smithsonian Books, 2001).
8 *Ibid.*, p. 3.
9 *Ibid.*
10 John R Boyd, *A Discourse on Winning and Losing*, 1987.
11 Colin S. Gray, *Modern Strategy* (Oxford: Oxford University Press, 1999), p. 91.
12 Grant T. Hammond, *The Mind of War* (Washington D.C.: Smithsonian Books, 2001), p. 139.
13 Hammond, 142.
14 U.S. Marine Corps 1997.
15 U.S. Marine Corps, 73.
16 *Ibid.*

CHAPTER 13
MAO

1 *Selected Military Writings of Mao Tse-tung*, pp. 86-87.
2 See Mao Tse-Tung, *On Protracted War* (Peking, China: Foreign Language Press, 1960); Mao Tse-Tung: An Anthology of His Writings, Anne Fremantle, (ed.) (New York: New American Library, 1972).
3 Jung Chang and Jon Halliday, *Mao: The Unknown Story* (New York, NY: Alfred A. Knopf, 2005), p. 4.
4 For example, in *On Guerrilla Warfare*, Mao quoted Sun Tzu, Clausewitz and Lenin.
5 Mao Tse Tung, *Report on an Investigation of the Peasant Movement in Hunan*. Vol. I, in *Selected Works of Mao Tse-tung* (Peking: Foreign Languages Press, 1975), pp. 23-29.
6 Mao Tse Tung,. *On Guerrilla Warfare*. Translated by Samuel B. Griffith. (Champaign, IL: University of Illinois Press [1937] 2000), p. 68.
7 Mao Tse Tung, "Problems of Strategy in Guerrilla War Against Japan," *Selected Works of Mao Tse Tung*.
8 *Ibid.*
9 *Ibid.*
10 *Ibid.*
11 *Ibid.*
12 *Ibid.*
13 Benjamin I. Schwartz, *Chinese Communism and the Rise of Mao* (Cambridge, MA: Harvard University Press, 1968), p. 189.
14 Bard E. O'Neill, *Insurgency and Terrorism: From Revolution to Apocalypse* (Washington, D.C.: Potomac Books, 2005), pp. 99-103.
15 "Some Questions Concerning Methods of Leadership" in *Selected Works of Mao Tse-tung*. Marxists.org. 1 June 1943.
16 Mao Tse Tung, *On Guerilla Warfare*. Translated by Samuel B. Griffith (Champaign, IL: University of Illinois Press [1937] 2000), p. 92.
17 Mao Tse Tung [1937] 2000, p. 41.
18 *Ibid.*, p. 46.
19 A Single Spark can Start a Prairie Fire' in *Selected Works of Mao Tse-tung*, PFLP, 1965, Vol. I, p. 124.

20 Mao Tse Tung, "Problems of Strategy in Guerrilla War Against Japan" in *Selected Works of Mao Tse Tung*. May 1938.
21 Mao Tse Tung, *On Protracted War*, 1938.
22 *Ibid.*
23 *Ibid.*
24 *Ibid.*
25 *Ibid.*
26 Mao Tse-tung and Che Guevara, *Guerrilla Warfare*. Trans. and Introduction by Samuel B. Griffith. 1961, Cassell; London, pp. 31-32, 41-42.
27 Mao, in one of his earthy metaphors, used to compare the need for a base area with an individual's need for buttocks. "If an individual didn't have buttocks, he ... would have to run around or stand around all the time.His legs would get tired and collapse under him, and he would fall down." Cited in Douglas S. Blaufarb, *The Counterinsurgency Era: U.S. Doctrine and Performance 1950 to the Present* (New York. The Free Press; 1977), p. 4.
28 Gann, Lewis, *Guerrillas in History* (Stanford, California: Stanford University Press, 1971), pp. 64-65.
29 *Ibid.*, pp. 65-67.
30 See Bard O'Neill, *Insurgency and Terrorism* (Dulles, VA: Potomac Books, 2005), pp. 49-55.

CHAPTER 14
SUMMATION

1 Bernard Brodie, *Strategy in the Missile Age* (Princeton, NJ: Princeton University Press, 1959), p. 408.
2 C. von Clausewitz, *On War*, ed. and trans. M. Howard and P. Paret (Princeton, NJ, 1976), p. 149.
3 P.A. Crowl, 'Alfred Thayer Mahan: The Naval Historian', in P. Paret (ed.), *Makers of Modern Strategy: From Machiavelli to the Nuclear Age* (Princeton, NJ, 1986), p. 468.
4 Giulio Douhet, *The Command of the Air* (Rome, 1921, trans. D. Ferrari, Washington, DC, 1983), p. 3.
5 From Clausewitz's note of 10 July 1827, in *On War*, edited and translated by Michael Howard and Peter Paret (Princeton: Princeton University Press 1976), p. 69.
6 T.R. Phillips (ed.) *Sun Tzu: The Art of War* (Harrisburg, PA, 1944), p. 55.
7 M.T. Sprout, 'Mahan: Evangelist of Sea Power', in Earle, *Makers of Modern Strategy*, op. cit., p. 416.
8 *Ibid.*, pp. 461-2.
9 Julian Corbett, *Some Principles of Maritime Strategy*, ed Eric Grove (Annapolis, MD, 1988; 1st edition London, 1911), p. 308.
10 J.F.C. Fuller, *The Reformation of War* (London: Hutchison, 1923), p. 218.
11 J. Shy and T. W. Collier, 'Revolutionary War', in Paret, *Makers of Modern Strategy*, op. cit., p. 817.
12 Samuel B. Griffith, 'Introduction', *Mao Tse-tung on Guerrilla Warfare* (New York: Frederick A. Praeger, 1961), p. 4.

13 Carl von Clausewitz, *On War*, ed. and trans. Michael Howard and Peter Paret, ind. ed. (Princeton: Princeton University Press, 1984), p. 89.

14 Michael Howard, "The Use and Abuse of Military History," in *The Causes of War* (Cambridge, MA: Harvard University Press, 1983), p. 194.

15 Andrew Millett and Williamson Murray, "Lessons of War," *National Interest* 14 (Winter 1988), pp. 83–95.

16 Bernard Brodie, 'The Continuing Relevance of Clausewitz', in Carl von Clausewitz, *On War* (trans. Michael Howard and Peter Paret), (London: David Campbell Publishers Ltd, 1993), p. 62.

17 *Ibid.*, p. 732.

18 Colin S. Gray, *Strategy and History: Essays on Theory and Practice* (London: Routledge, 2006), p. 6.

19 Colin S. Gray, *The Future of Strategy* (Cambridge: Polity Press, 2015), p. 117.

20 See Eliot Cohen, *The Big Stick: The Limits of Soft Power and the Necessity of Military Force* (New York: Basic Books, 2016), pp. 200–6.

21 Bernard Brodie, *Strategy in the Missile Age* (Princeton, NJ: Princeton University Press, 1959), p. 408.

Bibliography

Books

Adda Bozeman, *Politics and Culture in International History: From the Ancient Near East to the Opening of the Modern Age* (Princeton: Princeton University Press, 1960).

A.J. Echevarria II, *Clausewitz and Contemporary War* (Oxford: Oxford University Press, 2007).

Air Vice-Marshal E.J. Kingston-McCloughry, *War in Three Dimensions: The Impact of Air Power upon the Classical Principles of War* (Oxford: Alden Press, 1949).

Alfred Thayer Mahan, *The Influence of Sea Power Upon History 1660-1783* (New York: Dover Publications, Inc., 1987).

Alfred Thayer Mahan, *From Sail to Steam: Recollections of Naval Life* (New York: Harper Bros. Press, 1907; repr., New York: Da Capo Press, 1968).

Alfred Mahan, *Naval Strategy Compared and Contrasted with the Principles and Practice of Military Operations on Land* (Westport, CT: Greenwood Press, 1975).

Alfred Mahan, *Interest of America in Sea Power, Present and Future* (Boston, MA: Little-Brown, 1897).

Andrew D. Lambert (ed.), *21st Century Corbett: Maritime Strategy and Naval Policy for the Modern Era* (Annapolis, MD: Naval Institute Press, 2017).

Anne Fremantle (ed.), Mao Tse-Tung: An Anthology of His Writings (New York: New American Library, 1972).

Bernard Brodie, *Strategy in the Missile Age* (Princeton, NJ: Princeton University Press, 1959).

Baron De Jomini, *Excerpts from The Art of War* (Greenwood Publishing Group, Inc., Rightsholder Public Domain, 1971).

B.H. Liddell Hart, *Strategy* (New York: Meridian, 1991).

B.H. Liddell Hart, *Thoughts on War* (London: Faber & Faber, 1944).

B.H. Liddell Hart, *The British Way in Warfare* (London: Faber and Faber, 1932)

Benjamin I. Schwartz, *Chinese Communism and the Rise of Mao* (Cambridge, MA: Harvard University Press, 1968).

Bard E. O'Neill, *Insurgency and Terrorism: From Revolution to Apocalypse* (Washington, D.C.: Potomac Books, 2005).

Boone Bartholomees Jr., "A Survey of the Theory of Strategy," in *The U.S. Army War College Guide to National Security Issues, Cases* (New Delhi: Routledge, 2014).

Carl von Clausewitz, *On War* trans. Michael Howard and Peter Paret (London: David Campbell Publishers Ltd, 1993).

Chester G. Starr, *The Influence of Sea Power on Ancient History* (New York: Oxford University Press, 1998).

Christopher S. Celenza, *Machiavelli: A Portrait* (Cambridge, MA: Harvard University Press, 2015).

Colonel J.J. Graham (trans.) Carl von Clausewitz, *On War* (New York: Barns & Noble, Inc., 2004).

Colonel Sir William F. Butler, *Charles George Gordon* (London: MacMillan & Co. 1889).

Colin S. Gray, *Modern Strategy* (Oxford: Oxford University Press, 1999).

Colin S. Gray, *The Strategy Bridge: Theory for Practice* (Oxford: Oxford University Press, 2010).

Colin S. Gray, *Strategy and History: Essays on Theory and Practice* (London: Routledge, 2006).

Colin S. Gray, *The Future of Strategy* (Cambridge: Polity Press, 2015).

Colin S. Gray, *The Airpower Advantage in Future Warfare: The Need for Strategy* (Maxwell Air Force Base, AL: Air University Press, 2007).

David Jablonsky (ed.) *Roots of Strategy* (Mechanicsburg, PA: Stackpole Books, 1999).

Douglas S. Blaufarb, *The Counterinsurgency Era: U.S. Doctrine and Performance 1950 to the Present.* (New York. The Free Press; 1977).

Donald Dale Jackson and the Time-Life Editors, *The Epic of Flight: The Aeronauts* (Alexandria, VA: Time-Life Books, 1980).

Edward M. Collins (trans. and ed.) *Carl von Clausewitz, War, Politics, and Power: Selections from On War and I Believe and Profess* (Washington, DC: Regnery Publishing, 1997).

Edward Meade, *Makers of Modern Strategy, Military Thought from Machiavelli to Hitler* (Princeton NJ: Princeton University Press, 1943).

Eliot Cohen, *Supreme Command: Soldiers, Statesmen, and Leadership in Wartime* (New York: Anchor Books, 2003).

Eliot Cohen, *The Big Stick: The Limits of Soft Power and the Necessity of Military Force* (New York: Basic Books, 2016).

Everett Carl Dolman, *Pure Strategy: Power and Principle in the Space and Information Age* (London: Frank Cass, 2005).

Geoffrey Blainey, *The Causes of War* (New York: The Free Press, 1973).

George J. Gilboy and Eric Heginbotham, *Chinese and Indian Strategic Behavior: Growing Power and Alarm* (Cambridge: Cambridge University Press: 2012).

Giulio Douhet, *The Command of the Air* (Washington, D.C.: Office of Air Force History, 1983).

Grant T. Hammond, *The Mind of War* (Washington D.C.: Smithsonian Books, 2001).

Harry G. Summers Jr., *On Strategy: A Critical Analysis of the Vietnam* War (Novato, CA: Presidio Press, 1982).

Hew Strachan, *European Armies and the Conduct of War* (Boston: George Allen & Unwin, 1983).

Hew Strachan and Sibylle Scheipers (eds.), *The Changing Character of War* (Oxford: Oxford University Press, 2011).

J. Boone Bartholomees Jr. (ed.) *The U.S. Army War College Guide to National Security Issues* (Carlisle Barracks, PA: Strategic Studies Institute, US Army War College, 2012).

J.F.C. Fuller, *The Reformation of War* (London: Hutchison, 1923).

James R. Holmes and Toshi Yoshihara, *Chinese Naval Strategy in the Twenty First Century: The Turn to Mahan* (London: Routledge, 2008).

John R Boyd, *A Discourse on Winning and Losing*, 1987).

Julian S. Corbett, *Some Principles of Maritime Strategy* (Annapolis, MD: Naval Institute Press, 1988).

Julian S. Corbett, *England in the Seven Years' War: A Study in Combined Strategy*, vol. 1 (London: Forgotten Books, 2015).

John F. Beeler, *British Naval Policy in the Gladstone-Disraeli Era, 1866–1880* (Palo Alto, CA: Stanford University Press, 1997).

Jung Chang and Jon Halliday, *Mao: The Unknown Story* (New York, NY: Alfred A. Knopf, 2005).

Kanti Bajpai, Saira Basit and V. Krishnappa, *India's Grand Strategy: History, Theory, Cases*, Routledge.

L.N. Rangarajan, *Arthaœstra* (New Delhi: Penguin Books, 1987).

Lawrence Freedman, *Strategy: A History* (New York: Oxford University Press, 2013).

Leo Strauss, *Thoughts on Machiavelli* (Chicago: The University of Chicago Press, 1984) Lewis Gann, *Guerrillas in History* (Stanford, California: Stanford University Press, 1971).

Lee Kennett, *A History of Strategic Bombing* (New York: Scribner, 1982).

Mao Tse Tung, *On Guerrilla Warfare*, (Champaign, IL: University of Illinois Press, [1937] 2000).

Mao Tse Tung, *Selected Works of Mao Tse-tung*, (Peking: Foreign Languages Press, 1975).

Mao Tse-Tung, *On Protracted War* (Peking, China: Foreign Language Press, 1960).

Michael I Handel, *Masters of War* (Frank Cass Publishers, Great Britain, 2001).

Michael Howard and Peter Paret, *Carl von Clausewitz, On War* (London: David Campbell Publishers Ltd, 1993).

Michael Howard, *Clausewitz* (New York: Oxford University Press, 1983).

Michael Howard, *The Causes of War* (Cambridge, MA: Harvard University Press, 1983).

Niccolò Machiavelli, *The Art of War* (trans.) Ellis Farneworth (New York: De Capo Press, Inc., 1965).

Peter Paret (ed.), *Makers of Modern Strategy: From Machiavelli to the Nuclear Age*, (Princeton, NJ: Princeton University Press, 1986).

Philip Crowl, *Alfred Mahan, Armaments and Arbitration, or the Place of Force in the International Relations of States* (New York, NY: Harper and Brothers, 1912).

Phillip S. Meilinger, *The Paths of Heaven: The Evolution of Airpower Theory* (Maxwell AFB, AL: Air University Press, 1997).

R.P. Kangle, *Kautilya Arthaœstra* (Bombay: University of Bombay, 1972).

Robert Coram, *Boyd: The Fighter Pilot Who Changed the Art of War* (New York: Little, Brown, 2002).

Samuel B. Griffith, *Mao Tse-tung on Guerrilla Warfare* (New York: Frederick A. Praeger, 1961).

Sir Walter Raleigh, *The Works of Sir Walter Raleigh*, vol. 8 (Oxford: Oxford University Press, 1829).

Sun Tzu, *The Art of War* (trans.) S. B. Griffith (Oxford: Oxford University, 1963).

T.R. Phillips (ed.), *Sun Tzu: The Art of War* (Harrisburg, PA, 1944).

William Livezey, *Mahan on Seapower* (Oklahoma City, OK: University of Oklahoma Press, 1981).

William Mitchell, *Winged Defense* (New York: G.P. Putnam's Sons, 1925).

Periodicals

Andrew Millett and Williamson Murray, "Lessons of War," *National Interest* 14 (Winter 1988).

Bernard Brodie, 'Clausewitz: A Passion for War', *World Politics* 25/2 (1973).

Bernard Brodie, "The Heritage of Douhet," *Air University Quarterly Review* VI, No. 2 (Summer 1953).

Edward J. Villacres and Christopher Bassford, "Reclaiming the Clausewitzian Trinity," *Parameters* (Autumn 1995).

James King, "On Clausewitz: Master Theorist of War," *Naval War College Review* 30 (Fall 1977).

Jon Robb-Webb, "Corbett and The Campaign of Trafalgar: Naval Operations in their Strategic Context," *Defense Studies*, Vol. 8, No. 2 (June 2008).

Raymond Aron, "Clausewitz' Conceptual System," *Armed Forces and Society* 1, No. 1 (Fall 1974), p. 56.

Roger Boesche, "Kautilya's Arthaœstra on War and Diplomacy in Ancient India," *The Journal of Military History*, 67:1 (January 2003).

Index